MODERN TEACHING OF ECONOMICS

MODERN TEACHING OF ECONOMICS

[Strictly According to the UGC Syllabus for B.Ed. Course]

By
SEEMA SHARMA

ANMOL PUBLICATIONS PVT. LTD.
NEW DELHI - 110 002 (INDIA)

ANMOL PUBLICATIONS PVT. LTD.
4374/4B, Ansari Road, Daryaganj
New Delhi - 110 002
Ph.: 23261597, 23278000
Visit us at: www.anmolpublications.com

Modern Teaching of Economics

First Published, 2004

ISBN 81-261-2025-8

PRINTED IN INDIA

Published by J.L. Kumar for Anmol Publications Pvt. Ltd., New Delhi - 110 002 and Printed at Mehra Offset Press, Delhi.

Contents

Preface

Education is a vast discipline and Teachers' Training is a vital part of it. The responsibilities of the educationists and educators are focused on the task of providing better training to the future teachers for their better learning and proper development. Needless to say that this responsibility can only be exercised, if the trainers are equipped with the required knowledge of the subject concerned. That's why it becomes essential for making adequate provisions for each course to the student-teachers or teacher trainees. The present series is designed for providing a solid workable base for all course-papers. It has been prepared strictly according to the syllabus of the B.Ed class, prescribed by the UGC for different universities

No doubt, there are so many other books on the subject, available in the market, written by worthy authors. However, every writer has his or her own style and way of presentation. The present work also has its own features and characteristics.

In preparation of this series of texts, the editor had to refer to the works of other authors and information sources. The editor feels a deep sense of gratitude for incorporating their ideas in the text. Hopefully, this series would serve as a 'ready to refer' tool for all teachers, teacher-students and others.

—Editor

1

Significant Subject

Special Place

The place of importance that Economics enjoys is evident from the fact that this is perhaps the only discipline in the social sciences in which a Nobel Prize is awarded. Economics is increasingly used for a broad array of decision-making matters within business, government sectors and departments, United Nations Organisation and its subsidiary organisations and several other organisations.

In developed countries, developing countries, the least developed countries, people want better civic facilities, educational facili-ties, defence services. Economists while studying the way a society uses scarce resources such as land, labour, raw materials and machinery to provide goods and services, analyse their findings to determine costs and benefits of using resources in a particular way.

The study of economics emcompasses the most effective means of utilising available resources in virtually every sector including household management.

Study of economics has now assumed great importance as the modern society cannot be comprehended in isolation. It has close links with production, arrangement and distribution of goods and services of a variety of nature not only national but also at international fronts.

The study of economics has become all the more important as the modern Economics now deals with multifarious socio-economic and financial matters of an individual as well as of a society. It studies systematically and methodically the economic network of society including agriculture, business, money and banking, international trade, transportation, planning, growth and development. On account of such an intimate relationship with nation's developmental aspects, subjects like chartered accountancy, cost accountancy, operational research, industrial relations, labour relations, social administration, statistics, sociology, public administration, social work and social welfare which cumulatively contribute to the gross national product have become an integral part of Economics.

Economists are constantly engaged in analysing and interpreting a number of economic phenomena occurring at a rapid pace and influencing all aspects of human life. At this critical juncture economists come forward and contribute subsequently to arrive at decision fairly quickly and intelligently.

Functional Aspects

Gone are the days when economists held that it was not the business or function of Economics to solve practical problems. As observed by Eraser, "An economist who is only an economist is a poor pretty fish." Armed-chair economists or theoreticians do not have a very significant place in the present scenario and especially in the case of developing and least developed countries or economies. Tugwell has very rightly observed that it is only a 'Premature flowering of Economies', which is responsible for its separation from practical life. Likewise Wosten laments, "We spend too much time forging theoretical tools and too little time in trying to make practical use of them." As pointed out by Pigou when we study economics, "Our impulse is not the philosopher's impulse, knowledge for the sake of knowledge but rather the physiologist's knowledge for the healing that knowledge may help to bring." Again he has observed, "Economics is chiefly valuable neither as an intellectual gymnastic, nor as a means of winning truth for its own sake, but as a housemaid of Ethics and a servant of practice."

Economics is helpful in finding appropriate solutions to economic problems – individual, national and global. It is the science that studies various activities concerning wealth, its consumption, production, its consumption and distribution.

Economics develops deep insight to understand economic problems.

Economics develop the capacity to make the proper use of economic resources.

Expertise in economic issues leads to economic and social planning.

Economics helps to develop a viable economic structure.

Economics is very helpful to understanding the working of trade and industry and financial institutions.

Economic planners suggest ways and means of increasing national income.

Common Aspects

1. Economics acquaints the child with the general economic, social and geographical environment of the society.
2. Economics in schools helps the students to take a keen interest in the ways people live through various socio-economic institutions.

3. The teaching of Economics enables the students to recognise what is undesirable in the economic system and how to get rid of it.
4. The teaching of Economics develops a broad outlook among students and they become sensitive to the needs of the underprivileged sections of the society.
5. The teaching of Economics endeavours to develop in the students the ability and will to participate in the task of the reconstruction of the economy and society with a sense of social commitment.
6. Teaching of Economics aims at developing a faith in the minds of the students in the destiny of the nation as they learn that if the other nations can achieve a higher standard of life, there is no reason for them to remain backward.
7. The teaching of Economics promotes the values of socialism in students as enshrined in our constitution.
8. The teaching of Economics inculcates attitudes and skills for maximization of economic welfare.
9. The teaching of Economics prepares students for a vocation.
10. The teaching of Economics enables the students to become socially efficient individuals.
11. The teaching of Economics develops in the student an awareness to make the proper use of natural and human resources.
12. The teaching of Economics acquaints the students with the problems of globalization in economic matters.
13. The teaching of Economics enables the students to understand the main features of capitalism, mixed economy and socialism.
14. The teaching of Economics is helpful to the students understanding the mechanism of the working of the financial institutions.

15. The teaching of Economics enables the students to appreciate the phenomenon of interdependence of the various regions of the country. Thus it helps in the development of the values of emotional and national integration.

QUESTIONS

Essay Type Questions

1. Make out a case for the introduction of Economics in the curriculum, especially at the school stage.
2. Why has the teaching of Economics received so much importance in the modern times ?
3. What is the practical utility of the teaching of Economics?

Short Answer and Objective Type Questions

4. Mention any three categories of people for whom the study of Economics has practical importance.
5. List any two theoretical advantages of the study of Economics.
6. Write 'yes' or 'no' against each statement given below :
   (i) Teaching of Economics is helpful to the student. ( )
   (ii) Knowledge of Economics has no utility for a trader. ( )
   (iii) Teaching of Economics acquaints the students with the working of financial institutions. ( )
   (iv) Teaching of Economics is closely related to the teaching of Biology. ( )

2

Fundamental Issues

The educators and philosophers have emphasised certain principles of teaching which the teachers are expected to bear in their mind the principles of teaching which the educators have emphasised for making their teaching effective, efficient and inspirational. Sometimes these principles are classified as psychological and general principles. This classification is however very arbitrary and both types overlap.

Following are the important considerations which necessitate the use of principles and maxims of teaching in the teaching-learning process including Economics :

1. The child is the agent in his own learning. Out of the three components of a learning situation : the child, the teacher and the environment, pride of place is to be given to the child. He must become the most important agent in his learning. It means that teaching-learning must be thought of in terms of activities and experiences which appeal most to the child.

2. Children learn best when they are active. When we consider the child an agent in his own learning, we must provide for him to be active. The medium of learning is the activities undertaken by the child. Learning take place through a continuous process of interaction between the learner and his environment.
3. Knowledge or information is not the goal. Self-realization is the goal. Personality and character are more important than the subject matter. To possess all the knowledge of the world and lose one's own self is an awful fate in education.
4. Child-centred approach is more psychological than logical. It emphasises the process rather than the product.
5. Child-centred approach gives freedom to the child under the creative and sympathetic direction of the teacher.
6. One single exposure to an experience does not develop the necessary co-ordination of the physical and mental faculties of a child. Hence there has to be repetitive exercises and drills to give a certain knowledge and the efficiency and tenacity of a skill and value. It is here the child becomes a trainee and the teacher becomes a trainer or the child an educand and the teacher as an educator.
7. A child is a unique being and can function only by remaining in the world in which it has a specific role to play. The teacher's role is to help the child to conform to its unique role, both in its spirit, habitual values, choices and consistent behaviour patterns.
8. The child's sense of wonder and astonishment and his natural curiosity lead to a learning process which should be encouraged by teachers.

The role of principles and devices of teaching-learning may be summed up as under :

1. Motivating children.

2. Developing trust and confidence in children's capacity to learn.
3. Becoming as a resource for creating meaningful learning experiences.
4. Accepting the individual and the group.
5. Participating as a member of the group in guiding learning.
6. Becoming sensitive to the child's needs and interacting in a way that would provide a sense of feeling and security.
7. Recognising and reinforcing the individual contribution.

General Rules

1. Principle of Activity or Learning by Doing.
2. Principle of Play-way.
3. Principle of Motivation.
4. Principle of Self-Education.
5. Principle of Individual Differences.
6. Principle of Goal Setting.
7. Principle of Stimulation.
8. Principle of Association.
9. Principle of Readiness.
10. Principle of Effect.
11. Principle of Exercise or Repetition
12. Principle of Change and Rest.
13. Principle of Feedback and Reinforcement.
14. Principle of Training of Senses.
15. Principle of Group Dynamics.
16. Principle of Creativity.
17. Principle of Correlation.

While discussing various principles of teaching, it must be kept in mind that these principles overlap and there is no thin line of demarcation. Moreover they are complementary and supplementary to each other.

Academic Rules

Principle of Activity or Learning by Doing—Children are active by nature and any process or method that is not based upon the student activity is not in accord with the progressive educational theories. Rousseau considers the child as a 'hero' in the drama of education and as such he must be allowed to play the dominant role. So the first principle is to keep the class active.

Children have been endowed by nature with tremendous vitality. In the words of T.S. Avinashilingam, "The Great Ganga of life flows majestically on. But if anyone tries to retain and dam it, the dam will break unless attempts are simultaneously made to divert it into other channels. These waters can only be diverted, but cannot be dammed indefinitely. If anyone tried to do the impossible, it would be at his peril, for the dam will break, sooner or later. So is the nature of children. The great vitality of our children cannot be permanently restrained without providing a positive purpose. Thus, providing for various types of activities which will interest the children and give them opportunities for observation and the use of their hands is to offer them the fulfilment and satisfaction, which nothing else confers."

Activity does not mean mere physical activity. If a pupil is to develop all sides of his personality, then it is necessary for him to be active in all ways, to exercise all the powers he has.

Principle of Playway—This principle is closely related to the principle of learning by doing. According to Froebel, play is the chief activity of childhood. It gives joy, freedom, contentment and inner and outer peace. It holds the source of all that is good. But "without rational conscious guidance", says Froebel, "childish activity degenerates into aimless play instead of preparing for those tasks of life for which it is designed."

Play is a natural activity. Just as a poet cannot refrain himself from writing a poem, a musician from singing, a dancer from dancing and an actor from acting, so too a child cannot refrain himself from playing. Play comes from within. It is a voluntary activity and is the manifestation of creative urge. It gives joy, freedom, contentment, inner rest and peace with the world. This implies that a spirit of playway should prevail in the classroom work.

Principle of Motivation — The teacher will do his best to motivate all the children in the lesson. Motivation arouses the interest of children and once they become interested, they are willing to concentrate and work. Motivation is developed by the following techniques :

(i) Utilising the instinctive tendencies of the children in an effective manner.

(ii) Satisfying the curiosity of children.

(iii) Utilising all the senses of children.

(iv) Relating closely body and mind.

(v) Linking teaching-learning with life.

Principle of Self-education — Best teaching is enabling the child learn by his own efforts. Teachers must fire the imagination of their students. Children, we are told, must be left free to express themselves, for the best education is self-education. Teachers, we are told, must stand aside. They must talk less, explain less and direct less. Adamson states, "The whole business is between the individual and his world's and the teacher is outside it, external to — if he may facilitate it, turning his attention to one or other member of the wedded pair. He may approach the individual and his avenues of approach will be one or other of the instincts or emotional dispositions, which are the prime movers of mental life. He may try fear, pugnacity, curiosity, or sympathy, or a combination of them, to quicken the current which seems to him sluggish or he may approach the fact or truth, whichever of the three words it belongs to, and see whether anything can be done by lighting it up, or lining in main features and blotting out detail to facilitate adjustment. But whatever he tries, subject or object or both together, he remains outside the process, a spectator, a manipulator, perhaps a distributor; he is never in it and of it. Within that mysterious synthetic activity through which the individual is at once appropriating and contributing to his environment, forming and being formed by it. ......the teacher has neither place nor part." The statement implies that the essential activity in teaching is not the adjustment of child to teacher but is to enable him to adjust himself to the environment and also to change the environment to adjust himself. Teaching must enable the child to work independently and without the teacher at a later state.

Dr. A.G. Hughes and Dr. E.H. Hughes remark, "It must be emphasised however, that teachers are not as superfluous as some enthusists suggest, teaching is not the baneful evil it is sometimes represented to be. It is true that children are by nature curious, assertive and creative, but they are also submissive, imitative and ready to appeal for help. It follows, therefore, that we are not necessarily working contrary to child nature when we teach. We must, however, know when to teach and when to stand aside, when to explain and when to leave children to make discoveries, when to demonstrate and when to leave children free to experiment, when to require children to listen and when to give them scope for free expression." The two important aspects of teaching are, stimulation and inspiration. The teachers must fire the enthusiasm of their pupils. They must encourage them in the development of their natural desire to work and to be active and guide these desires into worthwhile channels. The late President Eliot of Harvard once said, "The supreme value of a teacher lies not in the regular performance of routine duties, but in his power to lead and inspire his students through the influence of his own mental and moral personality and examples."

Principle of Individual Differences—No two children are alike. Teaching to be effective must cater to individual differences of children.

Principle of Goal Setting—A definite goal must be set before each child according to the standard expected for him. Short-term or immediate goals should be set before small children and distant goals for older ones. It must be remembered that goals should be very clear and definite and the children must understand these goals.

Principle of Stimulation—Burton has said, teaching is the stimulation, guidance, direction and encouragement of learning. Ryburn emphasises this aspect in these words, "the guidance of the teacher is mainly a matter of giving the right kind of stimulus to help him to learn the right things in the right way."

Principle of Association—Throndike points out that things we want to go together should be put together. Many different things or ideas which we want to go together should be associated with each other. They should form a part of one process. Then it becomes easier to make the students understand their relationship.

Principle of Readiness—This principle is indicative of learner's state of mind to participate in the teaching-learning process. Readiness is preparation for action. A teacher must be alive to this principle.

Principle of Effect—This principle states that a response is strengthened if it is followed by pleasure and weakened if followed by displeasure.

Principle of Exercise or Repetition—According to it, the more a stimulus induced response is repeated, the longer it will be retained. Other things being equal, exercise strengthens the bond between situation and response. Conversely a bond is weakened through failure to exercise it. Thus the principle has two sub-parts: (i) Principle of use and (ii) Principle of disuse.

Principle of Change and Rest—Psychological experiments in learning have demonstrated that fatigue, lack of attention and monotony can be overcome by making appropriate provision for change, rest and recreation. While framing the time table it is kept in view that subjects and activities are provided in such a way that the students do not experience boredom and fatigue. Usually two consecutive periods of a subject are not provided in a class.

Principle of Feed-back and Reinforcement—Learning theories point out that the immediate knowledge of the results and positive reinforcers in the form of praise, grade, certificates, token money and other incentives can contribute to make the task of learning joyable.

Principle of Training of Sense—Senses are said to be the gateways of knowledge. The power of observation, discrimination, identification, generalisation and application can only be appropriately developed through the effective functioning of senses.

Principle of Group Dynamics—Under the influence of group behaviour, appropriate changes in the behaviour of the members of the group can take place. Individuals composing the group think and feel as the group feels, do as the group does. A suitable climate for group dynamics is to be created in the classroom environment.

Principle of Creativity—Opportunities should be provided to the students to explore things and events and find casue-effect relationships. This principle envisages that every student possesses some element of creativity which must be explored and developed to the maximum extent.

Principle of Correlation—Gandhiji was of the firm view that correlation should be the basis of all work. He advocated that correlation of the learning task should be established with the craft, physical and social environment.

Common Rules

Successful teaching necessitates that the teacher comes down to the level of the pupils and at the same time assists them in rising above it. To a great extent, the principles of teaching to be followed depend upon the age of the pupils, the subjects and topic of the lesson. However, there are certain general principles which should underline the teaching of all subjects. As already stated, there is no clearcut dividing line between psychological and general principles of teaching.

Principle of Definite Goals or Objectives. Destination or goals of teaching-learning must be clear to the teachers and students. Goals and objectives keep the teachers and students on the track. Definiteness of goals helps in planning, executing and evaluating every step, phase or act of the teaching-learning process.

Principle of Child-centredness. The entire teaching endeavour is for the child. Therefore, it is essential that teaching strategies should cater to the aptitude, interest and abilities of the students. In the drama of education, child should be assigned to the role of 'hero'.

Principle of Linking with Life. Teaching can never be performed in a vaccum. It is always in a social context. In the teaching of all the school subjects,' examples from everyday life should be given their due place.

Principle of Correlation. Knowledge is one 'whole'. Various ideas and events are interrelated. There exist links among various subjects. Correlation of the present events can be made with the past. Similarly future can be visualised on the basis of the present happenings or state of affairs. Gandhiji propounded his system of Basic education with correlation as its cornerstone—correlation with the craft, correlation with the physical environment and correlation with social environment.

Principle of Active Involvement and Participation of Students. Teaching-learning is a two-way traffic. Traditional teaching was almost teacher-centred. There was very little scope for the involvement of the students. The teacher taught and the students listened to him passively. The new teaching emphasises that the students must actively participate in all the stages and steps of teaching-learning.

Principle of Cooperation. Classroom environment becomes lively when the teacher and the taught work in unison, helping each other in carrying out the task of teaching and learning. All the participants have the same common interest. Naturally, they must cooperate with teacher.

Principle of Remedial Teaching. All students do not learn with the same speed and accomplishment. Some lag behind and need extra coaching. The teacher has to find out where the fault lies and think for positive measures. He may have to arrange for remedial or compensatory or extra teaching for any particular group of students for removing their specific difficulties.

Principle of Creating Conducive Environment. Physical as well as social environment of the classroom plays a vital role in motivating the learners. Arrangement of light and furniture etc. should be properly attended to. There should be proper discipline and order. The teacher should be sympathetic but firm.

Principle of Planning. Planning determines the quality or success of any task. Planning in teaching involves the preparation of the lesson notes, provision of teaching aids, and working out strategies to be adopted in the delivery of the lesson.

Principle of Effective Strategies. Teaching process to be effective must adopt proper means, strategies and tactics. A teaching strategy is a generalised plan for a lesson which includes structure, desired learning behaviour in terms of goals of instruction and an outline of planned tactics necessary to implement the strategy.

Principle of Flexibility. Strategies should serve as guides for effective teaching. Strategies may have to be changed if the classroom situations so warrant. Teaching is a complex task and a live phenomenon. The possibilities of alternation in planned strategies cannot be ruled out at the execution stage. A teacher must be quite imaginative and resourceful for adapting himself and his teaching to the requirements of the teaching-learning environment.

Principle of Variety. A variety of teaching aids and strategies should be adopted to motivate and sustain the interests of the students. Variety serves as great tonic for creating fresh environment and checking boredom and lethargy.

Ideal Teaching Method

The maxims of teaching are very helpful in obtaining the active involvement and participation of the learners in the teaching learning process. They quicken the interest of the learners and motivate them to learn. They make learning effective, inspirational, interesting and meaningful. They keep the students attentive to the teaching learning process. A good teacher should be quite familiar with them. Now we proceed to discuss them.

From the Known to the Unknown—The most natural and simple way of teaching a lesson is to proceed from something that the students already know to those facts which they do not know. What is already known to the students is of great use to the students. This means that the teacher should arouse interest in a lesson by putting questions on the subject matter already known to the pupils. The teacher is to proceed step by step to connect the new matter to the old one. New knowledge cannot be grasped in a vacuum. A civic lesson on the powers of the President of India may start from the powers of the President of Municipal Boards or of the President of Village Panchayat. A lesson on profit and loss in arithmetic can easily be taught to the pupils by referring to the shopkeepers who make profit. A history lesson on Lord Rama may be taken up with the celebration of Ram Lila.

From Simple to Complex—The simple task or topic must be taught first and the complex one can follow later on. The word simple and complex are to be seen from the point of view of the child and not that of an adult. We would be curbing the interest and initiative of the children by presenting them complex problems before the simpler ones are presented. In a lesson on nature study, for instance, a child will understand the concept of a flower first and thereafter its various parts. Similarly in a geography lesson the teacher will take up the general study of a region or country first and later on a detailed and specific study.

From Easy to Difficult—We must graduate our lessons in order of ease of understanding them. Students' standard must be kept in view. This will help in sustaining the interest of the students. In determining what is easy and what is difficult we have to take into account the psychological make-up of the child. Logically viewed one skill may be easy but psychologically it may be difficult. There are many things which look easy to us but are in fact difficult for children. The interest of the child has also to be taken into account. Lines are very easy to draw but a child may not like to draw lines. He may try to draw an animal. There is no doubt that it is difficult, but it is more interesting to him and so is easy for him. We should encourage him to do so and our approach will be psychological instead of logical.

From the Concrete to the Abstract—A child's imagination is greatly aided by a concrete material. "Things first and words after" is the common saying. Rousseau said, "Things. Things. Things". Children in the beginning cannot think in abstractions. Small children learn first from things which they can see and handle. Very young pupils learn counting with the help of pebbles etc. A child understands an aeroplane with the help of a model. Actual visits to canals and rivers provide a clear idea of them.

A lesson in geography can be made interesting with the help of models, pictures and illustrations of bridges, rivers and mountains etc. Care must be exercised to ensure that the students do not remain at the 'concrete stage' all the time. This is only the initial step for children with a view to reach the higher stage of 'abstraction' as they advance in age.

From Particular to General—Before giving principles and rules, particular examples should be presented. As a matter of fact a study of particular facts should lead the children themselves to frame general rules. The rules of arithmetic, of grammar, of physical geography and almost of all sciences are based on the principle of proceeding from particular instances to general rules.

From Indefinite to Definite—Ideas of children in the initial stages are indefinite and very vague. These ideas are to be made definite, clear, precise and systematic. Effective teaching necessitates that every word and idea presented should stand out clearly in the child's mind as a picture. For classifying ideas, adequate use must be made of actual objects, diagrams and pictures. Every possible effort should be made to make the children interested in the lesson.

From Empirical to Relational—Observation and experience are the basis of empirical knowledge. Rational knowledge implies a bit of abstraction and argumentative approach. The general feeling is that the child first of all experiences knowledge in his day to day life and after that he feels the rational basis. For instance, plane geometry makes better sense when taught in the context of everyday life instead of it in the format of a highly abstract theory. It is always better to begin with what the children see, feel and experience than arguing and generalising.

From Psychological to Logical—Logical approach is concerned with the arrangement of the subject matter. Psychological approach looks at the child's interest, needs, mental make up and reactions. When we treat a subject logically, we are usually thinking of it from our own point of view and not from the point of view of the child. In psychological approach, we proceed from the concrete to the abstract, from the simple to the complex and from known to unknown. We start reading by teaching the child to read a whole sentence, as for him, the unit is the sentence, not the word or the letter as it is for the adult. This is psychological approach. In a drawing lesson a child has little sense in lines and curves. Logically we start with simple lines and curves but psychologically we start with drawing a whole animal.

From Whole to Parts—Whole is more meaningful to the child than the parts of the whole. J.P. Guilford, E.B. Newman and May Seagoe conclude after their research that the 'whole' approach is generally better than 'part' learning because the material to be learnt 'makes sense' and its part can be seen by the learner as interrelated. The learner sees a relationship between the central idea of the material to be learned. The 'whole' unit or passage for slow learners should be smaller than the 'whole' for the fast learners.

From Near to Far—A child learns well in the surroundings in which he resides. So he should be first acquainted with his immediate environment. Gradually he may be taught about things which are away from his immediate environment. In a geography lesson we start from the local geography and then take up tehsil, district, state, the country and the world gradually.

From Analysis to Synthesis—Analysis means breaking a problem into convenient parts and synthesis means grouping of these separated parts into one complete whole. A complex problem can be made simple and easy by dividing it into units.

From Actual to Representative—When actual objectives are shown to children, they learn easily and retain them in their minds for a long time. This is specially suitable for younger children. Representative objects in the form of pictures, models etc. should be used to the grown ups.

Proceed Inductively—This maxim includes almost all the maxims state above. In the inductive approach, we start from particular examples and establish general rules through the active participation of the learners. In the deductive approach, we assume a definition, a general rule or formula and apply it to particular examples. An example will make this distinction very clear. 'The farmers in India are very poor' is a general statement in the deductive type of reasoning. The inductive will follow thus : Ram is a farmer. He is very poor. Shyam is a farmer. He is very poor. Krishan is a farmer. He is very poor. In this way from several such examples it will be concluded that farmers are poor. Thus we concluded generalisations.

It must be accepted that in the ultimate analysis maxims are meant to be our servants and not masters. Moreover, by and large, they are interrelated. Different maxims suit different situations. It is, therefore, essential that of each maxim a judicious use should be made.

QUESTIONS

Essay Type Questions

1. Why do we need principles of teaching-learning ?
2. Explain any five principles of teaching with suitable examples.
3. State the significance of any five maxims of teaching.
4. Explain the meaning of proceed from 'known to the unknown', from 'simple to complex' and from 'general to specific' in the context of maxims of teaching. Cite examples.
5. What is meant by psychological principles of teaching ? Explain the implications of any four principles of teaching in Economics.
6. What is meant by general principles of teaching ? Explain the implications of any four principles in the teaching of Economics.

Short Answer and Objective Type Questions

7. Classify the following into principles of teaching and devices of teaching.
   (i) Play-way.
   (ii) Proceed from concrete to abstract.
   (iii) Self education.
   (iv) Individual differences.
   (v) From easy to difficult.
8. Some statements are given below. Write 'True' if the statement is correct and 'False' if it is not true.
   (i) Planning helps to prevent wastage in teaching-learning. ( )
   (ii) Pupil wastes his time in self-study and does not learn anything. ( )

3

Basic Ideas

Human economic activity is as old as human history. In ancient India, 'Artha' (wealth) was considered as an important means of achieving the ultimate goal of human life which was termed as Moksha' (liberation from the suffering of the cycle of birth and death). 'Artha' however was to be earned through 'Dharma (right actions or righteous) and to be used for 'Karma' (satisfaction of worldly needs in accordance with 'Dharma', i.e. right action). Of course there were other means also prescribed for the attainment of 'Moksha'.

A systematic study of Economics was done in India as early as the later half of the fourth century B.C. by Kautilya, also known as Chanakya or Vishnugupta who was the Prime Minister of the Emperor Chandragupta Maurya. His treatise captioned 'Arthshastra' is regarded as a monumental work on the art of administration, economy and polity.

Coming to the modern times, mercantilism was the first comprehensive economic theory. It developed in France and England in the 16th and 17th centuries. Mercantilists defended the economic policies that nations were following to increase their wealth. At that time, national wealth was considered to constitute gold and silver accumulated within a country. The commerce of the nation was treated like the finances of the household. Great efforts were made to protect domestic industries and many restrictions were imposed on international trade.

The credit of establishing Economics as a major field of study goes to Adam Smith (1723-90). In 1776 his book 'An Inquiry into the Nature and Causes of the Wealth of Nations' appeared which is still widely quoted. Economics became a recognized field of study during the 19th century. In colleges departments were created to teach economic theory. Economists, such as Alfred Marshall (1842-1924) at Cambridge University, attracted many students.

History and Background

Economics began as a British subject and remained so for many years. It became a recognised field of study during the 19th century. In colleges departments were created to teach Economics theory. Economists, such as Marshall (1842-1924) at Cambridge University attracted many scholars and students. Today it is an international discipline including scholars from most countries of the world and from all regions. Its chief centre is in the USA and papers originating from here account for a sizeable proportion of those appearing in the major journals.

Economists everywhere advise governments and private institutions and they frequently write in newspapers and appear on the radio and television.

Another important development particularly since the Second World War has been the use of Economics in new fields. Thus the Economics of Medicine, to cite one example has now become a specialised area with its own practitioners. Likewise Economics of Education emerged as a new area of studies.

Almost all political parties in all countries include economic issues in their election manifestos.

Classification of the Definitions

1	2	3	4	5
Wealth Centred Definition	**Walfare Centred Definition**	**Scarcity Centred Definition**	**Wantlessness Centred Definition**	**Growth Centred Definition**
Prominent Advocates	Prominent Advocates	Prominent Advocates	Prominent Advocates	Prominent Advocates
1. Adam Smith	1. Marshall	1. Robbins	J. K. Mehta	1. Samuelson
2. J. B. Say	2. Pigou	2. Stigler		2. Henry Smith
3. J. S. Mill	3. Cannon	3. Oscar Lange		3. K. G. Seth
4. F A. Walker	4. Beveridge	4. Scitovasky		4. Peterson
5. Caimes	5. Penson	5. Milton Friedman		
6. Chapman				

The Concept

Economists have expressed divergent views on the definition and meaning of Economics. In this regard, the 'Dictionary of Economics' (1998) has very rightly observed, "Economists have never been wholly satisfied with any definition of their subject. In fact, no short definition can convey to the beginner the scope and flavour of the whole subject as it was evolved." J. M. Keynes in his publication 'Scope and Method of Political Economy' has stated, "Political Economy is said to have strangled itself with definitions." Mrs. Barbara Wosten's views also echo the same voice, "Where ever six economists gather, there are seven opinions." Prof. Viner's views also reflect this, "Economics is what economists do." Writing about the nature of Economics, Durbin has remarked, "Certainty will always escape us."

Monetary Science

Adam Smith, Ricardo, J.B. Say and F.A. Walker are the prominent economists who regard Economics as a study of wealth. Adam Smith (1723-99), who is known as the 'father of Economics', named his famous book on Economics as 'An Enquiry into the Nature and Causes of Wealth of Nations' (1776). The emphasis of Adam Smith on wealth is clear when he writes in this book, "The great object of Political Economy of every country is to increase the riches and power of that country." (It may be remembered that earlier Economics was called as Political Economy.)

According to J. B. Say, a French classical economist, "Economics is the science which treats of Wealth."

Likewise F.A. Walker writes, "Political Economy or Economics is the name of that part of knowledge which relates to wealth."

J.S. Mill states, "Economics is the science of wealth related to man."

Cairnes has observed, "Political Economy is the science which studies the law of production and distribution of wealth."

Chapman states, "Economics is the science which studies wealth earning and wealth spending activities of man."

Main Features

1. Economics is the study of wealth.
2. Economics deals with the production and distribution of wealth.
3. Only material goods which are scarce and useful constitute wealth.
4. To increase wealth, production of material goods will have to be stepped up.

Analytical Review

Justification of Wealth Centred Definition – The 'Wealth definition' of Economics is justified on the ground that by studying the laws of production, exchange and distribution of wealth – useful goods or commodities, Economics makes an important contribution to the promotion of social welfare. Therefore it is unjust to dub Economics as a mean and sordid science.

It is also argued in favour of this definition that the abject poverty, huge magnitude of unemployment and under-employment prevailing today in developing countries like India cannot be removed without expanding the production of wealth and its equitable distribution.

Criticism of Wealth Centred Definition – The definition of Economics as a 'Science of Wealth' has received severe criticism from a number of scholars like Ruskin, John, Dickens and William Morris. Carlyle Ruskin dubbed it as a 'Gospel of Mammon'. Others call it 'Dismal Science', 'Science of Selfishness' and a Pig Science' etc.

Following types of criticism are generally levied against this definition :

1. This definition ignores the higher values of life.

2. It assigns man a secondary place.
3. It misses the central point that wealth is only a means to an end – the end being the welfare of man and the society.
4. It fails to lay due emphasis on man's behaviour towards wealth.
5. The concept of wealth in Economics involves the acceptance and justification of property right in various forms of wealth. The Indian constitution included it earlier as a fundamental right but subsequently deleted it.
6. Since the meaning of wealth is subject to different interpretations, it is not a scientific definition.

Physical Science

Marshall, Pigou, Cannon, Beveridge and Pension are the chief protagonists of this definition.

Prof. Marshall (1842-1924), the most prominent of welfare economists has observed, "Economics is the study of man's action in the ordinary business of life. It enquires how he gets his income, and how he uses it.....Thus, it is on one side the study of wealth and on the other and more important side a part of the study of man. He further states, "Economics is a study of mankind in the ordinary business of life. It examines that part of individual and social action which is most closely connected with the attainment and with the use of the material requisites of well being".

Marshall's view has been supported by Pigou. According to him, "Economics is a study of economic welfare, economic welfare being described as that part of welfare which can be brought directly or indirectly into relation with the measuring rod of money."

In the words of Penson, "Economics is the science of material welfare." In the views of Cannon, "Economics is a study of the causes of material welfare."

Perception of Benefit

1. It is a study of 'man as such' and a 'man of wealth'.

2. It implies that Economics is concerned with a particular aspect of man's life, i.e., material. There are several other aspects of man's life – political, religious, social etc.
3. The primary objective and end of Economics is the promotion of welfare.

Marshall's definition of Economics has been criticised by L.Robbins on the following grounds:

1. In Economics we study not only material things but also immaterial things. He argues, "A theory of wages which ignored all those sums which were paid for immaterial services or were spent on immaterial ends would be intolerable."
2. The concept of welfare is not definite and fixed. It differs in different countries and at different times. Welfare is a subjective concept.
3. Economics studies several activities and also is concerned with goods which are generally considered harmful to human welfare. Examples are studies of goods like cigarette, liquor or opium. Economists study the pricing problems and other aspects of such goods whether they promote welfare or not. Thus observes Robbins. "Why talk of welfare at all ? Why not throw away the mask altogether ?"

Dearth Problem

Robbins is the propounder of the theory of Economics as a science of scarcity. After criticising Marshall's definition of Economics as a science of material welfare. He in his book Nature and Significance of Economic Science (1931) gave the following definition, "Economics is the science which studies human behaviour as a relationship between ends and scarce means which have alternative uses."

Scholar's View

This definition is based on the following premises :

1. Wants are unlimited.
2. Resources for the satisfaction of wanted are limited.
3. There are alternative resources or means that can be put to various uses. It is because of the various alternative uses of the resources that we have to decide about the best allocation of resources.

An important point to note about Robbins' definition is that Robbins does not distinguish between material and non-material and between welfare and non-welfare. What ends or wants should be selected for satisfaction is not the concern of the economists. Thus according to Robbins, Economics is neutral between ends.

Robbins has further remarked, "When time and means for achieving ends are limited and capable of alternative application and the ends are capable of being distinguished in order of importance, then behaviour necessarily assumes the form of choice." It, therefore, means that Economics is the science of choice. Likewise Wicksteed, Stigler and Erich Roll also define Economics in terms of scarcity of resources and choice.

In the words of Stigler, "Economics is the study of the principles governing the allocation of scarce means among competing ends when the object of allocation is to maximise the attainment of ends."

Cair defines Economics in these words, "Economics is the study of the influence of scarcity on human conduct in circumstances where men have freedom of choice in allocating scarce and competing wants."

Robbins' definition is criticised on the following grounds :

1. Robbins' definition makes Economics neutral between ends. As observed by Thomas, "The function of the economist is not only to explain and explore but also to educate."

2. The scope of Economics is definitely wider than the allocation of resources.
3. The determination of national income does not fail within the purview of Robbins' definition as it lays stress on the allocation of resources.
4. Robbins definition is defective because it does not cover an important subject like economic growth.
5. Economists study the problem of choice if it has social implications that is when an individual's choice affects other members of the society. In the case of Robbins' definition, even a 'Sadhu' living in the Himalayas face as the problem of choice as how to distribute his time between various ends.
6. Robbins does not define the term resources which can be both material as well as human or non-material.
7. Robbins is silent regarding the objective for making choice between ends and scarce means.
8. The distinction between 'means' and 'ends' is not clear in Robbins' definition.
9. Some scholars are of the view that Robbins has reduced Economics merely to a valuation theory and has thus neglected other important aspects of the study of man.
10. According to Professor Schultze of the University of Maryland, Robbins' definition of Economics is misleading. "In particular it does not fully reflect two of the major concerns of modern Economics, growth and stability."

No Needs Status

Dr. J. K. Mehta, an eminent Indian economist defines Economics in somewhat philosophical terms. He states, "Economics is the science of human activities considered as an endeavour to reach the state of wantlessness."

Main Features of Wantlessness-Centred Definition: This definition leads to the following :

1. The chief objective of life is to obtain happiness or prosperity,
2. The real happiness or prosperity lies in wantlessness.
3. The stage of wantlessness is reached gradually.
4. The stage of wantlessness is the stage of bliss – a spiritual point of view.

Criticism of the Definition

1. This definition unnecessarily establishes the relationship of Economics with ethics, philosophy and religion.
2. The stage of wantlessness seems to be a 'Utopian' stage. It is rather impossible to reach that stage.
3. Economics loses its significance when man reaches the stage of wantlessness.

Progressive Status

Henry Smith, Paul Samuelson, K. G. Seth Boulding and Hicks are the chief advocates of this definition. Henry Smith in his book entitled A Prospect of Politico Economy (1968) defines Economics as, "Economics is the study of how in a civilized society one obtains the share of 'what' other people have produced and of 'how' the total product of the society changes and is determined."

A. Samuelson defines Economics as, "Economics is the study of how men and society choose, with or without the use of money, to employ scarce productive resources which could have alternative uses to produce various commodities over time and distribute them for consumption, now, and in the future, among various people and groups in society."

In this context, K. G. Seth has observed, "Economics studies human behaviour concerned with changes and growth in capacity to produce in relation to demand."

Main Features of Growth-Centred Definition

1. Like Robbins' definition it relates to choices.
2. It is also concerned with means which are scarce.
3. The resources have alternative uses.
4. It is concerned with production as well as its distribution.

Evaluation of Growth-Centred Definition

1. The word 'civilised' used in relation to society may mean different things to different people.
2. Money in the present economic scenario seems to be indispensable. This definition, by and large, has found more acceptability as all the important elements of Economics, namely the determination and distribution of national income and output, employment and the theory of economic growth are incorporated in it.

In view of divergent and conflicting meanings attached to the study of Economics, it is not possible to define Economics in a language that could be universally accepted. Jacob's observations provide a pragmatic approach : "Economics is what economists do.' Like the proverbial parable of the elephant and the blind men, each thinker seems to have his own concept of Economics which is influenced by his own outlook on his life experiences in the field.

The term 'Economics' is derived from two Greek words 'Oikos' and 'nemein' meaning to manage a household. A household requires management because a family's resources are limited and choice must be made. A family must decide what it will produce. What goods it will buy and how these goods will be shared. Likewise businesses and governments must also make choices concerning allocation of limited resources for production, consumption and distribution. Economists and planners study the different ways in which resources are used to fulfil society's needs. They also seek better ways for society to allocate its resources for achieving optimum results.

QUESTIONS

Essay Type Questions

1. "Economics is the science of wealth." Discuss this statement.
2. Mention some important definitions of Economics. Explain anyone definition in detail.
3. What is the difference in the definition of Economics given by Adam Smith and Marshall ? Which of these do you like most ? State reasons in support of your answer.
4. Explain the definition given by Robbins. State its merits and demerits.

Short Answer and Objective Type Questions

5. Match the contents of column 'A' with that of column 'B'

	A	B
(i)	Wantlessness Centred definition of Economics	Adam Smith
(ii)	Welfare Centred definition of Economics	Robbins
(iii)	Scarcity Centred definition of Economics	J. K. Mehta
(iv)	Wealth Centerd definition of Economics	Marshall

6. Write 'Yes' and 'No' against each statement.
   (i) Kautilya is called the 'Father of Modern Economy'.
   (ii) Paul Samuelson's name is associated with the growth definition of Economics. He defines Economics in terms of scarcity, means and ends.
7. Who is the author of the following statement? "Economics is the science of human activities considered as an endeavour to reach the state of wantlessness."

4

Motives and Goals

Practical Significance

According to Srivastava and Shouri (1989), the educational objectives serve the following functions :

1. Provide the desired directions to educational activities.
2. Determine the nature of educational activities.
3. Provide a basis for systematising or planning an educational programme.
4. Decide the points of emphasis in an educational activity.
5. Give unity and coherence to an educational programme.
6. Provide the basis for the measurement of growth and thus guarantee valid evaluation.
7. Help distinguish between various aspects of learning.
8. Help focus attention on proper attributes of teaching and evaluation.

9. Help grade learning experiences and also evaluation material.
10. Help maintain a balance between different aspects of an educational programme.
11. Help fix priorities in an educational programme.
12. Guide educational decisions in curricular and co-curricular areas.
13. Guide in the selection of relevant content.
14. Guide in bringing about improvements in education.
15. Give meaning to and clarify the structure and content of curriculum.
16. Help make learning functional.
17. Help articulate learning in various fields.
18. Help discover or evolve proper learning situations.
19. Help define educational processes.
20. Help make the intangible in education tangible.
21. Help identify weaknesses and strengths of pupils in learning.
22. Facilitate communication among educational workers.

Teaching Aims

Objectives provide the needed motivation and enthusiasm to take up any activity. They are the undisputed starting point of all ventures including educational ventures. They are the 'crux' and 'keys' of all educational activities.

A lot of confusion regarding the use of terms like aims, goals, outcomes, objectives etc. Quite a large number of educators use these terms synonymously. However, some educators use it differently. Following points of comparison will make the distinction clear between aims and objectives.

Educational aims and objectives provide direction to instructional aims and objectives.

Aims in Education	*Objectives in Education*
1. Aims are the directions in education. They are the end-view of the possible achievement.	1. Objectives are points showing the possible achievement in directions.
2. Aims are the directions given to the entire educational system within and without the classroom.	2. Objectives are confined to the class-room and the school or an educational institution.
3. The aims of education cannot be changed from subject to subject.	3. Objectives may be changed from subject to subject. Objectives of teaching social science, will differ greatly from the objectives of natural and physical sciences.
4. The achievement of aims of education is beyond the scope of school programmes. There are other agencies of education also.	4. Objectives of instruction can be achieved.
5. Aims are broader.	5. Objectives originate from aims.
6. In the day-to-day work aims being broad and wide, hence have little significance.	6. Objectives being specific become meaningful.
7. Aims being very broad and wide are not very helpful in selecting the content of a subject.	7. Objectives being quite specific help in the selection of the subject matter and also teaching-learning activities.

Some Examples of Aims and Objectives

Aims	*Objectives*
1. To develop international brotherhood.	1. The pupils acquire the knowledge of the cultures of other countries.
2. To eradicate illiteracy.	2. The adults acquire the knowledge of 3 R's.
3. To create good and intelligent citizens.	3. Pupils understand the relationship between rights and responsibilities.
4. To establish a harmonious balance between	4. Pupils acquire basic knowledge of arts, literature and science.
5. To develop spiritualism among students.	5. Pupils learn how to lead a virtuous life.

Study Objectives

Professor C.E.M. Joad in his book 'About Education' has laid down the following objectives of education :

(i) To equip a boy or girl to earn his or her livelihood.

(ii) To equip him or her to play his or her part as the citizen of a democracy.

(iii) To enable him or her to develop all the latent powers and faculties of his or her nature to enjoy a good life.

For the achievement of these objectives, teaching of Economics can play an effective role.

Prof. Pigou, in his book entitled 'The Economics of Welfare' states the following two objectives of education :

(i) Acquisition of knowledge.

(ii) Solution to the practical problems of life.

The objectives of education suggested by Prof. Pigou can very easily form the basis of the objectives of study of Economics. The study of Economics provides us with knowledge and also helps us to solve the practical problems of life.

Prof. Marshall has very appropriately observed, "The aims of study of Economics are to gain knowledge for its own sake and to obtain guidance in the practical conduct of life and especially social life."

In their book captioned Teaching of the Social Studies in Secondary Schools, H. C. Binning and D. C. Binning have laid down the objectives of teaching Economics in these words :

"The aim of Secondary School Economics should be to teach modern economic principles by observation and through an understanding of current practices."

Pupils should be trained to apply sound economic theory to every day life of the economic problems of the present day, those connected with industry, tariff, taxation, the expenses of Government, and the cost of living, are but a few of the many that the citizen has to face continually. A thorough appreciation of these problems and a clear insight by pupils into the social and economic environment are aims that, when achieved, are worthwhile and contribute largely to the main aims of education." Thus the aims of teaching of Economics are :

(1) To study of the modern principles and theories of Economics.

(2) To train the students to make a practical use of knowledge of Economics in their day-to-day life.

(3) To equip the students to solve their day-to-day problems with the help of Economics.

(4) To develop in the students the insight to understand the social and economic environment.

O. Lipstreu in his book titled Experts Look At Consumers has pointed out following aims of the study of Economics :

(1) To promote wiser purchasing and consumption of food, clothing, shelter and help.

(2) To provide experiences that will improve the ability of students to make rational choices.

(3) To develop intelligent consumer citizenship.

(4) To acquaint the students with agencies and sources of information that are helpful to the consumer.

(5) To develop in the consumer a philosophy about the use of his leisure time as well as good 'buymanship' in satisfying his vocational interest.

(6) To cultivate an appreciation of the role of consumer in a profit economy.

(7) To develop high standard of values and tastes.

(8) To develop a broad social intelligence in economic problems.

(9) To promote co-operative attitudes so as to increase the economic well-being.

(10) To provide means of evaluating the techniques of advertising.

(11) To develop an understanding of the significance of public expenditures.

Prof. M. P. Moffat in his book Social Studies Instruction has formulated the following objectives of the teaching of Economics :

1. To acquaint the students with those general economic conditions and benefits which may help them in choosing a career.
2. To develop an intelligent consumer citizenship.
3. To develop the capacity of the students to increase national income.
4. To develop the practical understanding of the students regarding budget.
5. To develop the ability of the students to raise higher standard of living.

Norman Lee in Teaching of Economics has suggested the follwing objectives of Economics Teaching :

1. To provide intellectual training.
2. To prepare students for citizenship.
3. To provide vocational training.

Indian Teaching Norms

There are several paragraphs in the report of the Education Commission (1964-66), that clearly express national and economic concerns in the context of national development. These concerns form the basis of the teaching or study of Economics. In other words, these determine the aims and objectives of the study of Economics. Here it must be emphasised that economic concerns cannot altogether be separated from national concerns. In fact economic concerns play a major role in the reconstruction of the society as envisaged in the Indian Constitution.

The Education Commission 1964-66 has very clearly stated the principal national objective and the role of education in the opening paragraph of its report in chapter one entitled 'Education and National Development' : "The destiny of India is now being shaped in her classrooms. This we believe, is no more rhetoric. In a world based on science and technology, it is education that determines the level of prosperity, welfare and security of the people. On the quality and number of person coming out of our schools and colleges will depend our success in the great enterprise of national reconstruction the principal objective of which is to raise the standard of living of our people." Among the important problems in this regard, it laid emphasis on 'Economic Growth and Full Employment'. While discussing the role of education it observed, "In our opinion, no reform is more urgent than to transform education, to endeavour to relate it to the life, needs and aspirations of the people and thereby make it a powerful instrument of social, economic and cultural transformation necessary for the realization of our national goals. " This according to the Commission can be done if education

- is related to productivity;
- strengthens social and national integration; consolidates democracy as a form of government and helps the country to adopt it as a way of life;
- hastens the process of modernisation and
- strives to build character by cultivating social, moral and spiritual values. The Commission emphasised that all these aspects are interrelated in the complex process of social change. We cannot achieve even one without striving for all.

Accordingly, the Commission suggested the following two main programmes:

1. The Development of Physical Resources through the modernization of agriculture and industrialization. This requires the adoption of a science-based technology, heavy capital formation and investment and the provision of the essential infrastructure of transport, credit, marketing and other institutions.
2. The Development of the Human Resources, through a properly organized programme of education.

Again the Commission observed, "The realisation of country's aspiration involves changes in the knowledge, skills, interests, and values of the people as a whole. This is basic to every programme of social and economic betterment of which India stands, in need." For the fulfilment of all these objectives, teaching of Economics can go long way. Thus at every stage of Economics teaching, these national objectives must be kept in view.

In the light of above discussion, the aims and objectives of the teaching Economics are :

1. To enable the students to understand overall concerns of national development.
2. To enable the students to understand the role of economic development in the context of overall national development.
3. To enable the students to understand the economic problems facing the nation.
4. To enable the students to understand the role of planning in economic as well as national development.
5. To enable the students to understand the basic principles and practices of a socialism as envisaged in the constitution.
6. To enable the students to understand the principles and practices of mixed economy.
7. To enable the students to understand the need for increased productivity.
8. To enable the students to understand the need for providing equality of opportunity.
9. To enable the students to understand the economic theories and practices.
10. To enable the students to increase productivity in every endeavour.
11. To enable the students to take up some vocation suiting their abilities, aptitudes and interests when they complete their schooling.

12. To enable the students to start their own enterprise when they complete their schooling.
13. To enable the students to develop intelligent citizenship.
14. To develop in the student the skill of 'learning while earning' or 'earning while learning'.
15. To develop in the students a broad social intelligence in economic problems.
16. To develop in the students an understanding of the significance of public expenditure.
17. To promote cooperative attitude in the students to increase economic well being.
18. To provide experiences to the students to improve their ability to make rational choices.
19. To develop in the students the sentiment of emotional integration and national integration by emphasising the aspect of economic interdependence of various regions of the country.
20. To develop in the students high standards of ethical, moral and spiritual values.
21. To develop in the students high standards of tastes.
22. To develop in the students scientific outlook on economic issues also.
23. To enable the students to develop the art of spending money.

Wider Aims

The job of describing and deciding upon the desirable objective of teaching of Economics is done by the UGC in India. The UGC Report (1979) on The Modernisation of the Syllabi in Economics, for the first time, outlined, on an all-India basis, the aim of the B.A. courses as follows :

It should provide a balanced education which should improve the quality of citizenship and help the student comprehend and appreciate the problems of his society.

In the U.K., the report of the Joint Committee of the Royal Economic Society (1973) listed the following aims of the Economics curriculum :

(i) a capacity to understand both in theory and application the principles upon which an economy, such as that of the U.K., works;

(ii) a general understanding of the more important economic institutions within which the national economy operates; and

(iii) a capacity to handle, interpret and present the statistical evidence on which economic decisions are reached.

Particular Aims

The UGC Curriculum Development Centre (1989) in this regard has made useful observations :

"Knowledge of Economics is essential in many basic fields of learning and it is desirable that one gives a thought to differential course-contents according to the needs of the students. The number of students presently opting for Arts and Commerce courses is very large. Bearing in mind this development, as also the fact that the motivating factors of these students are extremely diverse, a major change in the form of a separation of courses according to the needs of the students is called for. The system of education has to be set up in such a way as to produce a range of outputs appropriate to the needs of the country." The question then is, should all students study the same course or would it be preferable to provide a range of courses aimed at different ability and requirement levels. Depending on the requirements, we can have the following classifications :

(i) Economics as a part of general education;

(ii) Economics for those who wish to pursue a professional non-academic career in the subject; and

(iii) Economics for those who wish to be academics.

It is obvious that the quality and contents of the course-material should be different if it is to be relevant from the point of view of the respective groups of students.

Role of General Education

1. To provide the student with an understanding of basic economic problems.
2. To teach to acquire and develop logical expresssion of ideas. The aim of teaching at this level should be to provide a balanced education which would improve the quality of citizenship, and help the student comprehend, and appreciate the problems of society. Such a point of view would have four major implications :
   (a) There should be no specialisation at the B.A. stage in the sense that the student is exposed to a broad variety of subjects;
   (b) These subjects should have relevance to economics;
   (c) As far as possible, stress should be laid on basic theories with application to Indian scene rather than on sophistication and;
   (d) The syllabi of different universities need not be identical but still ought to have a basic common content.

Typical Professionals

While there does exist a potential demand for economists, it has to go largely unsatisfied because the economic graduates we produce are unsuited for the job. To overcome this obstacle in the employability of economics students, we have to link teaching of economics with the needs of business and industry. If we can do so, then not only will we make the teaching of Economics job-oriented, but we will also satisfy a need which has very real social importance. In the opinion of some, an economist should be regarded as a trained expert or an applied technologist who is proficient in:

(i) optimisation methods and decision-making.

(ii) relating his/her expertise to the total life situation, and

(iii) devise solutions acceptable to the clients.

Professionals in Education

It is common observation that a great majority of students take up employment or take to business after graduation and even those students desirous of further academic pursuits are attracted towards management and other job-oriented career courses. Hence, we do not necessarily get the best of students joining up for post-graduation courses. Of these students, an even smaller number choose to become academics. Such students need to be given a thorough grounding in economic theory and in the handling of the tools of economic analysis. Economic theory, as it is taught to this group, should not be divorced from practical applications and should be allied and interwoven with the study of the organisation and structure of the economic system. The National Income approach which deals, qualitatively and quantitatively with the real causes which determine the wealth of nations, affords a good way to combine theory and reality. To cultivate the student's analytical faculty for understanding economic phenomena should be the prime objective here.

QUESTIONS

Essay Type Questions

1. Why do we need aims and objectives of education ? In what ways do these aims and objectives determine the aims and objectives of the teaching of Economics ?
2. What are the considerations in determining the aims and objectives of teaching Economics ?

3. What should be the aims and objectives of teaching Economics in the Indian context ?

4. State the significance of aims and objectives of teaching Economics at various stages ?

Short Answer and Objective Type Questions

5. State in brief the difference in aims and objectives.

6. Choose the correct alternative. The primary objective of teaching Economics is :
   (i) development of democratic ideals.
   (ii) development of scientific temper.
   (iii) development of economic efficiency.
   (iv) development of ethical values.

7. Tick (✓) the correct answer. For the development of consumer efficiency :
   (a) Philosophical perspective is needed.
   (b) Scientific perspective is needed.
   (c) Psychological perspective is needed.
   (d) Economic perspective is needed.

5

Area and Sphere

So far as its subject matter is concerned economics has a very extensive field. In fact all the activities of human beings have some bearing on economic activities. Economics tends to pervade all disciplines in one or the other form. Thus its scope is very wide.

The Sphere

The scope of Economics is determined by the way the economists look at it. Since economists have different views on the concept of Economics, its scope is naturally affected accordingly.

According to Milton Freidman, all economic problems come under the scope of Economics. He has stated, "Economics is the science of how a particular society solves its economic problems. An economic problem exists whenever scarce means are used to satisfy alternative ends." This approach confines the scope of Economics to a particular society only. But the present emphasis on globalisation extends the scope of Economics.

Samuelson's definition of Economics indicates that it is concerned with the production, distribution and consumption of commodities.

J. M. Keynes is his book "The Scope and Methods af Political Economy" has mainly included the following elements in the scope of Economics :

1. Subject matter of Economics.
2. Nature of Economics.
3. Relationship of Economics with other sciences.

Generally speaking, following elements are included in the scope of Economics :

1. Subject matter of Economics.
2. Nature of Economics.
3. Limitations of Economics.

The subject matter of Economics has been divided into two parts – Micro Economics and Macro Economics. Ragner Frisch of Oslo University (Norway) was the first economist to use these terms in 1933 which now have been adopted by economists all over the world.

The term Micro Economics is derived from the Greek word mikros meaning small and the term makros meaning large. Thus Micro Economics deals with the analysis of small individual units of the economy such as individual consumers, individual firms and small aggregates or groups of individual units such as various industries and markets. On the other hand, Macro Economics concerns itself with the analysis of the economy as a whole and its large aggregate such as total marginal output and income, total employment, total consumption, aggregate investment.

Macro Economics

Meaning. The word macro is derived from the Greek word 'makros' meaning 'large' and therefore Macro Economics is concerned with the economic activity in its 'largeness', i.e., it analyses the economic system in its totality. In the words of Professor Boulding, "Macro Economics deals not with individual quantities as such but with the aggregate of these quantities, not with the individual prices but with the price level, not with individual outputs but with the national output." Therefore, Macro Economics is also known as 'Aggregative Economics'.

According to Shapiro, "Macro Economics deals with the functioning of the economy as a whole." In the words of Gardner Ackley, "Macro Economics deals not with individual quantities as such but with aggregate of these quantities, not with individual incomes but with the national income, not with the individual prices but with the price level, not with the individual output but with the national output".

According to the 'Dictionary of Economics' (1998), Macro Economics is "The study of whole economic system aggregating over the functioning of individual economic units. It is primarily concerned with variables which follow systematic and predictable paths of bahaviour and can be analysed independently of the decision of the many agents who determine their level. More specifically, it is a study of national economics and the determination of national income".

Salient Features

1. It focuses on sectors of the economy but not those that function on separate units; instead those sectors run across the entire economy.
2. These sectors are the industrial sector, the personal sector, the financial sector, the government and overseas sector.
3. The main topics covered by Macro Economics are :
   (a) The determination of nations' income
   (b) Prices
   (c) Employment
   (d) The role of fiscal and monetary policy.

(e) The determination of consumption and investment.

(f) The balance of payments

(g) Economic growth.

According to the Dictionary of Economics, in recent years the tendency in academic Economics has been for macro economic models to be laid on micro economic foundations, circular flow of income and economic doctrines.

Micro Economics

According to the Dictionary of Economics by Graham Bannock, R.E. Baxter and Evan Davis (1998), Micro Economics is "The study of Economics at the level of individual consumer groups, or firms. No very sharp boundary can be drawn between Micro Economics and the other areas of the subject i.e. Macro Economics but its broad distinguishing feature is to focus on the choices facing, and the reasoning of individual decision makers." It further states that it is a long standing requirement of Micro Economics that it can justify the behaviour it ascribes to individual as being logical, given their preferences or prejudices.

The general concern of Micro Economics is the efficient allocation of scarce resources between alternative uses. But more specifically it involves the determination of price through the optimizing behaviour of economic agents, with cosumers maximising utility and firms maximising profit.

Area of Influence

The Micro Economics covers both the behaviour of individual sectors and the ways the sectors interact in equilibrium and disequilibrium in individual markets.

The Areas

The main areas of Micro Economics according to the Dictionary of Economics are:

1. Demand theory.
2. The theory of the firm.
3. The demand for labour and other factors of production.
4. Welfare Economics.
5. The study of the interaction between markets in general equilibrium analysis.

In the words of K. E. Boulding, "Micro Economics is the study of particular firms, particular households, individual prices, wages, incomes, individual industries, particular commodities."

Prof. A. P. Lamer in 'Micro Economics Theory' in Perspectives in Economics, edited by Brown Neuberger and Palmatier (1968) explains the concept of Micro Economics as. "Actually Micro Economics is much more intimately connected with the economy as a whole than is Macro Economics and can even be said to examine the whole economy microscopically."

According to Prof. Leftwitch, "Micro Economics is concerned with the economic affairs of such economic units as consumers resume owners and business firms."

The four basic issues namely :

1. What goods shall be produced and in what quantities ?
2. How shall they be produced ?
3. How shall the goods and services produced be distributed ?
4. Whether the production of goods and their distribution for consumption is efficients?

Importance and Uses of Micro Economics

1. Micro economic theory explains the consumption or allocation of total production.
2. It explains why somethings are produced more than others.

3. It provides depth in understanding as to how a free private enterprise economy operates.
4. It tells us how the goods and services produced are distributed among the various people for consumption, through price of market mechanism.
5. It shows how the relative prices of various products and factors are formed, that is, why the price of cloth is what and why the wages of an electrician are and so on.
6. It explains the conditions of efficiency in consumption and production.
7. It highlights the factors which are responsible for the departure from the efficiency or economic optimum.
8. It suggests suitable policies to promote economic efficiency and welfare of the people.
9. It teaches us that a completely 'direct' running of the economy is impossible, i.e., modern economy is so complex that no central planning authority can obtain all the information and provide appropriate directions necessary for its execution.

The Distinction

Prof. Gardner Ackley in his book 'Macro Economic Theory' (1961) explains the relationship between Macro Economics and Micro Economics in these words, "Macro Economics concerns itself with such variables as the aggregate volume of the output of an economy, with the extent to which its resources are employed with the size of the national income, with the 'general price level'. Micro Economics on the other hand, deals with 'division' of total output among industries, products and firms and the allocation of resources among competing ones. It considers problems of income distribution. Its interest is in relative prices of particular goods and services."

Macro Economics and Micro Economics both deal with 'aggregates' but there is a marked difference in the nature of 'aggregates' dealt with each. Macro Economics also uses aggregates smaller than for the whole economy but only in a context which makes them sub-divisions of an economywide total. Micro Economics also uses aggregates but not in a context which relates them to an economy wide total."

Actually Micro and Macro Economics are interdependent. As explained by Gardner Ackley, "The relationship between Macro Economics and the theory of individual behaviour is a two way street. On the one hand Micro Economics theory should provide the building blocks for our aggregate theories. But Macro Economics may also contribute to micro economic understanding. If we discover, for example, empirically stable micro economic generalisations which appear inconsistent with micro economic theories or which relate to aspects of behaviour which micro economics has neglected, Macro Economics may permit us to improve our understanding of individual behaviour."

Prof. Boulding, has observed, "It must not be thought because of the difference in their methods that Macro and Micro Economics are different. They are merely different ways of studying the same set of phenomenon." Prof. Samuelson has also stated, "There is really no opposition between Macro and Micro Economics. Both are absolutely vital. And you are only half-educated if you understand the one, being ignorant of the other."

Growth of Economy

The following characteristics of economic development would go a long way in explaining the meaning of economic development:

1. Prolonged and steady increase of national income.
2. Rise in the living standard of the people.
3. More equitable distribution of wealth among the population.
4. Improvement in the quality of life of the people.
5. Rise in the share of investment in national expenditure, leading to a rise in capital stock per person.

Comparative Study

Basis	*Micro Economics*	*Macro Economics*
1. Degree of Aggregate	Micro Economics studies individual units of the economy, like a firm like a firm oran industry etc.	Macro Economics deal with the aggregate of the economy, such as national income, total employment, general price level etc.
2. Objective	The objective of Micro Economics is to study the principles, problems, policies concerning the optimum allocation of resources.	The objective of Macro Economics is to study the problems, policies and priniciples relating to full employment of resources.
3. Method of Study	'Other things being equal' is the basis for the formulation of laws and principles. Effect of only one change and keeping other factors constant is determined.	In Macro Economics, mutual inter-dependence of different economic variables, e.g., total income, total consumption, total saving etc. is studied. This method of study is called 'general economic analysis'.
4. Paradox	Micro decisions may not hold true for the economy as a whole. For instance if an individual saves, he will be benefited.	But if the whole society starts saving it will reduce consumption, demand income etc. This paradox causes difference between Micro and Macro Economics.
5. Instrument	Demand and supply are its main instruments.	Aggregate demand and aggregate supply are its main instruments.
6. Alternative Nomenculture (name)	It is also called 'price theory'.	It is also called the 'income theory' or 'employment theory'.

6. Changes in the structure of national production, becoming more diversified as industry, utilities and services take a larger relative share, compared with agriculture and other forms of primary production.
7. Expansion in foreign trade sector relative to the whole economy, particularly as manufactured exports take a large share in an increased export total.
8. Population rising rapidly as death rates fall.
9. A demographic transition occurs in which improved living conditions in turn bring the birth rate down, to check the rate of overall population increase.
10. Population living in urban areas, changing from a small minority to large majority.
11. Rapid spread of literary skills and other forms of educational attainments.
12. Rise in the government budget relative to national income as the government undertakes expanded commitments to construct economic and social infrastructure.

Significance of the Subject

With a view to classifying Economics in the category of 'Science' or 'Art', we may explain in brief the characteristics of 'science'.

As propounded by Aristotle, science consist of a body of general truths.

Galbraith observes, "By science we mean a body of knowledge that seeks to tell the truth, the whole truth and nothing but truth."

According to Huxley, "By science, I understand all knowledge that rests upon evidence and reasoning."

Scientists are interested in particular truths as exemplified in general principles which have the following important characteristics :

1. Principles in science are arrived at as a result of the pursuit of methodical way and means.
2. The fundamental points are not random bits of information but are systematically related.
3. They repeat in the real sense of the word.
4. They are uniform.
5. They are available for observation and experimentation.
6. They are exact.
7. They are objective and free from personal bias and prejudices.
8. They have a practical value. Mastery of a field helps one to control the present and predict the future.
9. Measurability is an essential and strict characteristics of science.

Economics is a science in the sense that it pursues its techniques to establish and interpret facts. Like Physics, Chemistry or Natural Sciences, Economics is also an empirical field of study. It employs many methods of enquiry such as observation, classification, framing hypotheses and analysing evidence before interpreting facts. Though Economics uses scientific techniques, we must realise that as Economics deal with human affairs which are very complex, results in Economics cannot be so accurate and exact.

A scientist concentrates his attention on extracting general truths and is in a position to predict quite fairly. An economist on the other hand is engrossed in the peculiarities of a particular event. Economists cannot be prophets but a study of the economic history of a country or a movement does put them in a position to forecast its future. The fundamental difference is that the course of human history is influenced by uncertain events and therefore, it is rather impossible to anticipate the future and predict it with any amount of certainty.

Some scholars accordingly argue that Economics cannot be called a science in view of the following :

1. The facts of Economics are very complicated.
2. The facts of Economics seldom repeat in the real sense of the term.
3. The underlying facts of Economics have a very wide scope and they are so varied that they can seldom be uniform.
4. Economic data are normally not available for observation and experimentation.
5. Economic data are the product of economic activities which are constantly changing. They therefore, cannot provide dependable data for the formulation of general laws and principles.

The economist's work is concerned largely with the character and reliability of resources. Facts may be arranged in a systematic manner and in accordance with the established laws of research, but the information is inferior to the data available in natural or physical sciences. The economist does not have the direct experience of phenomenon which he tries to explain.

Human beings are made up of individuals and no individuals are alike. Every human being has something unique in spirit, if not in body.

There are two types of sciences—physical or natural and social. Economics is not a physical or natural science but is certainly a social science. It does employ the methods of social sciences in the following forms :

1. In Economics we collect data from different sources.
2. In Economics we use a variety of methods to collect the data.
3. In Economics we carefully and systematically analyse, classify and sort out the collected data.
4. The laboratory of Economics is the 'universe', the ingredients of which are obtained from various human beings.

5. In Economics, we lay down certain principles and theories on the basis of observation, analysis and comparative study of events.

In the absence of unanimity among economists as is clear from the following statements, the claim of Economics to be regarded as a science has been challenged.

1. According to Prof. Viner, "Economics is what economists do."
2. In the words of Wosten, "Whenever six economists are gathered, there are seven views." — 'In Lament for Economics' (1938).
3. Wosten has further observed, "Economists are under suspicion of being charlatans and they cannot afford to arrogate honourable titles to themselves..... In the increasingly common application by theoretical economists of the term science to their studies, there is an element of wishfulment... The zealous student of Economics science would do well from time to time to remind himself that of all the demand and supply, cost surveys or indifference curves that give so formidable appearance to his text book, not one (unless by accident) is founded upon fact.... The reader would search far and wide through the works of analytical economists before he came upon single prediction endorsed by the weight of authoritative opinion of the course of events to be anticipated in any concrete historical situations."
4. Bernard Shaw has remarked, "If the economists of this world were laid end to end, they would not reach a conclusion."
5. Poincare has stated, "Economics is built up of facts as a house is built of stones, but all accumulation of facts is no more a science than a heap of stones in a house."
6. To quote Durbin, "Certainty will always escape us and prediction miss the mark."

Economics as an Art

The answer to the question whether Economics is an art or not depends upon what we consider to be an art. An art is a systematised body of knowledge but unlike a science it lays down precepts or specific solutions for specific problems. The objective of art is the formulation of precepts applicable to policy. Applying this concept of art to Economics, we find that Economics is in certain respects an art as well. There are several branches of Economics which offer us practical guidance in the solution of economic problems.

The theory of consumption provides us the well known law of substitution which tells consumers how to maximise their satisfaction from expenditure.

The theory of production offers help in the task of industrial organisation and minimisation of costs.

The modern theory of employment affords practical guidelines to governments in combating cyclic unemployment. Examples can be multiplied.

Academic Science

Instead of considering Economics as a Science and an Art, some economists prefer to classify it into Pure Economics and Applied Economics. The view of such economists is that these terms are more scientific and conducive to better understanding of Economics. Pure Science confirms itself to accurate description of a phenomenon. It explains what it is, how it works and what its effects are. It, however, does not concern itself with what ought to be. It also does not tell us whether the effects are good or bad. On the other hand, applied science takes the knowledge acquired from pure science and applies it to economic problems. Pure science furnishes the tools with which applied science works with. Thus Economics is both a pure and an applied science.

Practical Aspects

Experimental approach or method is usually associated with physical sciences. It is also widely held that an experiment can only be conducted in a place known as 'Laboratory' where it is possible to control various factors so as to obtain objective results. Experiment method permits the formulation of various designs keeping in view the important characteristics of the experimental method. It is felt that this cannot be used in an economic study. We cannot do in Economics what the experimenter can do in Physics. We cannot take a portion of the community in our hands, view it in different aspects and place it in different positions in order to solve problems and satisfy our speculative curiosity.

It is true that the experiments of the types of physical sciences cannot be carried on in Economics. Nevertheless we can adopt experimental approach in the study of Economics. If we observe minutely, we realise that some experiments are made every moment in Economics also. Experiments in different forms of economic systems, are being conducted in different countries and in regions of the same country also. It is observed by Garner that enactment of every law, the establishment of every new situation, the inauguration of every new policy is an experiment in the sense that it is regarded merely as provisional or tentative until the results have proved its fitness to become permanent.

Rules and Regulations

Meaning of a Law. In the words of Marshall, "Economic laws, or statements of economic tendencies are those social laws, which relate to branches of conduct in which the strength of the motives chiefly concerned can be measured by money price."

Characteristics of Economic Laws

Lack of Exactitude – Marshall has compared economic laws to the laws of tides rather than to the simple laws of gravitation.

Hypothetical – Economic laws are conditional since their validity depends upon the fulfilment of certain conditions. They simply state that other things being equal, certain results will follow.

Statement of Tendencies – As observed by Moore and others, "There is no convenient yardstick by which to measure the currents in business affairs, for these are subject to gusts of fear or perhaps of fantastic optimism as unpredictable as earthquakes."

Limited Applicability – Laws of Economics have only a limited application to a given environment. For example, Bagehot has observed that Laws of Economics propounded in England were applicable to a grown up society of competitive commerce.

Fundamental Concepts

Principle of Maximisation – According to Mrs. Joan-Robbinson, "The fundamental assumption of economic analysis is that every individual acts in a sensible manner and it is sensible for the individual to balance marginal cost and marginal gain." In actual practice, this assumption may not work.

Constant Consumer Behaviour – It is assumed that the consumer's tastes remain unchanged for fairly long periods of time. This, however, has limited validity in the fast changing scientific and technological scenario which affects all types of behaviour including consumer behaviour.

Perfect Competition – The economists proceed on the basis of a perfectly competitive model. This again is not based on reality.

The Concept of Equilibrium – Equilibrium implies a situation from which no departure is desired. It is a point of maximum satisfaction for the consumer, firm, industry or entrepreneur.

'No Other Change' – Most of the statements of economic laws are qualified by the statement 'Other things being equal'.

Existence of Certain Institutions – It is assumed that in a capitalist order of society the institution of private property exists. Likewise there are assumptions regarding the existence of political stability, law and order and markets etc.

Miscellaneous Assumption – It is assumed that technical factors put a limit to industrial output. Geographical factors are also assumed. It is accepted that harvest time is influenced by nature and the most important assumption is that goods are at a premium.

QUESTIONS

Essay Type Questions

1. Explain the various dimensions of Economics.
2. Into how many divisions would you divide the subject-matter of Economics ? Explain each division in brief ?
3. What main elements would you include in the scope of Economics ? Write brief note on each.
4. Differentiate between the traditional approach and the modern approach to the division of the subject matter of Economics.
5. Explain the concepts of Micro Economics and Macro Economics. State the subject matter included in each.
6. Make a comparative study of Micro Economics and Macro Economics.
7. Explain the relationships of economic knowledge.
8. "Economics is what the economists do." In this context explain the definition and scope of Economics.
9. "Whenever six economists are gathered, there are seven points." In this context explain the nature of Economics.
10. Discuss the nature of Economics as normative science. What is its practical importance?
11. What are the characteristics of economic laws ? State their basic assumptions.

Short Answer and Objective Type Questions

12. Write short notes on – (i) Macro Economics, (ii) Micro Economics, (iii) Economics as a science.

13. Write 'Yes' or 'No' against each statement :
    (i) Macro Economics includes theory of demand. ( )
    (ii) Micro Economics includes theory of income. ( )
    (iii) Macro Economics includes economics of welfare. ( )
    (iv) Micro Economics includes fiscal economics. ( )
14. Give the origin of the word 'Mirco Economics' and 'Macro Economics'.
15. Write two points to show that Economics is not a science.

6

Aims of Teaching

Tests, examinations or evaluation are the mileposts along the road of learning and are supposed to tell the teacher and the learner (student) the degree to which both have been successful in their achievement of the course objectives. An instructional objective may be defined as an intent communicated by a statement describing a proposed change in a learner—a statement of what the learner is to be like when he has successfully completed a learning experience. There are several objectives to be achieved through instruction and accordingly several learning experiences are provided. The statement of objectives of a teaching programme must denote 'measurable' attributes 'observable' in the learners. As Robert E. Mager has said, "An instructor will function in a fog of his own working until he knows just what he wants his students to be able to do at the end of the instruction."

The Pereptions

Specification of educational objectives in concrete and practical terms implies that emphasis shifts from teaching the subject to that of teaching the pupil. It is specified in terms of pupil's behaviour.

As instructional objective serves the following purposes :

1. It makes the instructional goal very clear.
2. It delimits the scope of each objective.
3. It indicates the depth of each objective.
4. It helps in determining the instructional strategy.
5. It makes instruction meaningful by pinpointing the behaviour or desired change.
6. It provides the basis for the selection and application of education procedure.
7. It provides insight into the linkages to be forged in the whole teaching-learning process thereby integrating instruction and evaluation.

Objectives Compared

Educational Objectives	*Instructional Objectives*
1. Philosophy determines educational objectives.	1. Psychology is the basis of instructional objectives.
2. Educational objectives are very broad.	2. Instructional objectives are very specific.
3. All schools subjects may have common educational objectives.	3. Each school subject has specific teaching or instructional objective.
4. Educational objectives include instructional objectives.	4. Instructional objective form a part of educational objectives.
5. Examples of educational objectives are : development of character, emotional and national integration, democratic values, secularism etc.	5. Examples of instructional objectives are : Behaviour patterns of a man of character-characteristics of a man of character-how he conforms to a situation in honesty etc.

Fundamental Objectives

1. The statement of an objective should include both (a) the kind of behavioural outcome expected and (b) the content. The former is sometimes called competence or modification part. The term modification implies that it is at the level of the individual's behaviour that the change occurs as a result of learning. Content on the other hand is the medium for the realisation of the desired behaviour . It does not acquire any direction unless it is harnessed to mental processes. It is the question of activising a product through the application of processes using various communication symbols. For example, Summer monsoon is just an item of knowledge but educationally it becomes meaningful only when we say : the pupil explains the causes of the reversal of wind movement during the monsoon season.
2. An objective should be conceived and stated in terms of pupil's behaviour.
3. Objectives should be worked out at the right level of generality (specificity) which are to be neither so vague nor so specific or atomistic as to be non-functional. Complex or compound objectives need particular attention in this respect.
4. Objectives should be stated non-compositely, so as to avoid confusion, repetition and contradiction.
5. Objectives in a list should not overlap. It may be helpful to group together similar objectives.
6. Objectives should be so stated that there is a clear indication and even distinction among learning situation required for realising different behaviour changes. For example, learning situations for memorizing certain facts would be basically different from the ones needed for developing critical thinking.

7. Objectives need to be conceived in terms of continuity of growth over a period. They should essentially be developmental in their purport representing roads to travel rather than the terminal points.
8. Worthwhileness of objectives should be carefully judged from various points of view particularly their social acceptability.
9. Objectives should be realistic. They should be attainable through available or pi-ocurable resources and testable through available or manipulable tools.
10. The list of objectives as a whole should be comprehensive enough to cover different outcomes expected of an educational programme in the cognitive, affective and the psychomotor domains.

The Tasks

The work of identifying well-defined behavioural changes requires that broader objectives should be broken down into more specific ones to a limit where they stand fully clarified and delimited. This step is often known as specifying objectives and its product comes to be known as 'specification(s)'. The specifications are thus the 'behavioural outcomes' expected as a result of learning experiences emanating from a learning situation. It is an exercise in meaningful analysis.

A practical way of getting at the specifications of an objective is first to state the objective, comprehend what we mean by it and then to seek answers to the question "what the students will be able to do to exhibit to us the achievement of the particular objective on their part." The answers will be specifications.

The Relationship

In order to clearly visualise the relationship between objectives and pupils' activities, let us for a while study the following table, giving the activities and the corresponding objective that each can help achieve and try to draw some conclusions from it :

Pupils' Activities	*Objective*
Practical work	Understanding, Skill
Organising an exhibition	Interest, Appreciation, Application, Skill
Excursion	Knowledge, Understanding
Discussion	Understanding, Critical Thinking
Lecture	Knowledge, Understanding
Dramatisation	Comprehension, Interest

Classification of Instructional Objectives in Economics

(1)	(2)	(3)	(4)	(5)
Development of Knowledge (Information)	Development of Scholastic Abilities	Development of Practical Skills	Development of Interest in the Subject	Development of Personal and Social Qualities

Academic Development

Objective—To acquire the knowledge (information) of facts, terms, concepts, conventions and trends, principles and generalisations, assumptions, hypotheses, problems, processes etc. in Economics.

Specification of the Objective—To demonstrate the achievement of the above objective the pupil :

(a) recalls facts, terms, concepts, principles, trends, etc.

(b) recognises facts, terms, concepts, principles, trends etc.

(c) reads information from various forms of representation of data, i.e., charts, diagrams, graphs, maps, tables etc.

Scholar's Capabilities

Objective 1—To develop an understanding of facts, terms, concepts, conventions and trends, principles and generalisation, assumptions, hypotheses, problems, processes etc. in Economics.

Specification of the Objective—To demonstrate the achievement of the above objective the pupil :

(a) discriminates

(b) classifies

(c) compares and contrasts

(d) identifies relationship

(e) detects the points of emphasis and the trends of arguments

(f) cites illustration

(g) detects errors and fallacies and rectifies them

(h) explains (analyses or gives meaning or clarifies or elucidates)

(i) gives reasons or advances arguments.

(j) interprets data presented in different forms.

Objective 2—To apply the acquired knowledge and its understanding to unfamiliar situation.

Specification of the Objective—To demonstrate the achievement of the above objective the pupil :

(a) analyses the unfamiliar situation or problem,

  (i) finds out what is given and what is required.

  (ii) recalls knowledge relevant to the situation.

  (iii) judges sufficiency or unsufficiency, adequacy or inadequacy of data or any other evidence for solving the problem.

(b) establishes relationships.

(c) suggests alternative methods for solving the problem.

(d) establishes relationships.

(e) draws inference and makes generalisation.

(f) makes predictions regarding the probable outcome of a given situation.

Skill Development

Objective—To acquire practical skills essential for the study of Economics.

Specification of the Objective—To demonstrate the achievement of the above objective, the pupil :

(a) draws charts, diagrams, graphs, maps and tables etc. from the given data.

(b) translates data from one form of presentation to another.

(c) prepares models.

Subject Attraction

Objective—To develop interest in the subject and problems related to the economic life of the people.

Specification of the Objective—To demonstrate the achievement of the above objective, the pupil :

(a) voluntarily studies literature related to Economics and tries to know about the inherent issues and problems.

(b) spends leisure time in trying to know about economic problems and issues and exerts in finding out solutions to them.

(c) closely observes economic processes and changes at local, national and international level.

(d) discusses and is able to communicate various aspects of everyday economic problems and their implications.

(e) enthusiastically participates in excursions, visits and field trips to places of economic activity (farm, factories, fairs etc.).

(f) collects information about the economic systems and facts about the economy of other localities, regions and countries.

Characteristics : Individual and Collective

Objective—To develop desirable positive attitudes necessary for developing a broader outlook.

Specification of the Objective—To demonstrate the achievement of the above the pupil :

(a) respects the views, opinions and problems of others and displays sympathy and fellow feeling towards them

   (i) shows tolerance.

   (ii) controls emotions and displays restrains.

   (iii) discusses impartially issues of disagreement with others.

(b) unhesitatingly mixes with people of different economic strata.

(c) judges issues objectively and on their merits.

(d) assumes responsibility in cooperation ventures.

(e) displays abhorence towards

   (i) socio-economic moral practices like hoardings, profiteering, blackmarketing, evasion of taxes, smuggling etc.

   (ii) wasteful, showful and uneconomic expenditure.

(f) realises the importance and respects man's potential and his contribution to national economic development.

[Adapted from Teaching Units on Evolution of Indian Economy' NCERT, New Delhi. (1983)]

QUESTIONS

Essay Type Questions

1. State the meaning and significance of an instructional objective in Economics. What are the basic principles of stating instructional objectives in Economics ?
2. Differentiate between educational objectives and instructional objectives in Economics.
3. Give the meaning of instructional objectives in Economics. Classify them and write any one instructional objective and its specification.

Short Answer and Objective Type Questions

4. Mention any three instructional objectives in Economics,
5. Classify the following into the type of instructional objective in Economics :
   (i) The pupil recognises recalled facts in Economics.
   (ii) The pupil discriminates terms in Economics.
   (iii) The pupil establishes relations between causes and effects in Economics.
   (iv) The pupil discusses everyday economic problems.
   (v) The pupil controls emotions.

7

Methods of Teaching

Method is defined by Thut and Gerbersich in these words, "A method is a well defined pattern of procedures within which a variety of the techniques and devices may appear as circumstances may require."

The effect of recent developments in educational philosophy and educational psychology upon the methods of teaching has been revolutionary. Any process that is not based upon the 'student-activity' is not in accord with recent educational theories. Rousseau considers that 'child' is a 'hero' in the 'drama of education' and as such he must play the dominant role.

The Secondary Education Commission 1952-53 has emphasised the need for using right methods of teaching in these words, "Every teacher and educationist of experience knows that even the best curriculum and the most perfect syllabus remain dead unless quickened into life by the right methods of teaching and the right kind of teachers. Sometimes even an unsatisfactory and unimaginative syllabus can be interesting and significant by the gifted teacher who does not focus his mind on the subject-matter to be taught or the information to be imparted but on his students—their interests and aptitudes, their reactions and response. He judges the success of his lesson not by the amount of matter covered but by the understading, the appreciation and the efficiency achieved by the students." The Commission has further observed, "Any method, good or bad links up the teacher and his pupils into an organic relationship with constant mutual interaction, it reacts not only on the mind of the students but on their entire personality; their standards of work and judgement, their intellectual and emotional equipment, their attitudes and values. Good methods which are psychologically and socially sound may raise the whole quality of their life; bad method debase it. So, in the choice and assessment of methods, teachers must always take into consideration their end products, namely, the attitudes and values inculcated in them consciously or unconsciously."

James Welton has stressed the significance of good methods of teaching, "The teacher is like a guide and the pupil like a traveller in an unknown country. The traveller knows where he wanted to go, but knows neither the way not the exact character of the place he wishes to go.......... But unless the traveller that is that pupil takes the journey himself, nothing is accomplished. Many lesson is too much like a guide describing the journey to the would-be traveller who sits and listens but does not leave his chair to undertake it. In other lessons, the guide himself laboriously takes the journeys again and again, but the traveller that should be, remains inert. In short, no matter how admirably a lesson is planned, there is no really methodical teaching unless the pupils by their own efforts pass along the road tacit for them. True teaching is nothing but arousing and directing activity."

In the words of Herbard Ward and Frank Rosceor, "While it is true that good method is not merely a collection of artifices or mechanical devices and that every teacher must devise his own method, it is important to remember that good methods can result only from the constant observation of certain broad principles. These include orderly procedure in teaching, an arrangement of the subject matter which will avoid waste of time and of energy and a distribution of emphasis which will secure the greatest cooperation from the pupils and maintain their active interest."

Dynamic Methods

1. The origin of modern methodology may be traced to 'Great Didactic of Johann Amos Comenius who lived in the seventeenth century. Comenius believed that all instruction should be carefully graded and arranged in a natural order. He advocated that the teacher, in his methods, should appeal through sense perception to the understanding of the child. He set forth his principles in his 'Great Didactic'. The world of Comenius, however, like that of other educators of his time was buried beneath the sea of religious controversy and bigotry of his age.
2. 'Emile' of Rousseau in the second half of the eighteenth century laid the foundations of the methodology that became the inspiration of forward looking and progressive educators. Comenius provided some ideas, Rousseau improved and enlarged and others worked them and put them into practice. In his chief educational work 'Emile', Rousseau begins with his principle "Everything is good as it comes from the hands of the Author of Nature; but everything degenerates in the hands of man." He points out that there are three great teachers, 'nature, man and things'.
3. Johann Heinrick Pestalozzi attempted to 'psychologise instruction'. He declared that the basis of all education was a drawing out process and not a pouring in process and that the basis of all education lay in the nature of the child and that methods of instruction must be sought and constructed to that end.
4. Wilhelm August Froebel and Johann Friedrich Herbart, disciples and followers of Pestalozzi developed elaborate systems of education. The work of Froebel dealt largely with the Kindergarten stage. Herbart gave his

famous 'Herbartian Steps' which cast a flood of light on existing methods. Herbartian steps became the stimulators of various other movements in the field of education. Herbart condemned the rote method and stressed comprehension and association. The concept that the outcome of education was not the strengthening of the mental faculties but rather the building up of an 'apperceptiveness' of ideas was very revolutionary: Herbartian theory and practice became popular in Germany between 1865 and 1885. Teachers and students from many lands studied at Jena, a centre of Herbartian teaching. By 1890, these ideas were brought to America where they received an almost universal acceptance.

5. The period of Herbartian influence, on the whole, was a transitional one. It prepared the way for newer and better concepts of education. By 1910, Herbartian as a system of education was quite generally criticised. Herbartianism stressed the teacher and the formal procedure of teachings; the new theories of educational philosophy emphasised the pupils. Emphasis during recent years has been on individual instruction in the classroom but the socialisation of the individual is not to be negelected. Almost all modern methods and procedures can be used to promote both.

6. Dewey endeavoured to substitute bookish learning by experience. He strongly recommended investigation and experimentation. According to him the school is a 'special environment' where a certain quality of life and certain types of activities and occupations are provided with the object of securing children's development along desirable lines. "The teacher", according to him, "is a guide and director, he steers the boat but the energy that propels it must come from those who are learning."

7. Children have been endowed by nature with tremendous vitality. They have within them the springs of youth, joy and vigour. They possess curiosity and wish

> to know things for themselves. In the words of T.S. Avinashilingam, "The Great Ganga of life flows majestically on. But if anyone tries to retain and dam it, the dam will break unless attempts are simultaneously made to divert it into other channels. These waters can only be diverted, but cannot be dammed indefinitely. If anyone tried to do the impossible, it would be at his peril, for the dam will break, sooner or later. So is the nature of children. The great vitality of our children cannot be permanently restrained without providing a positive purpose. In ordinary bookish classroom education, the teacher teaches, students are but passive listeners. Their energy has not to be restrained by fear, inducement or punishment. This is against their nature and that is why we see much outbursts of so-called indiscipline. But, on the other hand, if we provide such activities in which the children themselves can take part we will find that discipline becomes natural. Thus, providing for various types of activities which will interest the children and give them opportunities for observation and the use of their hands is to offer them the fulfilment and satisfaction, which nothing else confers."

The principle of 'Learning by Doing' has been accepted by all the progressive educators and in all the progressive countries. All educationists recognise that activity as an important instrument of education.

Effective Methods

These may be listed as under :

1. They should aim at inculcating 'love of work'.
2. They should aim at developing the desire to do work with the highest measure of efficiency of which one is capable. The motto of every school and his pupils should be 'Everything that is worth doing at all is worth doing well.' Whether it be making a speech, writing a compo-

sition, drawing a map, cleaning the class-room, making a book, rack of forming a queue.

3. They should provide numerous opportunities of participation in freely accepted projects and activities in which discipline and co-operation are constantly in demand.
4. They should aim at developing the capacity for 'clear thinking' which distinguishes every truly educated person, "whether a student is asked to make a speech in a debating society or to write an essay or to answer a question in Commerce, History, Geography, or Science or an experiment, the accent should always be on clear thinking and on lucid expression which is a mirror of clear thought."
5. The methods of teaching should expand the range of students' interest. "We should urge all schools to provide in the time-table, at least one free period every day in which students may pursue their favourite hobbies and creative activities individually or in groups, preferably under the guidance of some interested teacher," recommended the Secondary Education Commission.
6. They should aim at providing opportunities to pupils to apply practically the knowledge that has been acquired by them. They should aim at transforming present bookish schools into 'work schools' or 'activity schools'.
7. They should aim at the quickening of interest and training in efficient techniques of learning and study.
8. They should train the students in the art of study. They should train the students in the use of reference material such as the list of contents and index in books, the dictionary, the atlas, and reference books like the encyclopaedia.
9. They should be adapted to suit different levels of intelligence.

10. They should be such as they balance the claim of individual work with co-operative or group effort. The training of emotions, attitudes and social capacities take place best in the context of projects and units of work undertaken co-operatively. The Secondary Education Commission has recommended that the teachers should be so trained that they are able to visualise and organise at least a part of the curriculum in the form of projects and activity units which groups of students may take up and carry to completion.

Classification of Methods of Teaching

There are a large number of ways of the classification of methods of teaching. Sometimes they overlap. Sometimes they include some techniques and devices of teaching also. As a matter of fact it is a very difficult task rather an impossible task to draw a line to distinguish these. Classification is also arbitrary.

Classification 1. Broad Classification

(1)	(2)	(3)
Telling Methods	Showing Methods	Doing Methods

Classification 2. Based on the Size of the Audience

(1)	(2)	(3)	(4)
Large Group Instruction	Medium Group Instruction	Small Group Instruction	Independent Study

Classification 3. Methods based Upon Equipment

(1)	(2)	(3)
Text Book Method	Library Method	Laboratory Method

Classification 4. Methods Based on Approach

(1)	(2)	(3)
Verbal	Specimen	Excursion

Classification 5. Methods Based on Organisation of Material

(1)	(2)	(3)	(4)	(5)	(6)
Chronological	Psychological	Topical	Integration	Unitary	Problematic

Classification 6. Methods Based on Specific Purpose

(1)	(2)	(3)	(4)
Explanatory	Reasoning	Diagnostic	Developmental

Contd.

Classification 7. Methods Based on Specific Student Purpose

(1)	(2)	(3)
Problematic	Project	Socialised

Classification 8. Methods based on Individual or Group Activity

(1)	(2)	(3)	(4)
Individual Activity	Committee Activity	Class Activity	Cooperative Activity

Classification 9. Methods Based on Teacher-Student Relationship

(1)	(2)	(3)
Assignment Method	Supervised Method	Freely Chosen Project Method

Classification 10. Methods Based Upon Pupil Participation

(1)	(2)	(3)
Systematic Participation	Socialised Recitation	Student Planned Activity

Classification 11. Methods Based on Physical Senses

(1)	(2)	(3)
Visual	Auditory	Both

Classification 12. Methods Based on Theories of Learning

(1)	(2)	(3)
Drill	Problem Solving	Activity

Classification 13. Methods Based Upon the Degree of Independence of Thought

(1)	(2)
Heuristic	Experimental

Classification 14. Methods Based upon Objectives of Education

(1)	(2)	(3)
Cooperative group work	Creative	Democratic

Classification 15. Miscellaneous Methods

(1)	(2)	(3)	(4)	(5)	(6)	(7)
Discovery Methods Methods	Encounter Methods	Expository Methods	Individualised Methods	Inspirational Methods	Natural Learning	Project Method

The Categories

Telling Methods—These include lecture method, debates and discussions, panel discussion, oral quiz, story telling etc.

Showing Methods—These comprise using demonstration, Charts, diagrams, observation of on-site operations etc.

Doing Methods—These consist of assignments, committee work, guided experiences, projects work, written tests etc.

Large Group Instruction—This includes descriptive method, lecture method, tele-lecture etc.

Medium Group Instruction—This denotes informal lecturing such as discussions in medium groups, dialogue, buzz groups, brain storming, role playing, demonstration, field trips etc.

Small Group Instruction—Seminars and discussions in small groups are the important methods covered in this category.

Independent Study—Under this mention may be made of the assignments, use of Dalton Plan, programmed learning, computerised instruction, committee work, work experiences etc.

Classification of Methods of Teaching: Methods of teaching Economics may be classified as under.

Discovery Methods—These methods are high on all the three dimensions; learner activity, experience and experimentation by the learner, and cognitive understanding. Simulations primarily come under this category. The main emphasis of methods in this category is on problem-solving and providing necessary framework to the learner, so that while solving the problem the learner is also able to learn the rationale and logic of what he has done.

Encounter Methods—Carl Rogers popularised the term 'Encounter'. Since the emphasis is on providing experience through confrontation or through encounter, and not through cognitive understanding, these methods are affective for change in basic behavioural patterns and developing new ways of looking at things. Role play also involves some amount of encounter.

Expository Methods—In these methods cognitive emphasis is very high, while emphasis on experience is low. One good example of expository method is the lecture method in which the main emphasis is on imparting cognitive information to the learners.

Individualized Methods—These methods are quite well known mainly through the popularity of programmed instruction. The main characteristic of these methods is the guided search encouraged by the instructor or the teacher. In addition to programmed instructions, self-study, computer-oriented instruction, case method, and prescribed experiments in science are other examples of individualized learning in which the main emphasis is for each learner to learn at his own pace.

Inspirational Methods—These methods are primarily based on high activity on the part of the instructor or the teacher. Giving a sermon to the students or to any group of learners is a good example of this methodology.

Natural Learning Methods—The main rationale of these methods is that learning takes place in a natural way and planning for learning is not necessary. Learners are left on their own, with free and unplanned activity. Thus, the emphasis on learning activity is high, whereas it is low on planned experience and on cognitive inputs.

Project Method—This is discussed in detail separately. Whether the method is activity-centred, life-centred, pupil-centred, teacher-centred or even subject-centred, there must be the abiding enthusiasm and interest of the teacher which would make teaching-learning efficient, enjoyable and pleasant.

Among the important methods, following deserve careful attention. However, it may be stated that these methods overlap in their treatment and it is not always possible to draw a clear-cut line.

1. Assignment Method
2. Case Study Method
3. Dalton Method
4. Discussion Method

5. Home Assignment or Home Task
6. Laboratory Method
7. Lecture Method
8. Note Dictation
9. Observation Method
10. Problem Method
11. Project Method
12. Question-Answers Method
13. Quiz Method
14. Review Method
15. Role Playing/Group Dynamics Method
16. Socialised Classroom Recitation Method
17. Source Method
18. Story Method
19. Supervised Study Method
20. Survey Method
21. Textbook Method

(*Note*—Sometimes some methods of teaching are also called techniques of teaching and vice versa. There is no water-tight compartment between methods and techniques. However, the Dalton Plan, the Problem Method and the Project Method are not used as techniques of teaching.)

Lecture Method

Significance of the Lecture Method—It is the oldest teaching method given by philosophy of idealism. As used in education, the lecture method refers to the teaching procedure involved in the clarification or explanation to the students of some major idea. This method lays emphasis on the presentation of the content. Teacher is more active and students are passive but he also used question answer to keep them attentive in the class. It is used to clarify matters, to expand content and motivate the students. By changing his voice, by impersonating characters, by shifting his position and by using simple devices, a teacher can deliver his lesson effectively. While delivering his lecture, a teacher can indicate by his facial expression, gestures and tones the exact shade of meaning that he wishes to convey.

Merits of the Lecture Method—Following are the merits of the lecture method :

1. It is economical as it needs no apparatus and no laboratory. A large number of students can be taught at a time.
2. It saves time and covers syllabus in a limited time.
3. It is very effective in giving factual information and in relating some of the thrilling anecdotes with historical lessons. The life stories of great adventurers, experimenters, investigators and thinkers can become very interesting and valuable talks by a teacher.
4. Lecturing makes the work of the teacher very simple. He need not make elaborate arrangements.
5. A good lecture not only stimulates the students but also lingers long in their imagination. It motivates students to become good orators.
6. It provides better scope for clarification and for laying stress on significant ideas.
7. It brings a personal contact and touch to impress or influence the pupils.
8. It provides flexibility. As the teacher is in close and intimate contact with pupils, he can adjust his technique in accordance with their abilities, aptitudes and interests.
9. It gives the students training in listening.
10. It gives the students training in taking notes rapidly.
11. It develops good audience habits.
12. It provides opportunities of correlating events and subjects.

13. It enables the linkage of previous knowledge with the new one.

Limitations—The limitations of this method are as follows :

1. There is very little scope for pupil activity.
2. It does not take into consideration individual differences.
3. Lecturing is against the principle of 'Learning by doing'.
4. It spoonfeeds the students without developing their power of reasoning.
5. Speed of the lecture may be too fast for the learner to grasp the line of thought.
6. An average student may not be able to fix up his attention to a lecture to forty to forty-five minutes.
7. A lecturer is likely to cover more content without realising that little learning takes place.
8. A lecture may become monotonous to the students after a while. Very few teachers can keep the interest of the student upto the end.

Guidelines for the Effective Use of the Lecture Method—The following points should be kept in view in using this device of teaching :

1. Matter should be arranged in such a way as to leave a single clear impression on the minds of the students.
2. Teacher should have pauses in between the lesson so that the students may learn the new knowledge bit by bit.
3. The rate of exposition should be slow when the class is backward. The teacher should utilise different ways of presenting the same information.
4. There should be abundant repetition but it should be in a new way so that the class may not feel dullness.
5. Children's way to looking at things should be considered in exposition. Language used should be familiar and suitable.

6. The lesson should be divided into sections which have logical sequence. This will enable the students to understand easily and will also train them in systematic thinking besides assisting them to put their own thoughts logically.
7. The rate of exposition and the size of the subject-matter are determined by the individual capacity of children and teacher's natural rate of speech.
8. Proper use of the blackboard should be made.
9. Actual objects, models, diagrams, sketches, etc., should be used.
10. The students should be encouraged to ask questions. This will enable them to get their doubts removed.
11. Verbal illustrations such as examples, comparisons etc., should be used to enable the student to grasp the exposition.
12. Pictorial illustrations such as pictures, maps and charts should be freely used as these help in motivating the students.
13. The aim of the lesson should be kept in view and the students fully made conversant with the aim.

Source Method

Source method implies the use of original material and documents in the teaching of commerce. A source method provides first hand experiences and leads to better understanding of the subject.

Sources may be divided into two categories :

(a) Primary sources

(b) Secondary sources

An act passed by the parliament or a state legislature on the commerce policy is a primary data whereas its extracts published in newspapers come under the secondary data.

The report of the Curriculum Committee or Curriculum Development Centre of the University Grants Commission is a primary source but extracts published in newspapers and journals fall under the category of secondary sources.

Use of the Source Method—It can be used at the following stages of the lesson :

Pre-lesson Use of Source—Visits to local markets, banks or exchanges etc. may be arranged before taking up a lesson on these topics. The teacher may also ask the students to read selected passages of an Act connected with the lesson before hand.

Mid-lesson Use of the Source—Extracts from the act may be read during the course of the lesson. This creates a real situation, provides vividness to the subject-matter and reinforces the impact of teaching.

Post-lesson Use of the Source—Pre-lesson use of a source can also take the form of post-lesson use of the source and vice versa. Students may be given assignments which need to make use of the sources.

Merits of the Source Method—Following are the main merits:

1. It provides a real situation.
2. It makes the subject-matter vivid.
3. It develops a sense of objectivity.
4. It arouses curiosity among the students.
5. It provides a motivating environment.
6. It develops elementary skills of collecting data, shifting the relevant and organising the same.
7. It provides opportunities for useful mental exercises—right thinking and imagining, comparing and analysing, drawing inferences etc.
8. It promotes interests in the study of the subject.
9. It initiates the students in research.

10. It provides functional knowledge. Even the slow and backward children feel interested when they see original sources. Their learning becomes functional because it is gained in the real context.
11. It supplements class-room lesson.

Limitations of the Source Method—Limitations are given below :

1. It is very difficult for the school teachers to have an easy access to original sources.
2. Utilisation of original sources is a very difficult task for the school students as they lack the requisite training.
3. The method is very complex and technical.
4. Contemporary authors and writers have given their own prejudices, preferences and limitations with the result that it becomes very difficult to sift fact from fiction. The students are, thus, lost in the maze of conflicting views about the same event or movement.
5. Source method of teaching Economics is very expensive.
6. Source method of teaching Economics is time consuming.

How to Make Source Method Effective—The students should be encouraged to study the resource books in the library. Educational tours to places of importance may be arranged. The students may be asked to write their own impressions and inferences about the places they visit. Copies of important extracts from the relevant records may be pasted on the blackboard for the use of students.

Dr. Keatings thinks that original sources can be used for creating suitable environment in the lower form. Well planned, purposive and well directed efforts have to made by the teacher in the use of this method. By suggesting the use of resource method, we do not aim at making our students research scholars. Use of the method in selected topics is likely to make the study of Economics more meaningful and real.

QUESTIONS

Essay Type Questions

1. "The teacher is a guide and director, he steers the boat but the energy that propels it must come from those who are learning." Comment upon this statement and give the main features of sound methods of teaching Economics.
2. "True teaching is arousing and directing meaningful learning." Elucidate the statement and bring out clearly the significance of dynamic and progressive methods of teaching Economics.
3. Why should the learner be involved in the teaching learning process of Economics ? What steps would you take to ensure his active involvement in the lesson ?
4. What is the significance of the lecture method in the teaching of Economics? How can we make this method effective ?
5. How would you adopt the approach 'Learning by Doing' in Economics ?
6. Explain clearly the use of source method in the teaching of Economics. What different sources would you use ? Write in brief.
7. How do modern methods of teaching differ from the traditional methods of teaching Economics ?

Short Answer and Objective Type Question

8. Classify the following methods into Telling, Showing and Doing :
   (i) Lecture Method

(ii) Project Method

(iii) Demonstration Method

(iv) Story telling Method

(v) Discussion Method

9. Give two methods involving independent study.

10. Write any two points of difference between lecturing method (lecture method) and doing method.

8

Techniques of Teaching

The term 'method' and 'techniques' are used as synonyms by several authors. For instance 'assignment' is used as a method as well as a technique. A method is a broad concept which includes several techniques of teaching.

Techniques of teaching are very valuable instruments in making teaching-learning efficient, meaningful and inspirational.

Importance and Implications

In order to facilitate the learning process the teachers resort to what have been called 'Devices' or techniques. A device implies the external mode or form which teaching may take from time to time.

According to John Mander, there are five main reasons which might justify the use of these expedients . They are given below :

(a) To teach something more thoroughly so that the children may retain the 'subject-matter taught, (b) To teach something more quickly. This will result in 'covering more ground' in a given time, and thus gives a better chance of "getting through the syllabus", (c) As a means of creating or sustaining interests, (d) As a means of integrating a number of separate pieces or work already learned by other means, (e) As a means of bringing with the experience and understanding of children something which is new to them. This often includes the presenting to children, in simplified form, of matters which can be appreciated fully only by adults.

Assignment Technique

Significance of Assignment—N.L. Bossing has observed, "The central position of the assignment in the techniques of teaching has remained unquestioned". G.H. Betts asserts, "Upon the proper assignment of the lesson depends much of the success of the recitation, and also much of the pupil's progress in learning how to study." W.N. Drum suggests, "Teachers generally do not appreciate the importance of the assignment, and the work of the pupils probably suffers as much from hasty or careless assignment as from any other single cause." H.R. Douglass and others are of the view, "The assignment represents one of the most important phases of teaching."

Types of Assignment and Homework—Following are the types of homework :

1. Writing of essay type answers to questions arising out of the subject-matter already done in the class.
2. Verbal memorising work pertaining to curricular and co-curricular activities. It may take the form of cramming facts, principles, memorising work in respect of debates etc.
3. Practical work, e.g., preparation of charts, maps and models, advance preparation for the coming lesson.
4. Problem assignment
5. Group assignment.

Purposes of Assignments in Economics – Following purposes can be stated:

1. To provide opportunities to work independently and thereby to develop in the students self-reliance and initiative.
2. To develop habits of reading regularly among the students.
3. To provide opportunities to the students to utilise their leisure time profitably. It is generally seen that our school children waste their precious time in loittering about or making mischief when no such work is given to them.
4. To give them opportunity to do practice what is done in the school.
5. To finish the prescribed courses in time. The syllabi is too heavy to be finished in the classroom work.
6. To serve as a link in the parent-teacher co-operation. It enables the parents to know that regular work is being done in the school.
7. To develop permanent interests and to train the students in the profitable use of leisure.
8. To enable the child to revise his previous lesson and prepare the next one.
9. To provide remedial measure for backward children.
10. To give chance to every child to progress at his own speed.

Essentials of an Assignment

1. The assignment should be clear and definite.
2. The assignment should be concise but sufficiently detailed to enable each student to understand the task assigned.
3. The assignment should anticipate special difficulties and suggest ways to remove them.

4. The assignment should relate the new unit to past experience.
5. Students should understand the importance of the assignment.
6. The assignment should arouse an interest in advance work.
7. The assignment should provide for differences in the ability and interest of students.
8. The assignment should be motivated chiefly by the hope of worthwhile achievements, rather than scholastic reward or the fear of punishment.
9. The assignment should stimulate thought.
10. The assignment should provide necessary and specific directions for the study of the lesson.
11. The assignment should be adjusted to the time and opportunity of the class.
12. Materials of the assignment should be varied and adaptable to the needs and interest of the students.

Difficulties in the Preparation of a Good Assignment— Fleming and Woodring have listed the following difficulties :

1. Insufficient thought and preparation in planning the assignment.
2. Inability to obtain an acceptance by the pupil of a worthy purpose for performance of the task.
3. Simulation of preparation of the assignments by appealing to the interests of the adolescents and by providing for real needs growing out of pupil experience.
4. Prevention of loss of interest due to too long phase of time between assignment and preparation.
5. Avoidance of assignments so long that successful accomplishment is impossible in the time available for preparation, with consequent loss of interest.

6. Guarding against too many and too varied activities, resulting in dividing interests with consequent bad habits of work, and unsatisfactory accomplishments.
7. Difficulty in presenting work to be done so that it is clearly understood by the pupils; also, the difficulty of ascertaining whether every pupil understands.
8. Gauging the difficulty of work so that success is possible for each pupil.
9. Determining essential requirements, and differentiation of assignment to suit the various levels and types of ability existing in the class.
10. Inclusion of challenges to mental exploration by the pupil, thereby simulating real thinking.
11. Provision for continuity of work by presenting new problems as a continuation of previous experience and anticipation of future problems.
12. Correlating with other subjects and outside activities.
13. Focusing attention on important elements in the new problem of task, and directing the attack in such a way as to increase interest rather than lessen it to stimulate effort, and to overcome seeming obstacles to accomplishment.
14. Providing the necessary tools for preparation by training in study procedures and techniques, and in selection, organization, and use of materials, thereby developing effective habits of independent work.
15. Giving to pupils devices for checking the mastery and performance of work undertaken.
16. Evaluating the effectiveness of an assignment by the equality of response during the presentation of the assignment, and by the adequacy of pupil preparation.
17. Providing sufficient time for adequate consideration of the assignment and determining the psychological moment for its presentation.

Suggested Assignment Procedure—The procedure suggested for the preparation of a good assignment is as follows :

1. Analyse the nature of the learning process required in the advance unit. This is without exception the first step in a good assignment procedure. Much of what follows in any good assignment depends upon this analysis.

2. Study the various types of assignment available and select the one, or modified form of it, that appears to fit best the learning situation. Some assignment types are admirably adapted to one form of learning for teaching but not to others.

3. Provide the essential background for the advance work where uncertainty exists that such background obtains. At this point too many teachers are likely to assume the adequacy of this background when in fact it may not exist. Scarcely can one emphasize too strongly the apperceptive preparation for the new.

4. Whether this is the next step in the assignment procedure or not, it is obvious that very early in the assignment phase the teacher must throw out a challenge to the student that will enlist his interest and maximum effort in the new unit.

5. Outline in sufficient detail the advance unit to be suited.

6. Suggest some plan of attack upon the new unit. It is well to remember one caution—do not do for the student that which he may be led to do for himself. This suggests the desirability of leading the class in a cooperative discovery of desirable leads for the general attack upon the new.

7. Where reference to source material other than the text-book is necessary, this should be made specific. The most satisfactory plan in the large unit assignment is to provide the select list of available sources in mimeographed or hectographed form with chapter or inclusive page references given.

Controversy Regarding Home Assignments — Whether or not homework should be given to the students is a controversial point. Extreme views have been expressed regarding the usefulness of the home work. The assignment of home task has been emphatically denounced by Bray. He writes, "Under normal conditions a reasonable day's work for a child has been done at the close of the afternoon and homework as it is generally organised does more harm than good as a rule in this country except perhaps from the point of view of examination success." On the other hand P.C. Wren commends the assigning of homework. An average guardian also feels that some work should be given to the student which he should do at home.

Disadvantages or Objections to Home Work

1. It deprives the children of participating in recreational activities when it imposes heavy demands upon them.
2. It is a great hindrance in the way of the students of enjoying family and social life.
3. It deprives children of the opportunity to help their parents in supplementing their income.
4. It imposes a great physical strain on small children and thus endangers their health.
5. It becomes a constant source of fear and worry to the students and therefore it endangers their emotional stability.
6. Children are tempted to copy whenever they find that the home task is difficult to do.
7. Sometimes children are tempted to tell a lie that due to certain reasons they have failed to do home task.
8. Unhealthy home conditions make study more harmful than profitable. There is a lack of adequate light and quietness in a large number of Indian homes and the atmosphere is not congenial for study.

9. Too much of homework develops an attitude of indifference on the part of the pupils and they become careless.
10. Lack of proper correction by the teacher, sometimes, gives rise to carelessness on the part of the pupils. It also develops wrong habits of work if the work is not properly checked.
11. Too much work is set by some over-enthusiastic specialist teachers in their subject completely disregarding what other teachers of the same class might have set for the same day.
12. The task is generally too academic in nature and ignores those activities which are needed most for an all-round development of the personality of the child.
13. It is not properly adjusted to pupils' needs and capacities.

Principles of Assigning Homework—Following are the principles of assigning homework:

1. The nature of homework should be such as it does not require any kind of assistance from a private tutor or guardian.
2. It should not be purely mechanical, i.e., requiring no general knowledge on the part of the child.
3. Homework should aim at developing the taste of the individual child. This purpose can be very conveniently realised if homework is in the nature of hobbies.
4. Homework should be very definite.
5. It should be supplementary rather preparatory as far as possible.
6. A single assignment for the whole class may not be considered as appropriate. It should vary according to the mental and physical makeup of the students.

7. Homework in different subjects should be co-ordinated. Homework time-table should be framed so as to avoid confusion.
8. Normally home assignment in Economics should not require more than one hour every day to complete it.
9. Home task should not be set as a punishment.
10. Home task should be properly checked.
11. Library books should be given for reading at homes as a home task.
12. Copies of the homework time-tables may be sent to the parents to seek their cooperation which is very important.
13. While assigning homework the teachers should take into consideration the home conditions of the child such as domestic employment, working conditions in the home etc.
14. 15% marks should be reserved for the evaluation of the student's work based on the assignments done throughout the year.

Methods of Correction—Following methods of correction may be adopted :

1. Correction by the teacher.
2. Correction with the help of the bright students in the class.
3. Correction with the help of the blackboard.
4. Correction by interchanging the exercise books among the students.
5. Glance checking and signing by teachers.

Brainstorming: Brainstorming is an activity which quickly elicits many ideas, reactions or points of information from a group. In this activity, a question is posed and the group members are asked to immediately give all the responses which occur to them without censuring or holding anything back. Everything is listed without any question, discussion or clarification. Later the ideas are screened, categorised, and analysed. This activity is undertaken when a group has been inactive or seems to be uninvolved in a discussion.

Brainstorming can be used to produce an overview of the dimensions of a problem (ask for causes : direct, indirect, remote, subtle and/or for consequences : immediate, long-range, probable or improbable) or solutions (ask for practical and imaginative) or of reactions and feelings.

Cartoon : Cartoon is pictorial representation of a message in an exaggerated and humorous manner to attract the quick attention of the students. It is an interpretative picture, usually a drawing, intended to convey a message or point of view about things, events or situations. For instance, an impact of poverty on people can be showed to the students through cartoons. Cartoons may be collected from different newspapers and magazines. Students and teachers may also prepare cartoons to illustrate the evils of population explosion.

Case-study Method : The case-study has been described by Harvey Newmen and D.M. Sidney in their book entitled Teaching Management in these words, "The name case study is a blanket term describing a selection of facts, either fictitious or drawn from real life, describing a technical or human relation situation usually in an industrial or commercial setting. It is a segment of history or a piece of reporting and like both history and journalism depends on selection and condensation for its effects." We may think of these case studies. 1. Success stories of Birlas or Tatas. 2. Role of Kurian in the promotion of Dairy Cooperative Movement in India.3. Case study of a sick mill or some other institution.

A case study involves an analysis of data to determine output, price, expenditure or some other aspect of business endeavour of an individual or institution. Analysis may be made through group discussion.

Merits of Case Study—The case study approach has the following merits :

1. It develops a scientific outlook and the ability to apply the scientific method to areas like business management.
2. It helps the students to apply theoretical principles on the job situations.
3. It develops in the students management skills from a practical stand point.
4. It provides a 'dramatic touch' to the situation.
5. It provides adequate experience in studying an actual situation.

Limitations of Case Study—Case study approach is not without limitations. Some of the important ones are given below :

1. It is not possible for the teacher to cover the entire course by the use of case study method.
2. The use of case study method puts on heavy demand upon the Economics teacher.
3. Case study method expects too much from the students.
4. Case study method gives the students an exaggerated idea of his own importance.
5. A prolonged exposure to case study method may develop in the students a too critical and negative approach of looking for what is wrong rather than developing a more constructive and positive approach.

Debate

Meaning of Debate—Debate implies giving arguments and counterarguments on some topic of importance. In a debate, speakers usually vehemently oppose each other's arguments. One group speaks for the topic and the other opposes.

Significance of Debate—Debate helps the students in developing habit of study, comprehending and critically analysing a topic, and expressing one's thought convincing, cogently and forcefully.

Debating qualities prepares students for facing audience effectively. Debating also enables students to become leaders. Debates supplement classroom teaching.

Organising Debates — Following points may be kept in view:

1. Topic of debate should be selected very carefully.
2. Sufficient time should be given to prepare students.
3. Adequate seating arrangement should be made.
4. Debate should be regulated systematically.
5. Judges should be chosen after due care.
6. Marking scheme should be scientifically prepared.

Description

Meaning of Description — Description and narration are quite similar and there is not much difference between these two terms. According to the dictionary meaning 'to describe' is 'to set forth, define, depict or portray in words' and 'Description' is defined as 'the act or representing a thing by words; account of the properties or appearance of something'.

More effective use of language is required in description than in narration. Description is needed in most of the lessons of almost all the subjects.

Guidelines for the Use of Descriptive Technique — The following points should be kept in mind while using this device of teaching:

1. The teacher should have a clear and strong visual image of the object. His information should not be mere theoretical. As far as possible the teacher should try to see the actual object. Of course, this will not be possible in all cases. Let it be borne in mind that without forming a clear visual picture of the object in mind, it will not be possible to describe the object in an effective manner.

2. Language employed should be very simple and clear.
3. It is better to give first a broad general effect of the appearance of the whole and then to fill in the details.
4. Description should be very brief and simple. Too many details at a time should be avoided as these baffle the children's imagination.
5. Important points should be repeated and stressed.
6. Description should be given in some definite arrangement.
7. Reliance should not be based on the words alone. Models, pictures or diagrams should also be used.
8. The aim of the description should be clear to the teacher and the taught.
9. The use of homely illustrations such as metaphors and similes help to verify description.
10. Important points may be explained on the black-board.

Comparison between Narration and Description

1. Presents fact in a logical sequence.	1. Presents fact in a logical as well as psychological points of view.
2. Used casually for clarification.	2. Used largely for presenting all round verbal picture.
3. Usually used in the oral form.	3. Can be presented both in oral and written form.
4. More analytical in nature.	4. More synthetic in nature.

Limitations of Description Technique

1. In the description technique, students usually remain passive.
2. The description technique makes the lesson dull and sometimes lifeless.

3. The students do not develop interest and motivation in the lesson.
4. The description technique to be effective needs expertise in the use of language, gestures etc. Every teacher does not possess the expertise needed.
5. Description technique does not develop adequate insight in the students.

Dramatization

Meaning—Dramatization has been described as 'a synthetic art', involving the purposive coordination and control of the delicate organs of speech and muscles of the body combined with a sense of rhythm, with a view to free and intelligent expression of emotions and ideas.

Dramatic art affords innumerable opportunities for the correlation of a large number of subjects. In the preparation of their roles, the students indirectly and unconsciously improve their speech habits and language. A systematic study of historical events has to be made when pageants of the life of great persons are prepared, i.e., pageant on the life of Buddha, Chandragupta, Vikramaditya, Gandhiji, etc. Children prepare costumes suiting different ages and thus comes to know about the dresses of the people during different periods of history. Dramatics also add to the economic and geographical knowledge of the students. Carpentry and other mechanical arts facilitate the work of construction of the stage. Dance and music add to the beauty of a drama.

Drama has its great social value. It is a cooperative enterprise and develops qualities of cooperation and social understanding. It helps in fostering espirit de corps among the students. In various school functions dramas form chief items of the programme. For the honour of the school, every student works to the best of his capacity.

Dramatics afford the student many opportunities for training in team work. They are very helpful in providing the students with opportunities for the release of the inhibitions to which they are subjected by the conventions of society.

There are many activities in a drama and as such students of diverse aptitudes get chances to choose items for which they are best suited and satisfy their urges, e.g., self-expression through the various activities of a drama.

Conditions for Success – A number of rehearsals bring grace and success to the play when it is staged. Pupils should prepare as much stage material as they can.

Children should be encouraged to write their own play. The usual participants in this activity should be given opportunities to play different roles. The same pupils as far as possible should, however, not be allowed to play the role of a villain.

Drill : This technique is also known as 'practice' or 'habit formation". This is a favourite device with the teachers. The purpose of drill is to increase proficiency in performance. In the words of Dr. Yoakam and Simpson (1957), "Drill is a serious work activity or the strengthening of association to make skills more permanent." The subject matter which demands drill for mastery exists more or less in all school subjects and has a wide scope in accountancy.

Important principles of effective drill are as under :

1. The students should understand the significance of the material which they are to repeat.
2. Appeal to the best motive of the students should be made.
3. The work should be of a graded nature. The child should get success in the early stages of practice.
4. Correct response should be secured from the very beginning.
5. Drill exercises should be short and distributed over a period of time.
6. The child's attention should be centred on definite improvement and on reasons of failure or lack of improvement

7. Drill is an individual affair and it is a wrong practice to ask the few to drill at the expense of many.
8. Right practice should be aimed at.
9. Drill should be varied. It should be of different forms, otherwise it is likely to become monotonous.

Association for Good

An Economic Association serves an important instrument of supplementing theory and practices of Economics. It may be formed to provide the students of Economics an opportunity to work cooperatively and understand each other.

The association may organise debates, symposiums, visits, film shows, lectures on topics of current economic interest or informal discussions. The association may maintain an Economics Room, bulletin boards, wall magazines and contribute a special section in the school magazine.

Office bearers of the Economic Association may be nominated or elected. Its membership can be voluntary or compulsory.

All activities of the Economic Association should be guided by the Economics Teacher.

Explanation

Meaning—The object of explanation is to enable the children "to take an intelligent interest in the proceedings, to grasp the purpose of what is being done, and to develop their understanding of how to do it."

To explain means "to make plain, manifest, or intelligible; to clear of obscurity; to expound; to lay open the meanings; to elucidate."

Panton observes : "Explanation forms a kind of bridge between telling and revealing knowledge to the learners, and it involves a number of techniques as well as narration and description. Throughout the process the teacher must keep in close touch with the minds of his pupil suggesting lines of thought, questioning them, answering their questions, setting them on practical work, examining the results obtained, discussing significant problems, etc."

Forms of Explanation

(1)	(2)	(3)	(4)	(5)	(6)	(7)
By acting	By using a sentence	By stating synonyms	By stating opposite words	By analysis	By telling brief history	By giving definition

Guidelines in the Use of Explanation—The following points may be noted in this connection:

1. Some definite aim must be kept in mind by the teacher and the students so as to remove obscurity.
2. The theme should be divided into different sections and must have logical sequence and a definite arrangement.
3. The capacity of the students to understand and assimi late the subject-matter should be given due consideration.
4. Too much of telling on the part of the teacher is likely to confuse the child instead of making things clear or intelligible.
5. The teacher should put the essential points on the blackboard.
6. The teacher would do well to ask questions from the students at different stages to ascertain whether they have followed him or not.
7. Illustrations both verbal and non-verbal; or audio-visual aids should be made use of.
8. A summary of the whole discussion should be given at the end of the lesson.
9. The teacher must be fully prepared to answer all questions of the students.

10. Students should be made active participants in the process of explanation.
11. Explanations should be done in simple language.
12. Correct language should be used.
13. Explanations should not be so lengthy so as to dampen the interest of the students.

Limitations of Explanation

1. The teacher should possess the needed expertise in the technique.
2. It is very difficult to set any limit to which explanation should be done.
3. Explanation is like to be more verbal in nature.

Exposition

Meaning of Exposition—To expose means to open, to exhibit, to display, to disclose or to subject to light. Exposition is making clear the new information. It is more than explanation. The purpose of exposition is to enable the children to grasp the sense or meanings of the subject-matter presented to them in an intelligible manner.

Effective teaching is based upon a clear exposition. The things must be explained fully to children. Hurried exposition results in faulty assimilation of knowledge.

Guidelines for Using the Technique of Exposition—The following points should be kept in view in using the technique of teaching :

1. Matter should be arranged in such a way as to leave a single clear impression on the minds of the students.
2. The teacher should have pauses in between the lesson so that the students may learn the new knowledge bit by bit.

3. The rate of exposition should be slow when the class is backward. The teacher should utilise different ways of presenting the same information.
4. There should be abundant repetition but should be in a new way so that the class may not feel dullness.
5. Children's way of looking at things should be considered in exposition. Language used should be familiar and suitable.
6. The lesson should be divided into sections which have a logical sequence. This will enable the students to understand easily and will also train them in systematic thinking besides assisting them to put their own thoughts logically.
7. The rate of exposition and the size of the subject-matter are determined by the individual capacity of children and teacher's natural rate of speech.
8. Proper use of the black-board should be made.
9. Actual objects, models, diagrams, sketches etc., should be used.
10. The students should be encouraged to ask questions. They will enable them to get their doubts removed.
11. Verbal illustrations such as examples, comparisons etc., should be used to enable the students to grasp the exposition.
12. Pictorial illustrations such as pictures, maps and charts should be freely used as these help in motivating the students.
13. The aim of the lesson should be kept in view and the students fully made conversant with the aim.

Limitations of the Technique of Exposition

1. It is a very difficult task to determine the various specific aspects of the lesson while exposing it.

2. It is not easy to decide about the appropriateness of exposition.
3. Exposition can only be effective when the teacher arranges the facts both in logical and psychological sequence.
4. For effective exposition, teacher needs to possess expertise in this.
5. Since there are individual differences among pupils, no definite opinion can be formed regarding the adequacy of exposition.

Exhibits : An exhibit is a collection of objects and materials arranged in a setting in order to convey a unified idea. An exhibit or collection of utensils, tools, art objects, or foods, may be used as a planned environment to introduce a unit. This type of teaching aid makes its best contribution during the lesson for clarifying concepts.

Students may also desire to exhibit models which they have made in connection with a topic of the lesson in the classroom. This provides an opportunity for them to present appropriate learnings. Different types of teaching aids may be combined in an exhibit. The exhibit should be placed in such a way that it attracts the attention of the students and ultimately develop thinking.

Annual school exhibitions may be arranged and the exhibits prepared by the students on different aspects relating to Economics displayed in the exhibitions.

Film Strips : Film strip is a short length of film containing a number of positives, each different but usually having some continuity intended to be projected as a series of still pictures by means of a film strip projector. They can be projected on a large screen for a group.

It is not essential that still pictures should have written captions.

In introducing a new learning material for teaching a lesson, the teacher can use film strips for large groups. Non-captioned strips should be used so that students may know their own ability to interpret picture.

Content of the film strips should be related to the content of the lesson under study.

The time factor should also be kept in mind for projecting film strips.

Group Dynamics

Meaning of Group Dynamics—Group dynamics is a method which aims at the socialisation of the pupils by developing in them the traits of initiative and responsibility within a group membership and in harmony with group interests. 'Cooperative' enterprise is the 'key-note' of this method. In this method, children are discussing, questioning, reporting, planning and working in natural ways. The teacher plays the role of an adviser, counsellor and guide in the best sense of the word, trying to get children discover things for themselves rather than to have them merely listening. Group dynamics method develops techniques useful in group work, to stimulate creative expression, to develop desirable social attitudes by providing practice in a large variety of socialised stimulus and above all, practice in the techniques of cooperative thinking. It develops social consciousness among the students.

Forms of Group Dymanics—This method has the following forms :

(1) Group Discussion

(2) Panel Discussion

(3) Seminar Technique

(4) Symposium

(5) Workshop

Group-Discussion

Meaning and Significance of Discussion—This method has been used in the teaching-learning process from time immemorial.

It was widely used at the famous Nalanda University. The Greek scholars in their walk used to discuss various problems and issues with their disciples. Discussion has been described as a thoughtful consideration of the relationships involved in a topic or porblem under study. It is concerned with the analysis, comparison, evaluation and conclusions of these relationships. It aims at uniting and integrating the work of the class. It is carried out by organising, outlining and relating the facts studied. It encourages the student to direct their thinking process towards the solution of a problem and to use their experiences for a further clarification and consolidation of learning material.

Discussion is to be distinguished from debate in which the participants seek to prove a point rather than to discover a truth. Debate may also be marked by uncontrolled exchange to verbalism.

Discussion is very important in stimulating mental activity, developing fluency and ease in expression, clarity of ideas in thinking and training in the presentation of one's ideas and facts. An exchange of ideas and opinions offers valuable training to students in reflective thinking.

Essential Parts or Constituents of Discussion—These are as under :

1. The leader—the teacher
2. The group—the students
3. The problem—or the topic
4. The content—body of knowledge
5. Evaluation—change in ideas, attitudes etc.

Organisation of Discussion—Following are the main techniques of organising discussion:

1. Introducing a topic or a problem by the teacher by giving points or explanations to serve as the basis of discussion.
2. Calling upon a pupil by the teacher to give facts, describe a sense or situation, explain an incident, event or happening for getting the discussion started.

3. Preparing an outline of points cooperatively by the teacher and a few students which may become the starting point for discussion.
4. Asking the students to describe their own experiences connected with the subject, topic or problem and making them points for discussion.
5. Presenting detailed papers by the teacher and discussions thereon.
6. Presenting detailed papers by the students and discussing them in the class.
7. Showing special works and projects to the class and discussing them.
8. Showing some pictures, charts, diagrams or any audio-visual material and discussion about them.

Merits of Discussion—Following are the merits of discussion:

1. It helps in clarifying issues.
2. It helps children in crystallising their thinking.
3. It helps students in discovering what they do not know and what they have overlooked.
4. It engenders more reflection. It is very different from note learning.
5. It represents a type of pooled knowledge, ideas and feelings of several persons.
6. It develops team spirit.
7. It engenders toleration of views which are at variance.
8. It affords opportunities to the students to learn together, make suggestions, share responsibility, comprehend the topic, evaluate the findings and to summarise results.
9. It provides opportunities to the students to speak distinctly, stand and sit correctly, respect the ideas of others, share interests, ask pertinent questions and comprehend the problem before the group.

10. It helps the teacher in discovering talented students who have potential for becoming good leaders.

Limitations of Discussion—Limitations of discussion are :

1. It is not suitable in all topics.
2. It is likely to be dominated by a few students.
3. It is likely to go off the track.
4. It may lead to unpleasant feelings.
5. It may create emotional tensions.
6. It may involve unnecessary arguments.

Directing Group Discussion—The teacher has to show immense patience and skill to ensure that discussion takes place on right lines and in the appropriate environment. Following points may be considered in this respect :

1. Students should be well acquainted with the significance of the topic, its nature and scope and causes why the class should discuss it.
2. Discussion should be confined to important aspects.
3. Students should be encouraged to participate in the discussion.
4. Ideas may be invited without pressure or embarrassment.
5. Explanations, where needed should be provided.
6. Personality cult should be avoided.
7. Cooperation rather than competition should be encouraged.
8. Efforts should be made to develop team spirit.
9. Doubts, mistakes and wrong interpretation should be made clear by the teacher.
10. Facts and points should be evaluated.
11. Facts and points should be summarised.

12. Students should be guided to appreciate difference of opinion and views.
13. Goals of discussion should be kept in view.
14. Only a few students should not be allowed to dominate the classroom discussion.
15. She students may be given training in discussion in small groups so that their hesitation is removed while participating in bigger groups.

Panel Discussion : In panel discussion three or four speakers discuss various aspects of a single topic in the class. One of them may act as chairperson to monitor discussions. A time schedule is drawn up. When the panel is ready to hold discussions the chairperson may explain the topic briefly. No one makes a speech. Rather, there is interplay back and forth among the panel members. The panel chairperson keeps the discussion to the point and ensure that all panel members participate equally. The panel members interact with each other with a good deal of a spontaneity. Once the panel members have made their presentation, students of the class may be invited to ask questions. Being a group activity in which students are directly involved, panel discussion enables them to reflect deeply upon an area of interest.

The teacher is behind the scene, motivating, encouraging and guiding the panel members and other students to derive the optimum benefit from this approach.

A panel discussion may be organised with the Managing Director of a Road Transport Corporation, Railway Zonal Manager, Managing Director of an Air Company, Incharge of a Shipping Company to give views on transport.

Seminar : A seminar is an advanced group technique which is usually used in higher education. It refers to a structured group discussion that usually follows a formal lecture or lectures often in the form of an essay or a paper presentation on a theme.

Individual students also prepare papers or reports and present them before a group of peers as part of the course work.

Duration of the presentation of papers at seminars varies from topic to topic and discipline to discipline.

Papers can be illustrated through projected aids (film strips, slides, transparencies) or non-projected aids (charts, diagrams, maps etc.).

Presentation of paper or papers is followed by general discussion by the entire group. Considerable student participation is expected.

As a seminar involves student preparation and participation and response from the peer group, it not only breaks the monotony of the lecture method but also motivates the students to probe into topic deeply. Understanding power and questioning ability in a relevant situation are developed. Self-reliance, self-confidence, sense of cooperation and responsibility are developed. The presenters of papers develop habits of sustained work, learn to collect and organise data in a sequential manner.

We can organise a seminar on bank organisation where the presenter can outline his theme followed by questions from the participants. He should keep in view the following points in this regard :

1. Selection of a meaningful and relevant topic.
2. Selection of students who are effective speakers to take lead.
3. Duration of the seminar – usually two hours.
4. Preparing the participants – providing them suitable guidelines for collecting and arranging the material.
5. Wise selection of the chairperson.
6. Framing suitable rules.

Seminar could be arranged by inviting experts on a topic and students asked to listen to their views and also provided opportunities to ask questions. Experts may be requested to keep in view the maturity level of the students. Time schedule for speakers may suitably be framed. Follow-up action on the seminar will enhance its utility.

Symposium : Symposium is a group discussion in which subject experts or speakers holding different points of view about the subject under discussion participate. Each speaker presents his ideas in a short speech. Generally the moderator or the chairperson and speakers discuss the various aspects of a theme in the symposium. The chairperson coordinates the different speakers' presentation. The total number of speakers usually does not exceed five excluding the chairperson. The audience very seldom participates as the chairperson and the speakers anticipate possible questions and incorporate these in their presentation.

The tendency among educators is to use the term seminar and symposium synonymously.

We can organise a symposium on business organisation with 3 speakers, each outlining a particular type, i.e., the partnership, joint stock company and cooperative organisation, with a moderator coordinating the symposium. We can also have a symposium in which experts on business organisation participate – a bank executive, a registrar of cooperative organisation and a leading partner in a business.

Workshop : Workshop procedure is a type of group procedure of teaching-learning where 'work' or 'doing' is the essence. In group discussions 'lecturing' or 'talking' is the key-note. A workshop is an activity-centred technique. It involves directly the skills of both cognitive and psycho-motor domains.

Making teaching and learning aids, charts and models, etc., preparing assignments, instructional designs, syllabi, manuals and critical reviews are the important activities of a workshop session under the guidance of experts. The participants work collectively and produce plans, solve problems, collect and organise resources, develop tests and find out ways and means of solving classroom problems faced by them. The experts help the participants to draw on their own experience.

Illustrations

Meaning of Illustration—To illustrate an idea or an object means to throw light on it. The term illustration is used in educational literature to mean the use of those aids which make various points, statements and arguments clear and vivid to students and assist them to acquire correct knowledge.

Types of Illustrations—There are several types of illustrations but we may divide them into two broad categories.

Concrete, Non-Verbal, Natural or Objective Illustrations—Under this head we may include objects, models, exhibits, demonstration, apparatus, pictures, diagrams, charts, maps, graphs, slides, films, radio, black-board, garden, museum, etc.

Verbal Illustration—These include anecdotes, stories, descriptions, incidents, comparisons, analogies, similes, dramatisation.

Advantages of Illustrations

1. They help to simplify explanations.
2. They make the instruction concrete.
3. They give vividness to explanations.
4. They assist in overcoming difficulties of understanding.
5. They create interest and curiosity in learning.
6. They help to strengthen the retaining and recollecting power of students.
7. They are valuable in developing the power of observations of students.
8. They help in the formation of good intellectual habits.
9. They are a ready means of fixing the attention of the students.
10. They lessen the knowledge load and set up associations which help in the economy of efforts.
11. They train the senses to greater acuteness of perception.

Relative Importance of Verbal and Non-verbal Illustrations — Their relative importance depends upon :

(a) The nature of the subjects.

(b) The level of pupils development.

Non-verbal Illustrations are more useful and should be frequently employed in the lower classes. Actual objects or their solid representations, models etc., should be used. Pictures, diagrams, sketches and graphs should be used in abundance in the higher classes. A high level of intelligence is required to understand verbal illustrations, such as analogies and similes etc., and, therefore, these should come at a higher stage.

It may not be possible in many cases to bring the common objects in class-room. Educational excursions may be planned to take the students to see real things.

Important Points regarding the Use of Illustrations : Illustrations are Means and not Ends — It must be remembered that illustrations are good servants but bad masters. Their misuse or overuse is likely to spoil the lesson. It is a wrong notion that without a paraphernalia of illustrative material, a lesson cannot be made effective. Following points may be kept in view in the use of illustrations of all types :

1. Illustrations should be relevant to the topic.
2. Illustrations should be simple and easily comprehensible.
3. Language used in verbal illustrations should be easy and simple.
4. Illustrations should be subordinate to the topic.
5. Illustrations should be accurate and exact.
6. Number of illustrations should be moderate.
7. Illustrations should be homely.

Laboratory Method

Laboratory method is usually associated with the teaching of science subjects. Nevertheless there is a tendency in certain quarters to use the term 'laboratory method' in the teaching of social sciences including Economics. The method may be explained as, "the greater part of the students will be studying and writing at their work tables. Two or three students may be having a quiet conference on some moot point. Others may be comparing notes or outlines of some phase of the work. One student may be busy at the dictionary, hunting for the explanation of some phrase or term; another may be consulting an atlas; a third may be sharpening a pencil or filling his fountain pen; a fourth may be making a map or preparing a graph; a fifth may be conferring with the teacher about some difficulty or asking for a criticism on his notes or outlines. Usually one or two students will be browsing among the volumes in the bookcases or going through tables of contents or indexes to find a clue to some obscure item. Now and then an idler or a dawdler will be observed. In general, however, the library room is a place of quite, disorderly order, in which students are busily engaged in profitable activities of one kind or another."

Narration

Meaning of Narration — Narration is one of the most important methods of communicating knowledge. It is not possible to elicit everything from the students. Narration implies giving account of events to others. According to Prof. I.H. Panton, "Narra-tion is an art in itself which aims at presenting to the pupils, through the medium of speech, clear, vivid, interesting, ordered sequences of events, in such a way that their minds reconstruct these happenings and they live in imagination through the experiences recounted either as spectators or possibly as participants."

Merits of Narration

1. Narration is an effective technique of presenting the subject matter relating to description.
2. Effective narration minimises the burden of books on students.

3. Narration presents a dear, comprehensive and vivid view of the subject matter.
4. Pupils gain information and knowledge through narration in lesser time and effort as compared to the study of books.
5. Narration develops interests in students in reading original books to gain more knowledge.

Requisites of Effective Narration—To be a good narrator, a teacher should know the skilful use of language. He should use appropriate language which should clearly depict situations and happenings. The speech or the language should also be appropriate to the level of the students.

Cultivating Art of Narration—The art of narration can be cultivated through four methods:

1. By observing the work of other skilful narrators.
2. By studying the work of successful writers of children's books.
3. By practising story-telling.
4. By critically observing one's own performance. The use of homely illustrations such as metaphors and similes relating the experiences with which children are familiar adds to the effectiveness of narration. The chief form of narration is story-telling.

Limitations of Narration

1. Students are likely to be passive listeners.
2. Effective narration technique needs expertise.
3. Students are occasionally discouraged to ask questions.
4. Effect technique needs logical as well as psychological approach.
5. Too much of narration tends to make lesson dull and dreary.

6. Appropriate language and gestures need to be developed for practising this technique.

The Dictation

Reasons for Note Dictating

1. Note dictating is resorted to on account of pressure of work upon the teacher and less time available for preparing the lesson.
2. Note dictating is a short-cut to prepare the students for examinations.
3. Note dictating is a short-cut to finish the heavy and overcrowded syllabi.
4. Sometimes note dictating is done when the teacher does not possess adequate power of expression.
5. Note dictating is done when there is non-availability of suitable textbooks.

Methods of Dictating Notes

1. Detailed notes on important topics after discussing the topic in the class.
2. Notes in the question-answer form primarily from examination point of view – guess questions and their answers.
3. Explanatory notes and summaries on the blackboard.

Defects in the Method of Note Dictation

1. It does not provide training in developing critical approach.
2. Note dictation makes Economics teaching synonymous with memorisation of facts communicated by the teacher.
3. Note dictation fails to develop proper insight into the subject.

4. Note dictation proves to be a great hindrance in developing the habit of consulting reference books and textbooks also.

Instead of dictating notes to the students, they should be encouraged to prepare their own notes.

Observation Technique

It is rightly observed that observation method under the careful observation of an Economics teacher proves very effective in the process of learning facts, skills, and behaviour which are retained for a longer period. Observation or direct experience or visits to actual place of work, i.e., banks, insurance companies, stock exchanges and transport enterprises etc. provide ample opportunities to students for 'seeing', 'hearing', 'examining', 'gathering data' and 'asking questions'. By visiting transport companies, students learn how people and goods are transported from one place to another. Pupils understand better the working of banks, cooperative stores, factories and markets etc., when they observe their working and this acquaint themselves with the process of production, distribution, exchange and consumption. Several organisational and managerial practices are learnt better through observation. Observation lends 'reality' to the subject-matter of Economics.

Among the important techniques mention may be made of field trips, educational excursions and community surveys etc.

Guidelines in the Use of Observation Technique in Economics

1. The teacher should prepare in advance an outline of the main points to be observed at the time of actual observation. For instance before taking the students to the factory, main points regarding working conditions etc. should be told to the students so that students observe these.

2. The things or processes or events to be observed should be closely related to the life situations which are studied in Economics.
3. Necessary guidelines and training in the technique of observation should be given to the students.
4. While taking students outdoor to observe some economic phenomenon, it should be ensured that reasonable freedom is given to the students.
5. After observation, students should be asked to explain the main points.
6. Gaps in the knowledge of students gained through observation should be filled up by the teacher.

Poster : Poster is a placard, usually decorative or pictorial utilizing an emotional appeal to convey a message aimed at reinforcing an attitude or urging a course of action. Many economic activities can be illustrated through the use of posters. They attract the attention of the students in a dramatic way. They create interest and become a source of motivation among the students. The teacher may use poster in introducing new materials to the students, in studying economic and industrial position in different geographical regions of the country, the posters may be used to arouse interest and motivate the students to raise question and problems from the posters. Posters may also be used to make summary of important learning material. The presentation of key ideas can be made through different posters in an effective manner. The most important merit of the poster is that one major idea can be presented to the students. The posters may be collected through industrial and government agencies. Posters may be prepared by the teachers and the students as well. Posters provide knowledge with respect to the resources of the country.

Review or Revision or Recapitulation

Review or revision is a 'retrospective view' of what has been learned or experienced. According to the literal meaning it means to 'view again'. In the words of Bossing, "The term review connotes not a mere repetition of facts or fixing them more firmly in mind, but rather a new view of these facts in a different setting that result in new understandings, changed atitudes, or different behaviour patterns." According to Rusk, "Review means getting a new view or renewal of an old view to assure a better view or grasp of relationships studied."

In the words of Dr. Yoakam and Simpson, "The review involves a recall for purposes of renewing the learning already passed and of carrying it on to mastery. It is the reorganisation and integration of experiences."

Purposes of Review

1. It helps in the fixation of relationship of facts by providing a restatement and organisation of facts.
2. It helps pupils to have a broader perspective of what is being taught.
3. It helps to reveal weakness in the teaching-learning process.

Types of Review

1. Review of a section of a lesson
2. Daily lesson review
3. Topical review
4. Cooperative review
5. Review by making charts, models etc.
6. Review by practical application.

Role Play

Role play is often referred to as 'practice in reality'. It provides practice in 'how to behave in certain situations'. It enables the learners to understand the attitudes, feelings or situations of those persons whose roles they assume. In it, participants are assumed to play realistic roles. They interact with each other in common economic and social situations.

Important objectives of designing role-play games are to enable the participants to learn to bargain, negotiate, compromise and make decisions.

In the 'Youth Parliament' or 'Student Parliament' one student may play the role of Finance Minister. Other students play the role of exeperts in economic and financial matters.

Other examples of games relating to Economics are the games of 'Business' and 'Monopoly' which the students generally play as hobbies.

Scrap Books

A scrap book is an exercise book which contains interesting materials pertaining the topics contained in the curriculum. The material may be in the form of charts, diagrams and graphs etc. Cuttings from periodicals, magazines and newspapers may also be pasted in it. It supplements class teaching.

Specimen

Specimen is a representative of a class of a thing removed from its natural setting. It is used for demonstration, analysis and study. It can also be examples of handwriting.

Specimens provide concrete and direct learning situation. They bring reality and vividness to instruction.

Springboard

Springboard are materials taken from the real world which draw attention to an issue or porblem and, thus, serve to stimulate inquiry.

Almost anything can be a springboard : documents, magazine or newspaper articles, graphs, maps etc. A news item relating to relaxation of ceiling by RBI on deposits of Non- Banking Finanacial companies may provide a springboard for discussion. A write-up about a selling spree may be the jumping ground for a discussion of bulls, bears and stags.

Story Telling Technique

Meaning of Story Telling—In simple words, as the name indicates story telling means telling a story.

Merits of Story Telling—Story telling is one of the most important methods of teaching. It is an art which enables the teacher to come very close to the heart of the students and thereby he attracts their attention. Some teachers are born story tellers and they are very fortunate in this respect. The art of story telling aims at presenting to the pupils, through the medium of speech, clear, vivid, interesting, ordered sequences of events, in such a way that their minds reconstruct these happenings and they live in imagination through the experiences recounted either as spectators or possibly as participators. Story telling enables the teacher to make lesson lively and interesting to the pupils. Stories of great reformers, writers, saints, discoverers etc. must be told to the students. Story telling helps in enhancing the interests of the students in the subject. It goes a long way in firing the imagination of the students.

Cultivating the Art of Story Telling—The art of story telling can be cultivated by :

1. Observing skilful narrators.
2. Studying the work of successful story writers.
3. Practising story telling.
4. Critically evaluating one's own performance and bringing about necessary changes.

Guidelines in Story Telling—In telling a story the teacher should be guided by the following points :

1. Suitable stories for the age of the students should be selected.

2. The stories should be short and the plot easy.
3. The teacher must know the story well that he wants to narrate. If he stops in the middle, it will detract charm from the story.
4. Language employed in telling a story should be very simple and easy.
5. A story should be told and not read. The story loses a great deal of its interest for the children if it is read.
6. The teacher himself should like the story and take interest in story-telling.
7. There should be plenty of action in the stories. Key sentences and phrases should be repeated as the children enjoy this repetition. The stories should be loaded with activities and experiences familiar to the children.
8. Conversation, if any, in the story should be given in indirect speech.
9. The method of introducing and developing the story should be thought out before-hand.
10. The story should be told in a natural way and very vividly.
11. Humour makes the story more interesting and should not be neglected.
12. To make the story more realistic, the teacher may use pictures and draw diagrams on the blackboard.
13. The story should suggest and inspire the students to action.
14. Ryburn suggests that well-known and familiar stories can be made fresh if they are told as though one of the characters in the story were telling it.
15. The story must have some aim besides mere enjoyment. The teacher must keep in mind the aim while narrating a story. The students too must know the aim.

16. The story should not be too lengthy.
17. The students should be encouraged to read it and tell stories.
18. After telling the story, students should be asked a few questions.

Special Study

Meaning and Significance of Supervised Study—Arthur C. Bining and David H. Bining describe the meaning of supervised study as, "By supervised study, we mean the supervision by the teacher of a group or class of pupils as they work at their desk or around their tables. In this procedure, we find pupils busy at work that has been assigned to them by the teacher. When they meet a difficulty that they cannot overcome, they ask the teacher for direction and assistance. The teacher, when not called upon, walks up quietly up and down the classroom or remains at his desk watching the pupils do their work continually, alert for any wrong procedures that the pupils may follow. He is always ready to direct and aid them."

Main Features of Supervised Study Technique

Individual Attention—Supervised study is an aid in helping to solve the problem of individual differences. Supervised study aids in preventing failures. The pupil works along his own mental level and at his own capacity. Assignments can be given to meet all levels of ability.

Better Pupil Teacher Relations—Another good feature of supervised study is seen in the better pupil teacher relations that it promotes. In the usual class teaching procedure, the teacher is frequently considered a hard task master and the procedure often produces a 'class versus teacher' attitude. Under the supervised study programme, he appears in the role of a helper and guide. There is greater opportunity for the display of sympathy and understanding. The teacher is able to understand the pupil and his difficulties better and is in a position to spurt him on to a greater effort.

Development of Skills—There are certain skills which can best be developed under this procedure. A thorough use of the supervised method would reveal weaknesses in the learner. Following skills can be developed easily :

(a) Skills as to how to read commerce material.

(b) Skills as to how to use encyclopaedias.

(c) Skills as to how to use dictionaries.

(d) Skills as to how to use maps, atlases, indexes and almanacs.

(e) Skills as to how to read graphs.

Forms of Supervised Study

(1)	(2)	(3)	(4)	(5)
Conference Plan	**Special Teacher Plan**	**Divided Period Plan**	**Two-Period Plan**	**Periodical Plan**
Conferences are organised from time to time to sort out the problems of students through mutual consultation.	Special teachers help students to solve their difficulties and problems.	Two teachers supervise the work of the students.	Two periods are provided to study the same subject matter.	Students are instructed to do pre-determined tasks. After some definite period their progress is supervised.

Guidelines for Using Supervised Plan

1. The teachers must possess great insight.
2. The teachers must be resourceful.
3. The teachers should plan the work in a rational, scientific and systematic way so as to develop appropriate attitude in the students.
4. Teachers should aim at developing self-confidence and self-dependence in the students.

5. The tasks assigned to the students should be graded according to their mental and physical abilities and interests.

Objections to Supervised Study—There are some objections such as :

1. Some investigations have concluded that the weak pupil is not helped by this method and in some cases is even hindered.
2. Supervised study requires the lengthened school day and which is not possible due to various pressures of co-curricular activities.
3. Supervised study is a costly method. It would necessitate an increase in the teaching force that would mean an increased cost of education.
4. Supervised study depends too much on the initiative and enthusiasm of the students which they seldom display.
5. Supervised study destroys the supremacy of the teacher as he plays a secondary role in the teaching learning process.

Student-motivated Techniques **:** "Don't do too much for the students", "Let students think and do" are the maxims that underline student-motivated techniques. Student-motivated techniques stress the value of analysis rather than the acquisition of facts. Group discussions, seminars, symposiums, workshops, individual assignments, surveys, paper reading contests—all come under the category of student-motivated techniques.

Wall-magazine

Wall-magazine is a type of bulletin board wherein various articles and essays or cartoons or write-ups etc. on a related theme in Economics are displayed. It provides training to work in a creative way.

Worksheet

Meaning of a Worksheet — A worksheet is basically a sheet containing content-based exercises, which is given to the students as class tasks in between the lesson, before the lesson or after the lesson. It may be given to the pupils along with the handout/book or separately. The main purpose of a worksheet is to promote content-based learning.

Structure and Preparation of a Worksheet — While preparing a worksheet, a teacher is, therefore, to keep in view the content and objectives of teaching the lesson.

A worksheet, usually, contains a variety of questions/exercises to be attempted by the students. The teachers generally go in for objective or short answer type questions as these enable one to cover a wide range of content and take less time to answer. Moreover, they leave enough time for the teacher to take teaching-learning activities in the post-worksheet completion phase.

The students are required to write the answers to the questions/exercises in the worksheet itself, in the space provided for the purpose. While preparing a worksheet, a teacher therefore, provides requisite space in the worksheet for the answers to be given or the exercises to be solved.

Classification of Worksheets

(1)	(2)
Open Book Worksheets	Closed Book Worksheets

In the open book worksheet, the students are provided freedom to consult the source material while attempting questions/exercises. In the closed book worksheet, however, the students are required to complete the exercises just as in an examination. They are not allowed to consult resource materials.

Precautions to be Taken while Making a Worksheet—The teacher needs to observe the following precautions while preparing a worksheet :

1. He should ensure that the worksheet does not become very lengthy and tedious and, thereby, look like an exami-nation question paper. It should normally, contain a variety of objective type or short answer type questions or both that can be solved or answered quickly.
2. He should prepare a worksheet only for the type of content for which the worksheet method is more effective. It is not suitable for the type of content that requires to be dealt with through interactive methods.

Use of Worksheet in the Teaching-Learning Process—A worksheet can be used as a method of teaching as well as an aid to teaching.

Worksheet as a Method of Teaching—When a worksheet is used as a method of teaching, the sequence of teaching-learning activities is as under :

1. The students are exposed to or provided with instructional material. The material may be presented through any one or a combination of the following modes : (i) oral, (ii) written, (iii) audio, (iv) visual, (v) audio-visual.

For presentation of the instructional material, the teacher may use traditional sources like books, handouts, posters, etc. or the modern one like tapes, films, video-tapes, video-disks, CD-ROM etc.

2. Worksheets are distributed among the students with precise directions about the assignment. The teacher states clearly (i) whether the students are to work individually or in groups of two or more than two, and (ii) whether or not they can consult the source material while completing the assignment.

3. On completion of the worksheet by students, the teacher provides the correct answers. One of the following procedures for evaluating the answers may be adopted as considered most suitable :
   (i) The teacher may provide the correct answers and the students evaluate their own answers themselves;
   (ii) The teacher may direct an exchange of worksheet among the students so that each student has his answers evaluated by a peer.
   (iii) The teacher himself may evaluate all worksheets;
   (iv) The teacher discusses the common errors with the students.

QUESTIONS

Essay Type Questions

1. Explain the meaning and significance of devices of teaching. State the role of narration in the teaching of Economics.
2. What is the meaning of assignments ? State their kinds and importance in Economics.
3. Write the merits and demerits of giving home assignments. What precautions should be taken so as to make this device effective in the teaching learning process of Economics ?
4. What is meant by exposition as a teaching device ? State its merits and demerits. Explain how would you make it an effective device in the teaching of Economics ?
5. What is the value of a text book of Economics ? State the qualities of a good textbook of Economics.
6. What are socialised techniques of teachings ? Explain their significance in the teaching of Economics.

7. State the meaning and scope of supervised studies in the teaching of Economics.
8. Explain the significance of narration, description, explanation and exposition as techniques of Economics teaching.
9. "Illustrations are good servants but bad masters." Comment upon this statement and state their significance in the teaching of Economics ?
10. Discuss the word 'illustration' as it is technically used in educational literature. What are the purposes and the uses of verbal illustrations in teaching Economics ? What are their limitations ?
11. What is the value of drill in teaching Economics ? How will you make this technique effective ?
12. Differentiate between a drill lesson and review. What is the purpose of review ?
13. "The modern concept of review is to make it new, deeper and broader overview." Explain how a teacher should plan review effectively.
14. What is the significance of the statement that "one learns best when he practices'.
15. Describe the meaning, nature and functions of this statement.

Short Answer and Objective Type Questions

16. Some statements are given below. Write 'T' if the statement is true and 'F' if it is false.
    (i) 'Doing' is more effective than telling. ( )
    (ii) Story should be told without any gesture. ( )
    (iii) Use of the technique 'Specimen' comes under telling. ( )
    (iv) Discussion is a one-way device of learning. ( )
    (v) Students should prepare charts. ( )

17. Write brief notes on :
    (i) Debates
    (ii) Note Dictation
    (iii) Drill
    (iv) Laboratory Method
    (v) Recapitulation.
18. Write a short note on observation as a technique of teaching in Economics.

9

Teacher's Responsibility

Dual Role

1	2
Role of the Teacher in the Overall Development of the student	Specific Role as a Teacher of Economics

Different Roles

Economics teacher has to perform several roles for the many-sided development of the personalities of their students. Broadly speaking, he is expected to work for the realization of four objectives nemely to enable the child 'to learn' or to gain information and knowledge, 'to be, 'to do' and 'to have a harmonious life'. Some of the important roles for the realisation of these objectives are listed below :

Confident—A teacher is expected to win the confidence of the students so that they express their feelings freely, if need be in private.

Democrat—He is expected to observe democratic values so as to prepare his students for a democratic way of life.

Equaliser—should treat all students on the basis of equality. He should work for developing an egalitarian outlook in students.

Facilitator of Learning—He works for the promotion of significant learning in his students.

Friend and Philosopher—He must perform the role of a friend and philosopher to his students.

Group Leader—As a leader to the social group in the class, he must develop a suitable climate and cohesion.

Guidance Counsellor and Helper—He provides academic, career and personal guidance to his students.

Initiator—He is supposed to play the role of an initiator by exploring the new technology to the best advantage of the students and the progress of education. He should play the role of an innovator of educational ideas, practices and systems.

Role Model—He is envisaged to behave in a manner whereby traits exemplified by him may be emulated by his students.

Detective—He acts as a detective to find out the shortcomings of the students—committing of offences and law breaking tendencies also if any.

Judge—He evaluates the academic and other performance of the students in an impartial manner.

Limiter or Reducer of Anxiety—He can help students control their impulses and reduce anxiety about their conduct and performance in different problematic situations.

Moral Educator—His important function is to inculcate attitudes and moral values cherished by society in the students.

Parent Surrogate (Parent Substitute)—He can play the role of ideal parents by treating students with affection and care.

Rationalist—He should set an example of a rationalist by basing his action on reason.

Referee—He is expected to settle disputes among students in an objective manner.

Reformer—His entire work consists of bringing about appropriate changes in his students for their full development.

Resource Person—He is expected to serve as a resource person for his students as he possesses knowledge of the subject-matter and skills, better than his pupils.

Secularist—He should play the role of a secularist by having an open mind on the beliefs of students.

Upholder of the Norms and Values—He must present the norms and values of society in a dignified manner.

Duties and Tasks

The following are his main functions and responsibilities :

1. Character development of students.
2. Effective teaching learning.
3. Adjusting individual differences.
4. Class-room management.
5. Evaluation of pupil performance.
6. Curriculum development and implementation.
7. Developing good family and community relations.
8. Total school effectiveness.
9. Professional growth and ethics.

Character Development—For this, the teacher :

1. Creates an atmosphere of purposeful order, enlists pupil's assistance in orderly, friendly, courteous and co-operative interpersonal relations.
2. Develops a respect for the rights, privileges and opinions of others.
3. Creates group situation which will develop desirable leadership and followership qualities in the pupils.

4. Sets a standard of class-room and school environment behaviour which conforms to socially acceptable behaviour.
5. Directs discussion and develops understanding on moral and other ethical issues in order to develop the understanding of the reasons for ethical standard.
6. Encourages each pupil's thinking and action.

Techniques of Teaching – (Effective teaching) This includes:

1. Selecting material, teaching aids and methods which will facilitate the learning process and stimulate students' desire for further learning.
2. Meeting the needs, background and capacities of the children being taught.
3. Teaching by use of a suitable variety of lectures, discussions, demonstrations, visual and oral presentations, recitation, directed group effort, experimentation, special projects and field trips.
4. Analysing and evaluating the effectiveness of various teaching techniques in order to improve the learning process.
5. Endeavouring to obtain and maintain pupil interest and attention so that teaching is done in a receptive environment.
6. Endeavouring to assure that material taught is applied in such a manner so as to develop a pattern of understanding in other areas.
7. Encouraging and guiding critical thinking by pupils.
8. Developing desirable work and study skills and habits.
9. Enlisting pupil participation in the lesson planning process.
10. Developing broad outlines and objectives to be attained within prescribed limits for a subject or skill area based upon the needs and interests of a specific group of pupils.

11. Assuring that preparation adequate to ensure purposeful and directed teaching precedes all actual class-room teaching.
12. Making suitable lesson plans and other necessary arrangements for substitutes.

Adjusting to Individual Differences and Development Levels—This calls for:

1. Drawing upon and applying the basic knowledge of the psychology of the child in order to establish readiness for learning.
2. Making an effort to know as much as possible about the background and out-of-school environment of each child in order to improve the teaching learning process.
3. Developing in each pupil a sense of personal growth and value.
4. Maintaining discipline by being consistent friendly, fair and firm.
5. Handling behaviour problems in a controlled manner.

Classroom Management—This means :

1. Assigning responsibility to pupils for the care and housekeeping of the classroom's physical assets.
2. Developing, preparing or providing material and equipment and displaying it in a manner so as to improve the learning situation.
3. Maintaining the school-room in a healthful and safe condition, assuring proper lighting, ventilation etc.
4. Preparing and maintaining orderly and accurately all required records, such as attendance register.

Evaluation and Reporting of Pupil Performance—This comprises :

1. Devising and administering appropriate tests to measure the level and quality of pupil learning.

2. Interpreting test results and relating findings to pupil progress or lack of it in order to improve the teaching and learning process.
3. Evaluating pupil performances through reports, recitations, homework and other types of assignment.
4. Reporting pupil achievements and progress to parents by means of conferences and progress reports.
5. Co-operating and enlisting the co-operation of school specialist in the process of pupil evaluation as required.

Curriculum Development and Implementation—This implies:

1. Participating in grade level or subject matter study of existing curricula and in the development of improved expanded curricula.
2. Determining the object, scope and methods of the grade and subjects to be taught.
3. Devising assignments, when necessary, in order to enrich the teaching programme for the pupils.
4. Correlating subject matter with the curriculum of other subjects.

Developing Good Family and Community Relations—This envisage :

1. Participating in parent-teacher associations and similar activities.
2. Participating in community affairs.
3. Making himself available to parents at scheduled times to discuss pupil progress and behaviour.
4. Evincing a sympathetic, helpful and understanding attitude towards parents and their children's schooling problems.
5. Establishing and maintaining a good relationship with parents and reporting of pupil progress, problems and needs from time to time.

6. Assuring through personal behaviour in the community that the school staff-image in the community is favourable.

Total School Effectiveness—This consists of:

1. Accepting responsibility for pupil discipline throughout the school and in the interest of the school as a whole.
2. Co-operating with all co-workers and exchanging ideas in order to improve and provide a variety of approach on the teaching situation.
3. Executing all required school regulations and assignments on time.
4. Accepting one's full share of pupil activity participation; such as attending athletic contest etc.
5. Contributing constructively to committees, faculty meeting and other school system groups.
6. Taking positive steps in developing and maintaining faculty and students morals.

Professional Growth and Ethics—This stipulates :

1. Keeping knowledge upto date.
2. Participating in in-service programmes like seminars and workshops etc.
3. Adhering to professional ethics, i.e., not compelling students to take tuition from him and his colleagues, not recommending instructional materials to students on some consideration etc.
4. Participating in the activities of professional organisations.

Basic Characteristics

These may be categorised as :

I. Scholarship.

II. Professional growth.

III. Personality.

IV. Teaching Skills.

V. Human Relations.

Scholarship—This includes :

1. Acquaintance with problems of present day life.
2. Background of a liberal education.
3. Reader of magazine and newspapers.
4. Reader of books on the subject taught.
5. Sound knowledge of the subject.

Professional Growth—This incorporates :

1. Desire for improvement.
2. Professional attitude.
3. Reader of professional books.
4. Reader of educational magazines.
5. Sound professional training.

Personality—It has three aspects :

(a) Physical aspects.

(b) Personal virtues.

(c) Executive abilities.

Physical aspects—These includes :

(i) Personal appearance include dress, carriage, social expression, and personal cleanliness.

(ii) Etiquettee including good manners, observance of social norms, courtesy and refinement.

(iii) Voice, rich and mellow.

(iv) Good language command including pronunciation, enunciation and grammar.

(v) Health.

Personal Virtues—These include :

(i) Enthusiasm.

(ii) Fairness.

(iii) Friendliness.

(iv) Optimism.

(v) Patience.

(vi) Self-control.

(vii) Sincerity.

(viii) Sympathy.

(ix) Tact.

(x) Understanding.

Executive Abilities—These include :

(a) Adaptability

(b) Directing ability

(c) Industriousness.

(d) Initiative.

(e) Organising ability.

(f) Resourcefulness.

(g) Self-confidence.

(h) Self-reliance.

Teaching Skills—The Core Training Programme Package (CTPP) of the NCERT (1979) aiming at enabling the teachers to acquire mastery of manipulative skills for making their teaching effective includes the following skills :

1. Skills of class management.
2. Skills of communication (Teacher's Acts).
3. Skills of Interaction (Teacher-Pupil Acts).
4. Skills of the use of Teaching Aids.
5. Skills of Attitude and Behaviour

Skills of Class Management—These include as below :

Control and Modification of Facial Expression. The teacher should enter the class as a balanced person. It is necessary to emphasise the need for neatness and simplicity in his dress and appearance. Gaudy dress and shabby appearance have to be avoided. The teacher must maintain his calm and confidence in the face of gesticulation and mimicking of the group.

Greeting and Taking up Proper Position in the Class. The teacher is expected to offer the greetings while entering the class and then take the central place when students are offering greetings orally or by standing up in their seats and then face the class and respond to the greetings.

Movements (Locomotive in the Class-room). Appropriateness of movement lies in providing a balanced supervision to the class and in being available at the right time to the students who needs help.

Use of Appropriate Gestures. Expressions of gestures of approval, appreciation and disapproval also have a great bearing on learning. The tendency of offering undue smile or encouragement or displeasure would form the negative points. Praise like gold and silver owes its utility to scarcity.

Skills of communication (Teacher's Acts)—This comprises five skills, narration, recitation, dramatisation, explanation and demonstration. These skills are teacher-dominated.

Skills of Interaction—These include :

(a) Questions and feedback.

(b) Discussion and

(c) Problem solving.

Skills of the Use of Teaching Aids—These consist of:

(a) Selection of teaching aids as per needs.

(b) Preparation of charts, models, maps and diagrams.

(c) Operation of mechanical aids.

(d) Positioning while writing on and explaining from the blackboard.

(e) Writing on the blackboard with reference to size, shape, boldness and colour of lettters.

(f) Drawing, sketching, preparing tables and graphs on the blackboard.

Skills of Attitudes and Behaviour – This comprises :

(a) Patient Listening.

(b) Suggesting.

(c) Guiding.

(d) Counselling.

Human Relations – This comprises amicable :

1. Relations with students.
2. Relations with colleagues.
3. Relations with parents.
4. Relations with school personnel.
5. Relations with administrators, inspectors, supervisors etc.
6. Relations with the community.
7. Relations with publishers, stationers, sports dealers etc.
8. Relations with professional organisations and workers.

Importance of the Word

E stands for Enthusiasm.

C stands for Clarity or Constructiveness.

O stands for Objectivity.

N stands for Novelty or New Ideas.

O stands for Observation.

M stands for Media User.

I stands for Interest in the subject or Interest in the students.

C stands for Character Constructiveness.

S stands for Scientific attitude.

T stands for Tact, Thirst for knowledge, Tolerance, Truth.

E stands for Efficiency or Emotional stability

A stands for Adaptability, Affection, Alertness.

C stands for Creativity

H stands for Hard work, Honesty, Humility, Human Relations, Humour.

E stands for Experimental attitude.

R stands for Rationality, Resourcefulness.

Particular Characteristics

A teacher teaching Economics is expected to possess the following specific qualities so as to make his teaching effective, fruitful and inspirational.

1. Interest in Economic problems.
2. Interest in current affairs, especially having an impact on economic issues.
3. Knowledge of statistics.
4. Knowledge of economic geography.
5. Knowledge of commercial economics.
6. knowledge of the principles and practices of teaching Economics.
7. Knowledge of sound evaluation procedures in Economics.
8. Skill in organising outdoor fieldwork like surveys and visits to places of economic, commercial and industrial importance.
9. Skill in preparing and presenting charts, curves, diagrams, graphs etc. on a variety of economic and statistical data.
10. Skill in correlating economic issues with other social issues.
11. Rational and scientific attitude towards controversial economic and social issues.

12. Skill in developing a comprehensive Question Bank in Economics.
13. Skill in the use of computer and Internet etc. for obtaining necessary facts and figures
14. Skill in organising economics club and association.

Teacher Education

Training of an Economics teacher involves the following :

1. University Degree in Economics
2. Training course including methodology of teaching commerce
3. In-service training through :
    (i) Seminars.
    (ii) Symposium.
    (iii) Workshops.
    (iv) Lectures.
    (v) Study of books, newspapers and journals related to commerce and allied subjects.
    (vi) Visits to commercial and industrial establishments.
    (vii) Visits to industrial fairs.
    (viii) Visit to book fairs.

QUESTIONS

Essay Type Questions

1. Explain the multifarious duties of the Economics teacher.
2. What specific teaching qualities should an Economics teacher possess to make his teaching effective as well as inspirational.
3. What types of skills are needed in an Economics teacher?

4. How can an Economics teacher develop his professional competence ?
5. Explain the system approach role of the Economics teacher ?

Short Answer and Objective Type Questions

6. List any three skills of an Economics teacher.
7. Mention any three methods of in-service education of an Economics teacher.
8. Give any three qualities of a teacher regarding effective class management.

10

Out of Classroom

The term 'Survey' is derived from the words 'sur' or 'sor', and 'veeir' or 'vieor' which mean 'over' and 'see' respectively. According to Webster's New Collegiate Dictionary, a survey is a 'critical inspection, often official, to provide exact information'. A survey deals with 'What is'. It describes and interprets what exists at present.

Importance of Survey

Whitney, F.L. – "The survey, according to recent social science terminology, is an organised attempt to analyse, interpret and report the present status of a social institution, group or area."

Yang Psin Pao—"A social survey is usually an inquiry into the composition, activities and living conditions of a group of people."

A survery is often conducted by collecting samples. Samples represent the entire population. For example, out of 10,000 families of a locality (population) we may select only 1,000 families. Thus

1,000 families will represent the characteristics of the 10,000 families. This is known as 'sampling'.

Teaching and learning in the outdoors implies teaching and learning outside the four walls of the classroom. It may also imply teaching and learning outside the school premises, i.e., from natural surroundings and from various community resources. This approach to education is based on the well-established principle of 'learning by doing'.

The principal premises underlying the implication of outdoor education for all subjects and at all levels are :

1. That which can be learnt inside the classroom should be supplemented by outdoor learning.
2. That which can be learnt in the outdoors through direct experience is more durable and effective.
3. That people and things are seen in their true relationships in the outdoor learning.
4. That school is not the only place of teaching-learning.
5. That the hidden curriculum outside the school should be taken note of.

Over the years, educator-philosophers like Comenius (1592-1670), Rousseau (1782-1852), Pestalozzi (1746-1827), Herbart (1746-1841), Froebel (1782-1852), Spencer (1820-1903), Dewey (1859-1952), Tagore (1861-1941) and Gandhiji (1869-1948) have pointed out the need for reinforcing abstract learning with concrete experiences. Going back to the Vedic and Epic periods, we find that Ashrams, mostly located at pleasing surroundings in the countryside/forests were the most important places of teaching-learning.

Lord Chesterfield (1694-1773) in a letter to his son away at school, aptly advised him, "The knowledge of the world can only be acquired in the world and not in a closet. Books will never teach you but they will suggest many things to your observation."

Gandhiji observed, "It is gross superstition to suppose that knowledge can be obtained only by going to schools and colleges.

The world produced brilliant students before schools and colleges came into being."

Outdoor education aims at enriching, vitalizing and complementing content areas of Economics by means of first hand observation and direct experience outside the classroom. By extending the classroom into the out of the doors, a setting can be provided for bringing deeper insight, greater understanding and real meaning to those areas of knowledge which ordinarily, are merely read and some-times discussed but seldom experienced.

The Merits : A Survey :

1. Provides the students a reliable evidence about the existing situation.
2. Motivates students through participation.
3. Makes the learning effective.
4. Helps the students to correlate their knowledge.
5. Develops practical skills of interpretation and presentation of data among the students.
6. Provides opportunities for human interaction leading to social growth.
7. Tends to develop initiative and responsibility among the students.
8. Provides an opportunity to the students to react to unexpected events, conditions or the actions of others.
9. Provides for a logical and psychological procedure.
10. Makes the students research minded.

The Limitations: The main limitations of survey method are as follows :

1. Requires great deal of time.
2. Is expensive.
3. If excessively used, it overburdens both the teacher and the students.

4. If data is insufficient, it leads to drawing of wrong generalizations.

The Sphere

There is a great scope for field activities in the teaching of Economics. Following are some of the activities that can be organised in this regard :

1. Survey of Economic Needs of a Community.
2. Land Used Survey.
3. Household Survey.
4. Survey of Sources of Irrigation for Farming in the Neighbourhood.
5. Survey Regarding Means of Personal Transport.
6. Survey of Agricultural Implements Used by Farmers.
7. Survey of Manures and Fertilizers Used by Farmers in a Village.
8. Traffic Flow Survey.
9. Working of a Bank.
10. Working of a Cottage Industry.
11. Visit to a Market.
12. Visit to Stock Exchange Market.
13. Visit to a Factory.
14. Visit to an Industrial Area.
15. Survey of Economic and Social Amenities Available in Two Different Areas.
16. Working of an Employment Exchange.

The Suggestions

The following instructions should be given to the students :

(i) They should establish proper rapport with the inhabitants of the area.

(ii) They should explain the objective of the survey.

(iii) Their questions should be simple and brief and should be of concern with their survey.

(iv) Such formalities as enquiring about the well-being of the person from whom the questions are to be asked will make the job easy.

(v) Questions should not be asked to a person whem he is busy in his own work.

(vi) The answers should be noted down immediately in record book so that they do not forget it later on.

The entire survey is divided into following five stages :

Preliminary Stage—At this stage, the surveyor prepares the plan of the field work. This is also known as planning stage.

Operational Stage—This stage comes when the surveyor completes his survey in the field according to the plan.

Tabulation Stage—After completing the survey the data collected are arranged in tabular form.

Mapping Stage—At this stage, maps of the concerned area are drawn on the basis of data collected during the survey.

Reporting Stage—Report is prepared after completing the entire survey process. Conclusions are presented in the report. Remedies to the problem are also suggested.

Various Kinds of Surveys

Introduction—Agriculture is the most important occupation in India. Therefore, it is very important for the students studying Economics to understand the land use. They can know about some of the drawbacks and suggest some measures to improve the situation.

Aim and Objective of the Survey—The main aim of the survey is to know about the land use in the agricultural area. For this purpose, the entire village or a part of it depending upon the size of the area can be taken.

Agricultural land can be found in the neighbourhood of big cities also. Our objective can be achieved by allotting numbers to fields, filling the crops grown in those fields and preparing a land use map of the concerned area. We are also required to collect information about soils, slope, drainage and irrigation.

Method—Required map is procured from the village official (Patwari). The teacher should divide the students into small groups of two or three students and allocate the area to be covered by each group. This will help in covering area in a short time.

Procedure of Survey—Going to the field on fixed date and time and establishing personal contact with the fanners. It is essential to collect the data and prepare the land use map. Often code numbers or abbreviations are used for plotting the land use.

On a separate map, marking the soil type according to colour and texture, and making notes about the general character of the field in terms of the slope and drainage whether the crop is irrigated or unirrigated, making enquiries from the farmers regarding the land use. For this purpose, students will need a schedule in which they will fill up various columns by gathering information from the farmers.

Tabulating and Processing the Data—After preparing the schedule as mentioned above, students tabulate and process the data as per requirement. The data are processed from the view point of land use and number of fields.

Analysis and Mapping—The entire information collected and mapped is analysed as follows :

(i) Total area of agricultural land.

(ii) Number of fields.

(iii) Average size of the fields.

(iv) Major soil types.

(v) Total kharif crops.

(vi) Area under kharif crops.

(vii) Area under rabi crops.

(viii) Total rabi crops.

(ix) Crops of inter season and area under such crops.

(x) Irrigated area – kharif, rabi and the seasonal.

Conclusion – Conclusion is given at the end. This includes an appraisal of land use. The defects in the land use, if any, are identified and remedial measures are suggested.

Introduction. The agricultural development in India depends to a great extent upon the agricultural implements used by the farmers. Personal means of transport also play an important role in agriculture.

Aim of Survey. The survey aims at knowledge about obtaining farm implements used by the farmers and it is also important to investigate about the quantity and types of manures and fertilizers being used by them.

Method of Survey. Following aspects of agriculture are investigated in this survey :

(i) Means of personal transport.

(ii) Agricultural instruments used.

(iii) Type of manures and fertilizers used.

(iv) Quantity of manures and fertilizers used.

These aspects are investigated on the following basis of information collected.

Procedure of Survey. The students will be divided into small groups. A map of the village will be prepared and different means of personal transport in different directions will be shown by a flow diagram. Various articles transported on different routes will also be shown on the basis of collected data. The sources of agricultural and transport and implements used will be shown by different diagrams such as bar diagram, pie diagram etc.

Conclusion. Conclusions will be drawn after completing the task. It will be found out whether these facilities exist in the village in sufficient quantity, what measures could be taken to provide these facilities, which type of fertilizers are used and also the quantity. Ways and means will be suggested to fulfil the demand.

Introduction—There are three types of occupations namely 'primary', 'secondary' and 'tertiary occupations'. The rural people are mainly agriculturist which is a primary occupation. People living in urban areas are mainly engaged in industry and trade which are secondary and tertiary occupations respectively. The occupational survey is done by personally going to the concerned areas.

Aims of Survey—Following are the aims of survey:

1. To know about the occupational structure of at least two or three localities.
2. To learn about the economic condition of people living in those localities.
3. To establish relationship between occupation and economic conditions of the people of these localities.
4. To compare the occupational pattern and economic conditions of at least two to three localities.

Method of Survey—Select two suitable localities for conducting the survey. Prepare questionnaire regarding occupational pattern in the following pattern :

Questionnaire

Sr. No.................. Name of the area ....

Village/Mohalla ....

1. Name of the head of the family ....
2. Educational qualifications ....
3. Number of the members of the family ....
4. Occupation ....
5. Monthly income ....

Procedure—Collect information on the basis of the questionnaire. Classify the occupational structure, divide people into different income groups and do the comparison of the occupation and income of different areas.

Conclusion—Prepare survey report on the basis of study.

Occupation Status

Occupation	*Number of People Engaged*	*Percentage of Total*
Primary		
Secondary		
Tertiary		
Total		

Income Status

Income status Annual Income (in Rs.)	*Number of families*	*Percentage of the total*
Less than 6000		
6,000-12,000		
12,000-24,000		
24,000-36,000		
above 36,000		

Societal Demands

Mariam E. Silcox under the caption 'Economic Life of Hartford', in Economic Education Experiences of Enterprising Teachers (New York : Joint Council on Economic Education, 1963) conducted the following survey. In West Hartford (U.S.A.), Connecticut, a study of sixth-grade class indicated the necessity for economic growth in their geographical area. For example, the growth of population in the community and all of the problems the community faced in providing additional and adequate educational facilities were examined, such as split sessions, temporary quarters, and other stopgap measures. The grumblings and complaints called for an answer. This was a personal dislocation, and the students were entitled to an explanation. Again, we see the motivation for a meaningful investigation in the area of Economics. The study revealed that growth in the community is affected by individual action and that the individual is affected by growth. Natural and human resources played a major role. Sources of capital investment were needed. Individual enterprise was a key to the development. Growth in West Hartford had to be associated with growth in the entire Hartforo area, in Connecticut itself, in New England, and the nation.

The factors of economic growth are the same in each of the geographical areas. The study also showed the interdependence of people in the community, the state, and the nation.

Interviews of town officials were conducted concerning the actions that were being taken to meet the challenge of growth and why it was impossible to institute certain remedies. Planning specialists came to the class along with local tax officials to explain their projections. The Chamber of Commerce officers were questioned on steps which they were taking to meet the challenge. Officials of manufacturing establishments and other business contributed insights into possible expansion plans.

The resources, after they were all investigated, the organizational patterns, and the effectiveness of West Hartford in meeting the growth were compared to problems which other communities were facing. The study was taken beyond national boundaries, and comparisons were made with areas in Latin America. Using the factors involved in the analysis of growth, the students were able to reach conclusions on the reasons and opportunities either for or against growth in other area. The question of why better use was not made of the available resources was raised; especially in regard to the Latin American countries. The students had come a long way from a concern with personal dislocation to an investigation of community and area development in their own as well as in other nations.

QUESTIONS

Essay Type Questions

1. Explain the meaning of a survey. What is its importance in the teaching of Economics? Explain this with the help of a survey.
2. What is the meaning of outdoor or field work ? State its significance in the teaching of Economics. Cite some examples of outdoor work in the teaching of Economics.
3. Explain the guidelines and steps in conducting a survey of some economic problem.
4. State the meaning of a survey in the context of the teaching of Economics. What are its merits and limitations. Explain the organisation of a survey in Economics.
5. As a teacher of Economics what type of surveys would you conduct to supplement classroom teaching.

Short Answer and Objective Type Questions

6. Differentiate between a sample and a population.
7. Fill in the blanks :
   - (i) A sample represents the......................
   - (ii) A survey provides......................learning experiences.
   - (iii) Learning is only confined to educational ....
8. Mention the names of any three educators who laid stress on concrete learning experiences.
9. List any three instructions that you will give to the students for conducting a survey.

11

Audio-Visual Aids

In someway or the other Audio-visual aids have been used in the teaching-learning process from time immemorial. In earlier times, since life was very simple, simple aids were used. With the development of science and technology and its use in all walks of life including education, a variety of teaching aids have come into vogue. Now it is universally accepted that without the adequate and proper use of aids, teaching-learning process cannot be inspirational and effective.

In the fifteenth century, Erasmus (1466-1536) a Dutch humanist, theologian and writer discouraged memorisation as a technique of learning and advocated that children should learn through the aid of pictures.

John Amos Comenius (1592-1670) prepared a book known as Orbis Sensulium Pictus (The World of Sense Objects) which contained about 150 pictures on aspects of everyday life. The book is considered to be the first illustrated textbook for childhood education. This book gained wide publicity and was used in childhood education centres all over the world. Jean Rousseau (1712-1778) and other educators stressed the need of pictures and other play materials. Rousseau condemned the use of words by teachers and he stressed 'things'. He pleaded that the teaching process must be directed to the learner's natural curiosity. Pestalozzi (1756-1827) put Rousseau's theory into action in his 'object method'. He based instruction on sense perception.

The term 'visual education' was used as early as 1926 by Nelson I. Greene.

Eric Ashby (1967) identified four revolutions in education : education from home to school, written word as tool of education, invention of printing press and use of books and lastly the fourth revolution in the use of electronic media, i.e., radio, television, tape recorder and computer in education.

Teaching Devices

'Audio-Visual Aids', 'Educational Communication Technology', 'Audio Visual Media', 'Learning Resources' and 'Instructional or Education Media', all these terms mean the same thing. Earlier the term used was audio-visual aids in education. With the advancement in the means of communication and that of technology, educators coined new terms. More specifically media refers to films, filmstrips, recordings etc. The use of the newer terms like Educational Technology or Instructional Technology is primarily due to the dynamic expansion of programmed learning, computer assisted instruction and educational T.V. This revolution in the field of audio-visual education is the outcome of the development in electronics, notably those involving the radio, tape recorder and computer.

Locatis and Atkinson (1984) define media as the means (usually audio-visual or electronic) for transmitting or delivering messages. Media includes such things as prints, graphics, photography, audio-communication, television, simulating games and computer.

Schramm, Wilber (1973) in his book Big Media—Little Media, included Aid Studies in Educational Technology, categorises computer, VCR, TV as 'Big Media' and 'radio, filmstrips, graphic, audio cassettes and various visuals as 'Little Media.'

The Concept

Bin-ton—Audio-visual aids are those sensory objects or images which initiate or stimulate and reinforce learning.

Carter V. Good—Audio visual aids are those which help in completing the triangular process of learning, i.e., motivation, classification and stimulation.

Edgar Dale—Audio visual aids are those devices by the use of which communication of ideas between persons and groups in various teaching and training situations is helped. These are also termed as multi-sensory materials.

Good's Dictionary of Education—Audio visual aids are anything by means of which learning process may be encouraged or carried on through the sense of hearing or sense of sight.

Kinder, S. James—Audio-visual aids are any device which can be used to make the learning experience more concrete, more realistic and more dynamic.

Mckown and Roberts—Audio-visual aids are supplementary devices by which the teacher through the utilization of more than one sensory channels is able to clarify, establish and correlate concepts, interpretation and appreciations.

Psychology of Using Teaching Aids/audio-visual aids in Teaching— Re-search done by Cobun (1968) indicated the following quantity of retention by the use of various senses : :

1 per cent of what is learned from the sense of TASTE.

1.5 percent of what is learned from the sense of TOUCH.

3.5 per cent of what is learned from the sense of SMELL.

11 percent of what is learned from the sense of HEARING.

83 per cent of what is learned from the sense of SIGHT.

Retention of what is learned is likwise related to sense experience.

Observation and research by Cobun tended to show, holding time as nearly constant as possible, that people generally remember:

10 percent of what they READ.

20 per cent of what they HEAR.

30 per cent of what they SEE.

50 per cent of what they HEAR and SEE.

70 per cent of what they SAY.

90 per cent of what they SAY as they DO a thing.

Popular saying on Audio-Visual aids

I hear, I forget.

I see, I remember.

I do, I understand.

The Importance

Audio-visual aids or devices or technological media or learning devices are added devices that help the teacher to clarify, establish, correlate and co-ordinate accurate concepts, interpretations and appreciations and enable him to make learning more concrete, effective, interesting, inspirational, meaningful and vivid. They help in completing the triangular process of learning, viz., motivation-clarification-stimulation. The aim of teaching with technological media is 'clearing the channel between the learner and the things that are worth learning'. The basic assumption underlying Audio-visual Aids is that learning—clear understanding—stems from sense experience. The teacher must 'show' as well as 'tell'. Audio-visual aids provide significant gains in informational learning, retention and recall, thinking and reasoning, activity, interest, imagination, better assimilation and personal growth and development. The aids are the stimuli for learning, 'why', 'how', 'when' and 'where'. The 'hard to understand principles' are usually made clear by the intelligent use of skilfully designed instructional aids.

According to Gandhiji, "True education of the intellect can only come through a proper exercise and training of bodily organs – hands, feets, eyes, ears and nose."

Commenting on the use of audio-visual aids, the Kothari Commission 1964-66 observed that it should indeed bring about an 'educational revolution' in the country. It further stated that the supply of teaching aids to every school was effective for the improvement of the quality of teaching.

The National Policy on Education, 1986 and as modified in 1992 has laid a great stress on the use of teaching aids, especially improvised aids, to make teaching-learning more effective and realistic.

In the words of Edgar Dale, "Because audio-visual materials supply concrete basis for conceptual thinking, they give rise to meaningful concepts enriched by meaningful association, hence they offer the best antidote for the disease of verbalism."

Some of the important advantages of the proper use of audio-visual aids in the teaching of Economics are :

1. Audio-visual aids are best motivators to learning.
2. They provide clear images of the subject matter.
3. They are antidote to the disease of verbal instruction.
4. They provide various learning experiences.
5. They provide a great variety of experiences.
6. They are helpful in fixing up new learning.
7. They provide vividness of ideas, processes and things.
8. They bring an element of reality in teaching-learning.
9. They provide lot of freedom to students.
10. They provide opportunities to students to handle and manipulate real things relevant to teaching-learning.
11. They increase the retentive power of the students.

12. They are based on maxims of teaching.
13. They are of a great variety and can be used in a variety of situations.
14. They save a lot of time and energy both of teachers and students.
15. They meet the individual differences of students.
16. They encourage healthy classroom instruction.
17. They are helpful in promoting education on a large scale.
18. They promote scientific temper.
19. They are helpful in developing higher faculties.
20. They provide effective reinforcements.
21. They lead to positive transfer of learning.
22. They provide positive learning environment.

Best Motivators—They are the best motivators. The students work with more interest and zeal. They are more attentive.

Clear Images—Clear images are formed when we see, hear, touch, taste and smell as our experiences are direct, concrete and more or less permanent. Learning through the senses becomes the most natural and consequently the easiest.

Antidote to the Disease of Verbal Instruction—They help to reduce verbalism. They help in giving clear concepts and thus help to bring accuracy in learning.

Various Experience—It is beyond doubt that the first-hand experience is the best type of educative experience. But it is not always practicable to provide such experience to pupils. Substituted experiences may be provided under such conditions. There are many inaccessible objects and phenomena. For example, it is not possible for the pupils living in India to see the Eskimos. Similarly, it is not possible for an average man to climb the Mount Everest. There are innumerable such things to which it is not possible to have direct access. So, in all such cases, these aids help us.

Helpful in Attracting Attention—Attention is the true factor in any process of teaching and learning. Audio-visual aids help the teacher in providing proper environment for capturing as well as sustaining the attention and interest of the students in the classroom work.

Helpful in Fixing up New Learning—'What is gained in terms of learning, needs to be fixed up in the minds of students. Audio-visual aids help in achieving this objective by providing several activities, experiences and stimuli to the learners'.

Vividness—Audio-visual aids give vividness to the learning situation. A film on Buddha provides a vivid picture of his life and teachings.

Realism—The use of audio-visual aids provides a touch of reality to the learning situation.

Freedom—When audio-visual aids are employed, there is great scope for children to move about, talk, laugh and comment upon. Under such an atmosphere the students work because they want to work and not because the teacher wants them to work.

Opportunities to Handle and Manipulate—Many visual aids offer opportunities to students to handle and manipulate things.

Retentivtty—Audio-visual aids contribute to increased retentivity as they stimulate response of the whole organism to the situation in which learning takes place.

Based on Maxims of Teaching—The use of audio-visual aids enables the teacher to follow the maxims of teaching like 'concrete to abstract known to unknown' and 'learning by doing'.

Variety—'Mere chalk and talk' do not help. Audio-visual aids give variety and provide different tools in the hands of the teacher.

Saving of Energy and Time—A good deal of energy and time of both the teachers and students can be saved on account of the use of audio-visual aids as most of the concepts and phenomena may be easily clarified, understood and assimilated through their use.

Meeting Individual Differences—There are wide individual differences among learners. Some are ear-oriented, some can be helped through visual demonstrations, while others learn better by doing. The use of a variety of audio-visual aids helps in meeting the needs of different types of students.

Encouragement to Healthy Classroom Interaction—Audio-visual aids, through their wide variety of stimuli, provision of active participation of the students, and various experiences encourage healthy classroom interaction for the effective realization of teaching-learning objectives.

Spread of Education on a Mass Scale—Audio-visual aids like radio and television help in providing opportunities for education to people living in remote areas. They also help in promoting adult education.

Promotion of Scientific Temper—In place of listening to facts, students observe demonstrations and phenomena and thus cultivate scientific temper.

Development of Higher Faculties—Verbalism promotes memorisation. Use of audio-visual aids stirs the imagination, thinking process and reasoning power of the students, and calls for creativity, and inventiveness and other higher mental activities on the parts of students and thus helps the development of higher faculties among the students.

Reinforcement of Learners—Audio-visual aids prove effective reinforcers by increasing the probability of re-occurrence of the responses associated with them and thus render valuable help in the teaching-learning process.

Positive Transfer to Learning and Training—Use of audio-visual aids helps in the learning of concepts, principles and solving the real problems of life by making possible the appropriate positive transfer of learning and training received in the classroom.

Positive Environment for Creative Discipline—A balanced, rational and scientific use of audio-visual aids develops motivation, attracts the attention and interests of the students and provides a variety of creative outlets for the utilisation of their tremendous energy and thus keeps them busy in the classroom work. In this way, the overall classroom environment becomes conducive to creative discipline.

The Qualities

1. They should be meaningful and purposeful.
2. They should be accurate in every respect.
3. They should be simple.
4. They should be cheap.
5. As far as possible, they should be improvised.
6. They should be large enough to be properly seen by the students for whom they are meant.
7. They should be upto date.
8. They should be easily portable.
9. They should be according to the mental level of the students.
10. They should motivate the learners.

Important Rules

Principle of Selection—Teaching aids prove effective only when they suit the teaching objectives and unique characteristics of the special group of learners. Following points may be kept in view in this regard :

(i) They should suit the age-level, grade-level and other characteristics of the learners.

(ii) They should have specific educational value besides being interesting and motivating.

(iii) They should be the true representatives of the real things.

(iv) They should help in the realization of desired learning objectives.

Principle of Preparation—This principle requires that following points should be attended to :

(a) As far as possible, locally available material should be used in the preparation of an aid.

(b) The teachers should receive some training in the preparation of aids.

(c) The teachers themselves should prepare some of the aids.

(d) Students may be associated in the preparation of aids.

Principle of Physical Control—This principle relates to the arrangement of keeping aids safely and also to facilitate their lending to the teachers for use.

Principle of Proper Presentation—This principle implies the following points :

(i) Teacher should carefully visualise the use of teaching aids before their actual presentation.

(ii) They should fully acquaint themselves with the use and manipulation of the aids to be shown in the classroom.

(iii) Adequate care should be taken to handle an aid in such a way as no damage is done to it.

(iv) The aid should be displayed properly so that all the students are able to see it, observe it and derive maximum benefit out of it.

(v) As far as possible, distraction of all kinds should be eliminated so that full attention may be paid to the aid.

Principle of Response—This principle demands that the teachers guide the students to respond actively to the audio-visual stimuli so that they derive the maximum benefit in learning.

Principle of Evaluation—This principle stipulates that there should be continuous evaluation of both the audio-visual material and accompanying techniques in the light of the realization of the desired objectives.

Classification of Teaching-Aids

Classification No. 1 : Projected and Non-Projected Aids

	Non-Projected Aids				
Projected Aids	*Graphic Aids*	*Display Boards*	*3-Dimensional Aids*	*Audio Aids*	*Activity Aids*
1. Films	1. Cartoons	Blackboard	Diagrams	Radio	1. Computer Assisted Instruction
2. Filmstrips	2. Charts	Bulletin	Models	Recordings	2. Demonstrations
3. Opaque Projector	3. Comics	Flannel Board	Mockups	Television	3. Dramatics
4. Overhead Projector	4. Diagrams	Magnetic Board	Objects	(Audio-visual)	4. Experimentation Films
5. Slides	5. Flash cards	Peg Board	Puppets	(Audio visual)	5. Field Trips
	6. Graphs		Specimens		6. Programmed Instruction
	7. Maps				7. Teaching Machines
	8. Photographs				
	9. Pictures				
	10. Posters				

Classification No 2 : Audio Materials, Visual Materials and Audio-Visual Materials

Audio Materials	*Visual Materials*	*Audio-Visual Materials*
(1) Language laboratories	(1) Bulletin boards	(1) Demonstrations
(2) Radio	(2) Chalk Boards	(2) Films
(3) Sound distribution system sets	(3) Charts	(3) Printed Materials with recorded sound
(4) Tape and disco recordings	(4) Drawings etc.	(4) Sound filmstrips
	(5) Exhibits	(5) Study trips
	(6) Filmstrips	(6) Television
	(7) Flash cards	(7) Videotapes
	(8) Flannel boards	
	(9) Flip books	
	(10) Illustrated books	
	(11) Magnetic boards	
	(12) Maps	
	(13) Models	
	(14) Pictures	
	(15) Posters	
	(16) Photographs	
	(17) Self-instructional	
	(18) Silent films	
	(19) Slides	

Classification No. 3 : Big Media and Little Media

Big media include computer, VCR and T.V. Little media include radio, graphics, audio cassettes and various visuals.

Classification No. 4 : Two-Dimensional and Three-Dimensional Aids

Two Dimensional Aids include—(1) Blackboard, (2) Bulletin board, (3) Flannel board, (4) Magnetic Board, (5) Peg Board, (6) Cartoon, (7) Charts, (8) Diagrams, (9) Flash cards, (10) Graphs, (11) Maps, (12) Photographs, (13) Posters.

Three Dimensional Aids include—(1) Models, (2) Diagrams, (3) Mock-ups, (4) Objects, (5) Specimens, (6) Puppets, (7) Samples, (8) Role play.

The Hindrances

1. Lack of enthusiasm for the use of teaching aids in teachers.
2. Non-availability of aids in schools.
3. Lack of facilities for the use of aids—electricity etc.
4. Lack of training on the part of teachers in the use of aids.
5. Costly nature of aids.
6. Lack of suitable storage facilities.
7. Non-availability of suitable teaching aids in the regional languages.

Value of Experience

Edgar Dale, the chief exponent of audio-visual aids in teaching is the originator of the 'Cone of Experience'. The diagram appears in his book Audio- Visuals Methods in Teaching (1964).

All the learning experiences which can be utilised for classroom teaching are shown by Edgar Dale in a pictorial device—

'pinnacle form'—which he called the 'Cone of Experience'. If we go up the pinnacle from its base, we find that every aid has been arranged in the order of increasing abstractness or decreasing directness. In a simple language, it may be stated that the 'cone' classifies the audio-visual aids according to their effectiveness in communication—aid at the base of the cone as 'most effective' relative effect gradually decreases.

The experiences included in the cone are as indicated below:

Direct, Purposeful Experience—The experiences gained through the senses are direct and purposeful. It has been amply observed, "An ounce of experience is better than a tonne of theory, simply because it is only as an experience that any theory has vital and verifiable significance." This, direct experience is gained through the aids mentioned at the base of the cone.

Contrived Experience—When the real thing cannot be perceived directly, its simplification become necessary. Contrived experience is like a working model which is an editing of reality and differs from the original either in size or in complexity. The real object may be too small or too big, may be confused or concealed. In such a situation, imitation is preferred for better and easier understanding.

Dramatic Participation—In dramatics, certain real events are presented through the play, the pageant (kind of community drama, usually based on local history), pantomine (actors do not speak, make movements), tablean (pictureline scene in which all the characteristics stand still, silently), and the puppets.

Different Kinds of Aids

Blackboard—Blackboard is a unique device which inspite of newer and better devices in vogue, is inapplicable as well as indispensable. It is the oldest and the best friend of a teacher. It is a mirror through which students visualise all about the teacher's mind, his way of explaining, illustrating and teaching as a whole. It is the cheapest and the most valuable teaching device and continues to be the *'sine qua non'* of our educational system. It is the most universally used aid. Writing on sand and clay was the ancient form of blackboard writing.

The use of blackboard in class teaching creates an informal atmosphere and motivates learning. Teaching no longer confines to anyone instructional device. It is a help to 'planning', to 'crystallizing' main points and to 'summarising' and 'reviewing' results. Blackboard being a simple means of dealing with the whole class as a unit, it is extensively used during the course of the lesson.

Uses of the Blackboard – Following are the uses :

1. The teacher can illustrate his lesson on the blackboard and draw the attention of the class to salient features in the lesson.
2. The lesson can be phased and summarized in the right manner. Abstract statement, can be clarified in the exposition stage and a summary containing important points can be given in the recapitulatory stage.
3. Questions and problems when planning class work or approaching a new subject can be listed by the teacher on the blackboard.
4. Pupils' interest in class work can be stimulated by blackboard writings and drawings.
5. It can be put to wide and varied uses. A teacher can use it for graphs, maps, graphic statistics, sketches, and various types of drawings.
6. It provides a lot of space for decorative and creative work.
7. The teacher can erase writings and drawings and start afresh.
8. It helps the teacher to focus the attention of his students on the lesson. It takes heed of varying capacities and rates of grasp of the students.
9. A teacher can review the whole lesson for the benefit of the class with the help of the blackboard.

Types of Blackboards

Fixed Blackboards—Fixed in the wall facing the class and normally made of wood or concrete cement.

Blackboards on Easel—A portable and adjustable blackboard on a wooden easel can be taken out of the classroom while taking classes in the open.

Roller Blackboards—Made of thick canvas wrapped on a roller mostly used for teaching higher classes.

Graphic Board—It has graphic lines and is used for teaching mathematics, science and statistics.

Magnu Board—A board which enables teachers to make 'three-dimensional demonstrations' with objects on a vertical surface. Small magnets are used to hold suitable objects fixed wherever they are put on this vertical surface.

Chalk Board of Different Types of Surfaces

1. Paint-coated pressed wood.
2. Dull finished plastic surface.
3. Vitreous-coated steel surface.
4. Ground glass board.

Chalk Board of Different Colours and Colour Chalks

Colour of the Blackboard	*Colour of the Chalk*
1. Green chalk board	White or Yellow chalk
2. Grey Chalk Board	Yellow
3. Red chalk board	Green, Yellow
4. Orange chalk board	Blue or light Green
5. Yellow chalk board	Blue
6. Rose chalk board	Purple, dark Blue
7. Black chalk board	Any colour

Effective Use of Blackboard : Skill in Writing on the Black-board—Following points may be kept in view while using the blackboard :

1. Blackboards should be kept clean so that writing on it could be easily read by the students from all parts of the room.
2. Writing on the board should be legible.
3. Letters and drawings should be large enough to be seen from all parts of the room.
4. Writing should be started from top left corner.
5. Writing should be in straight rows.
6. Extreme lower corner of the blackboard should not be made use of as writing on it cannot be seen easily.
7. Material on the blackboard should not be covered by standing in front of it
8. Only salient points of the subject-matter should be written on the black-board.
9. Diagrammatic visual presentation involving many processes should be prepared before the beginning of the lesson.
10. It should be ensured that the blackboard is well-lit by natural or artificial means.
11. Everything needed for the blackboard should be got together before the class begins, i.e., collection of chalks, rulers, T. square, compass, projector etc.
12. While writing on the blackboard, the teacher should ensure that the class is attentive.
13. Duster and not hand or handkerchief should be used in cleaning the black-board.
14. Occasionally students may be asked to write or draw diagram on the black-board.

15. Teacher should develop the ability to draw freely on the blackboard. The map or chart or diagram that grows before the very eyes of the students is much more useful and valuable than a well finished map, chart or diagram.
16. It should be ensured that the blackboard is periodically serviced.

Charts : A chart is a combination of pictorial, graphic, numerical or vertical material which presents a clear visual summary. The most commonly used types of charts include outline charts, tabular charts, flow charts and organisation charts. Other types of charts are technical diagrams and process diagrams. Flip charts and flow charts are also being used. Readymade charts are available for use in teaching in almost all areas in all subjects. But charts prepared by a teacher himself incorporating his own ideas and lines of approach of the specific topic are more useful.

Purposes of Charts – Charts serve the following purposes :

1. For showing relationship by means of facts, figures and statistics.
2. For presenting material symbolically.
3. For summarising information.
4. For showing continuity in process.
5. For presenting abstract ideas in visual form.
6. For showing development of structure.
7. For creating problems and stimulating thinking.
8. For encouraging utilisation of other media of communication.
9. For motivating the students.

How to Use Charts Effectively

1. Teacher-made charts should be preferred.

2. Students should be involved in the preparation of charts.
3. Charts should be so large that every detail depicted should be visible to every pupil in class wherever he is sitting.
4. A chart should display information only about one specific area in a subject.
5. A chart should not contain too much written material.
6. A chart should not contain many details.
7. A chart should give a neat appearance.
8. When a chart is to be used in the classroom, the teacher should make sure that there is provision for hanging the chart at a vantage point.
9. The teacher should have a pointer to point out specific facts in the chart
10. Straight pins, staples, pegboards clips, gummed hangers, paper-clips, folded making tapes may all be used for fastening charts without damaging them.
11. Charts should be carefully stored and preserved for use in future.

Types of Charts—The following is a list of basic types of charts in terms of arrangements and the kinds of ideas which they may express :

The Narrative Chart, an extended left-to-right arrangement of facts and ideas for expressing : (a) The events in a process such as shoe making, oil cracking, or the like, (b) The events in the development of a significant issue to its point of resolution or to present status (sometimes a time limit). Example : the events leading to the separation of the Bangladesh from Pakistan, the events leading to the establishment of the idea that an Individual should be free and that he should have a voice in his own government and the events leading to increased regulation of business by government, (c) Technological improvement over a period of years such as improvement in transportation, communication, manufacturing etc.

The Tabulation Chart, a left-to-right, top-to bottom arrangement of facts and ideas for expression : (a) Numerical data for making comparisons, (b) Lists of products, mountains, rivers, or the like in selected areas.

The Cause and Effect Chart, usually a limited left-to-right arrangement of facts and ideas for expressing : (a) Relationship between standard of living and such factors as economic system, availability of natural resources, level of technological advancement, (b) Relationship between a culture and neighbouring cultures, (c) Relationship between rights and responsibilities, (d) Relationship between a complex of conditions and change or conflict, (e) Relationship between the elected and the electors, (f) Relationship between community workers and the community which supports them.

The Chain Chart, a circular or semicircular arrangement of facts and ideas of expressing: (a) Transitions, such as the transition from raw materials to useful products, (b) cycles, such as the water cycle.

The Evolution Chart, a left-to-right arrangement of facts and ideas for expressing : (a) Changes in specific items from beginning to date, perhaps with projection into the future. Examples : origin of the automobile and its subsequent development, early basic homes and changes in basic homes to date, (b) Change in standard in food consumption, length of work, weak purchasing power of a rupee, or the like.

Display Boards : Display boards include bulletin board, flannel board, plastic graph board, magnetic board and peg board.

Bulletin Board— A bulletin board commends itself as a valuable source of information for vitalising our day-to-day practical activities and aspects of modern life. News items of current importance can be put along with other facts of importance like market trends.

Flannel Board— It is a rectangular board with flannel stretched over. Displays made of thin cardboard with coarse sand paper pasted in back may be shown on the flannel and changed with the progress of the lesson.

Plastic Graph Board—It is any smooth polished surface like plate glass rigid plastic sheet or laminated plastic sheet etc. with display material made of thin flexible sheets of different colours cut to required contours.

Magnetic Board—It is a thin mild steel sheet kept flat over a thin rigid wooden plank. Displays are cut-outs made with card-board or thin plastic sheets to the back of which are attached thin ceramic magnets.

Peg Board—It is a perforated painted hard board. Displays could be positioned at desired points by pegs.

Educational Films : Broadly speaking a film is a multiple media of communication. It presents facts in a realistic way, dramatizes human relations, arouses emotions and transmits attitudes. A good film on Economics and Commerce Education is very helpful in illustrating the working of an organisation, the qualities of leadership and several business operations.

The Children's Film Society was established in 1955 with the specific aim of undertaking and promoting the production of educational films.

Radio as an Instructional Aid : The potential of the radio as an instructional aid is being recognised more and more all over the world. R.G. Reynolds writes, "Radio is the most significant medium for education in its broadcast sense that has been introduced since the turn of the century. As a supplement to classroom teaching, its possibilities are almost unlimited. Its teaching possibilities are not confined to the five or six hours of the school day. It is available from early morning till long after midnight. But utilising the rich educational and cultural offerings of the radio, children and adults in communities, however remote, have access to the best of the world's stores of knowledge and art. Some day its use as an educational instrument will be as common place as textbooks and blackboards."

Frederic Wittis has rightly remarked, "I like to think of education by radio as a timely, vital and dramatic thing; a system of learning on acquiring more information; a means of widening one's horizons or enriching one's life and breaking down prejudices through inspiration and not perspiration; an education by desire and not by discipline; a pattern of swiftly changing pictures, events with keen interpretations, not statistics and formula; a moving panorama of the world in which we live right now, while we are living in it not a dreary drill of text books and tests. In short, I feel that one of broadcastings most helpful contribution to education and one of its real responsibilities to itself and its listeners is the popularising of education itself."

Television as an Aid

Availability of Direct Stimuli—Learning can be accomplished more effectively by televised instruction than by conventional methods. Proper use of television's illustrative technique can provide a more direct impact than a conventional lecture or textbook. This is accomplished through the direct pictorial interpretation of fact or theory, utilising static or dynamic visualisations, pictures provide stronger and more direct stimuli to personal thought and understanding than to words.

Consistency in Teaching-learning—Communication by speech is a learned skill, seeing and the thought stimuli provoked by sign begin shortly after birth and comprise the base of experience on which sensory reaction and knowledge are built. Through the use of visual media, consistency is built up into the instructional systems and thus it is more reliable for the student.

Economically Viable—Utilisation of video-assisted learning systems and internal video feedback technologies hold promise for meeting the pressure of information requests, while at the same time maintaining favourable cost benefit ratios especially if we allowed the use of INSAT.

Services of Super Teacher—Through television the 'Super Lecture' or 'Master Teacher' is available at a number of places simultaneously without the expenses of time and toil for travel.

Education of a Greater Number—Television is capable of providing the best possible instruction for the greater number of students.

Multiplication and Magnification—Television is an instructional tool that makes possible multiplication and magnification of distance and time factors and the storage of accomplished and tested instruction. Multiplication implies the exact reproduction of an instructive situation with transmission to an unlimited number of students, for example, the magnification and distribution of 'Live' surgical techniques and the magnification of minute biological reactions, specially in circumstances where normal observation would be difficult.

Efficient Use of Educational Television—Television, a complex tool for the possible development of excellent instruction, can be effective only if properly used by good craftsmen. The key to efficient, inspirational and practical educational television is cooperation among a progressive administration, a dedicated and sincere faculty and an educationally aware and technically knowledgeable staff. No other medium of instruction relies as heavily for quality on the interaction and interdependence of the team of experts : the manager, the educator, the artist and a number of other persons to be selected as much as for their ability to co-operate with others as for their competence in their respective fields.

It is of great importance that TV instructors are auditioned. The instructors appearing on the television must be capable of accepting and assimilating criticism which they would not ordinarily receive in the classroom.

The relationship between the instructor and the production expert determines the quality of presentations. The instructional expert, normally a qualified academician, too often tends to regard the production experts as the 'technician' without any academic stature. This tendency should be curbed before any worthwhile production can take place.

Television is a visual method and to attempt the production of a good instructional programme without a versatile artist is to attempt to produce dairy products without the source of milk.

Organization of the total effort should include, besides instruction and production specialists, an expert programme system analyist whose responsibility it would be to analyse the educational needs of the educational institutions and to recommend the most efficient use of the medium.

An educational psychologist should be an integral member of the team for testing and evaluating the result of the instructional methods as well as for advising on methods to be employed. A great deal of research is necessary to theories E.T.V.'s impact on learning processes.

Video Cassettes : Video Cassettes on different topics of Economics, Commerce and Management are available. The user simply attaches the cassette player to his television set, inserts a cassette and depresses a button. The obvious advantage of the cassette is that it is portable and can be used and reused at will and liking.

QUESTIONS

Essay Type Questions

1. Explain the meaning and significance of audio-visual aids. What is their role in the teaching-learning process of Economics ?
2. Classify audio-visual aids into projected and non-projected aids. Explain the importance of one projected aid and one non-projected aid in the teaching of Economics.

3. Classify aids into two dimensional and three dimensional aids in teaching-learning. State the significance of one aid of each category in the teaching of Economics.
4. "The black-board/chalk board is the most valuable teaching aid in the hands of the teacher." Elucidate this statement.
5. Explain the characteristics of good teaching aid in Economics. What are the principles in their use ? How can we popularise the use of teacing aids in the teaching of Economics in our schools ?

Short Answer and Objective Type Questions

6. Evaluate the teaching-learning value of
   (i) Models
   (ii) Charts
   (iii) Diagrams
   (iv) T.V.
7. Point out the significance of Edgar'Dale's cone of experience in teaching of Economics.
8. Under column 'A' names of some teaching aids are given. Under column 'B' are mentioned the type of aid. Match column 'A' with the type of aid, and write the correct answer under column 'C'.

A	B	C
(i) Specimen	Three Dimensional	
(ii) Exhibits	Two Dimensional	
(iii) Cartoons	Three Dimensional	
(iv) Charts	Two Dimensional	
(v) Sample	Three Dimensional	
(vi) Objects	Three Dimensional	

12

Educational Technology

Erish Ahsley (1967) talks of four revolutions in education :

(1) Revolution of shifting the task of educating young ones from parents to teachers and from home to schools.

(2) Revolution to adoption of the written word as a tool of education.

(3) Revolution as a result of invention of printing and availability of books and other teaching-learning material.

(4) Revolution on account of development in electronics, chiefly involving radio, television, cassette recorder and computer, and development of systems concept.

A very remarkable trend in the field of education during the last five decades in the advanced countries has been the tremendous use of educational technology in making education more productive, relating it to the individual, providing instruction (teaching-learning) on more scientific bases, making learning more powerful and lasting, making up the cultural handicaps of certain categories of pupils and for extending educational services in the remote areas.

The National Policy on Education 1986 and as modified in 1992 envisaged the role of media and educational technology as : Modern communication technologies have the potential to bypass several stages and sequences in the process of development encountered in early decades. Both the constraints of time and distance at once become manageable. In order to avoid structural dualism, modern educational technology must reach out to the most distant areas and the most deprived sections of beneficiaries simultaneously with the areas of comparative affluence and ready availability. Educational technology needs to be employed in the spread of useful information, the training and re-training of teachers, to improve quality, sharpen awareness of art and culture, to inculcate abiding values etc., both in the formal and non-formal sectors. In the villages without electricity, batteries or solar packs need to be used to run the programme.

Role of Technology

J. Bloomer—Educational technology is the application of scientific knowledge about learning to practical learning situations.

J.B. Gases—Educational technology has to be seen as part of a persistent and complex endeavour of bringing pupils, teachers and technical means together in an effective way.

Marilymn Nickson—Educational technology deals with the application of many fields of science to the educational needs of the individual as well as the society.

Michael J. Apter—The term educational technology can be interpreted in a rather narrow way to mean little more than the use of sophisticated hardware (like T.V., Projectors etc.) in teaching or in a broad but trivial way to mean the use of any new educational technique.

Michell—Educational technology could be helpful in educational innovation by considering new systems and materials along with inventing instruments and finding procedures and then thinking proper solutions for educational challenges.

National Council of Educational Technology, U.K.—Educational technology is the development, application and evaluation of systems, techniques and aids to improve the process of human learning.

National Academy of Engineering's Instructional Committee on Education : U.S.A.—Educational technology is the body of knowledge resulting from the application of the science of teaching and learning to the real world of the classroom, together with the tools and methodologies to assist in these applications.

Robert A. Cox—The application of scientific process to man's learning conditions to what has come recently to be called educational or instructional technology.

B.C. Mathis—Educational technology refers to the development of a set of systematic methods, practical knowledge for designing, operating and testing in schools.

De Ceoco—Educational technology is in the form of detailed application of the psychology of learning to practical teaching problems.

Department of Education and Science (DES) : U.K—Educational technology is the development, application and evaluation of systems, techniques and aids in the field of human learning.

Derek Rowntree—Educational technology is a rational problem solving appraoch to education, a way of thinking skeptically and systematically about learning and teaching.

Dieuziede—Director General of UNESCO's Division of Methods, Materials and Techniques—Educational technology implies all the intellectual and operational efforts made during recent years to re-group, re-arrange and systematise the application of scientific methods to the organisation of new sets of equipment and material.

D. Unwin—Educational technology is concerned with the application of modern skills and techniques to requirements of education and training. This includes the facilitation of learning by manipulation of media and methods, and the control of environment in so far as this reflects on learning.

E.H. Hadden—Educational technology is that branch of educational theory and practice which is concerned primarily with the design and use of messages which control the learning process.

G.O.M. Leith—Educational technology is application of scientific knowledge about learning, and the conditions of learning to improve the effectiveness and efficiency of teaching and learning.

I.K. Davis—Educational technology is concerned with the problems of education and training and is characterised by a disciplined and systematic approach to the organization of resources for learning.

Teaching Technology

A review of the above mentioned definitions of educational technology points out the following characteristics of educational technology :

1. Educational Technology is the application of scientific principles to the teaching of Economics.
2. Educational Technology lays stress on the development of methods and techniques for effective teaching-learning in Economics.
3. Educational Technology stresses the organisation of learning situations in Economics for the effective realisation of the goals of education.
4. Educational Technology emphasises the designing and measuring instruments for testing learning outcomes in Economics.
5. Educational Technology facilitates learning of Economics by controlling environment, media and methods.

6. Educational Technology involves input, output and process aspect of Economics of education.
7. Educational Technology is not confined to the use of electronic media in education. It includes systems approach also in the teaching and planning of Economics.
8. Educational technology is an important medium of communication in the teaching of Economics.
9. Educational technology is not to be taken as a synonym to audio-visual aids in the teaching of Economics.
10. Educational technology is a very comprehensive term and is not to be viewed in terms of its parts or processes. It includes instructional technology, teaching technology, programmed learning, micro learning and system analysis in the teaching of Economics etc.

Broad Aims

Hillard Jason has stated the following major objectives of educational technology :

1. Transmitting information,
2. Serving as role methods,
3. Assisting the practice of specific skills, and
4. Contributing to the provision of feedback. Mackenzie and others describe the following four main objectives of eductional Technology :
   (i) The need to reach more students,
   (ii) To reach them with an improved range of learning materials,
   (iii) To offer greater opportunities for independent study, and
   (iv) To permit at least a limited student response.

The U.S. Commission on Instructional Technology (1970) has listed the following important benefits of educational technology:

1. Technology can make education more productive.
2. Technology can make education more individual.
3. Technology can give instruction a more scientific base.
4. Technology can make instruction more powerful.
5. Technology can make access to education more immediate.
6. Technology can make access to education more equal.

Various Branches

Following are the five divisions of educational technology :

Educational Technology (I) – Here direct use of psychological principles is recommended. It deals with diagnostic assessments of pupils, educational objectives in behavioural terms, deciding for methods, devices for classroom instruction, and stimulus-control for self-instructional strategy.

Educational Technology (II) – Here instructional materials and communication means are produced after designing and examining them carefully. Emphasis is towards selection, processing and collections used for communication purposes.

Educational Technology (III) – The management aspects are considered here as planning, programming, budgeting, decision-making operations, research, system analysis and organisation of models for problem solving, computers and information system, and organisation of a man-machine system.

Educational Technology (IV) – It covers educational systems engineering, i.e., the planning, designs, construction and evaluation of instructional systems, administrative systems, operating systems (course, resource centre, curricular development work).

Educational Technology (V) – Educational planning is considered here just like the manifestation of educational systems engineering. The economic finances are the main basis here.

Audio-Visual Aids

Before the 1960s, the term audio-visual aids was very popular in teaching-learning. Generally audio-visual aids were used to make lesson interesting and to involve the use of more senses in learning process. Educational technology on the other hand is a wider part and audio-visual a part of educational technology. Scientific inventions have greatly influenced every aspect of human life. Our education process could not remain untouched with these innovations. The advent of teaching machines, radio, television, tape recorder, computer, language laboratory and internet gave a new dimension to the role of audio-visual aids. Educational technology is not confined to the use of aids. Educational technology makes a functional analysis of teaching-learning process and locates the various components that operate from the stage of input of that a output.

Educational and Instructional Technology

Educational Technology	*Instructional Technology*
1. It has a wider concept, including instructional technology.	1. It is a part of educational technology.
2. Goals are decided in the context of the needs of a nation.	2. Goals are determined in the context of the local needs.
3. Behavioural outcomes are determined keeping in view the ultimate needs of a nation.	3. Behavioural outcomes are determined keeping in view the specific expectations of the learners.
4. Attempts are made to discover the competencies and skills of learners all over the nation.	4. Competencies and skills of the learners of a locality are discovered.
5. Selection of educational media is made for making teaching-learning more effective in several schools of a region.	5. A given class or school is the unit for the selection of educational media for making teaching-learning more effective.
6. Teaching material is produced on a large scale.	6. Limited material is produced according to local needs.
7. Feedback is obtained at national level.	7. Feedback is obtained at local level.

Learning by Programme

Programmed learning is that part of educational technology that lays stress on a teaching-learning strategy based on self-instructional texts or auto-tutors. Programmed learning is usually associated with those programmes which individualise instruction. It is sometimes termed as 'software approach' to education.

Designs as Tools

Instructional designs is essentially a management approach that influence management decision-making in education. It has brought to educational management a scientific quantitative apporach for solving educational administrative problems. It involves three designs : (1) Training Psychology, (2) Cybermatic principles or theory of Reinforcement, and (3) Systems Analysis.

QUESTIONS

1. Explain the meaning of educational technology and its role in the teaching of Economics.
2. Differentiate between educational technology and audio-visual aids. State their implications for the teaching of Economics.
3. What is the difference between educational technology and instructional technology. State their role in the teaching of Economics.

13

The Interaction

It is a technique of teaching-learning which is used to establish a reciprocal relationship among the various subjects of the curriculum and between the school environment and the outside environment. Knowledge is 'One whole' and every source of knowledge is related to other sources in some degree. It is observed in this regard by Guyan, "Facts and ideas have a real and useful influence over the mind only when the mind systematises and coordinates them with other facts and ideas as they are produced." This is the basis of correlation.

The Requirement

Complex and Interrelated Problems of Life—The aim of education is to prepare an individual for life that is full of complex problems. The solution to these complex problems requires the study of a large number of subjects. Take for instance 'unemployment'. It must be studied not only in relation to economic activity and industry but in relation to education, politics and administration. A knowledge of these and other subjects is needed to understand this problem. The best method of education, would, therefore, be to study groups of subjects that are interrelated and help m the solution of various problems of life.

Crowded Curricula—In the past the child had to learn a few subjects but now the number of subjects has become large. It is not possible to have a sound knowledge of a subject without correlating it with the other or other subjects.

Artificiality of Treatment—Education through unrelated different subjects is detrimental to effective teaching-learning.. It becomes verbal, formal and artificial and isolates the individual from life. The work of different teachers remains isolatec and no attention is paid to the pupil's needs. The curriculum remains mere academic and its bearing on life is ignored. Thus correlation is needed.

Association of Ideas—The psychological principle of association of ideas gives rise to correlation. Any piece of knowledge, activity or experience is althought an isolated fragment, it is based upon, related to or is the product of informantion that we get from various subjects through various activities we perform either in school or outside. Education is a synthetic and not an isolated process. The task a teaching is a unifying and composite affair. Correlation is the technique which aim at imparting knowledge in a unified and integrated way.

Gestalt Point of View—Persons of this way of thinking maintain that the whole is greater than part and even different from the sum of its parts. Mind is not composed of different faculties. Cohesion is the power of the mind that integrate influences and impressions. An information related to one thing and again something related to the same thing should be put together.

New Trends in the Curriculum—New trends in education do not regard subjects in an isolated way. For example, social sciences includes history, geography, civics and economics and as such our methods of teaching should also present these subjects in a correlated way.

The Categorisation

Following methods are normally used in the classification of correlation :

Classification of Correlation I

(1)	(2)	(3)	(4)	(5)
Correlation with life.	Correlation of subjects with the craft.	Correlation of different subjects among themselves.	Correlation within the contents of subject.	Correlation of subjects round a project.

Classification of Correlation II

(1)	(2)	(3)
Multilateral Correlation	Unilateral Correlation	Collateral Correlation

Classification of Correlation III

(1)	(2)
Incidental Correlation	Planned Correlation

Classification of Correlation IV

(1)	(2)
Horizontal Correlation	Vertical Correlation

Classification of Correlation V

(1)	(2)
Correlation among subjects	Correlation among different topics of same subject

T. Raymond pleads for correlation as he thinks that, "total neglect of the natural affinities of the subjects of instruction undoubtedly increases the embarrassment caused by crowded curricula; it shuts out the light which one study often sheds upon another; it leads to artificiality of treatment and loss of interest; it deliberately trains the pupil to take a false view of knowledge of a mere agglomeration of independent parts, and to crown all, it leaves room for diversities of aim where the aim is essentially one."

Correlation with Life—This is an ideal type of correlation. School is said to be the 'Epitome' of life and our schools should be 'society or community in miniature'. The activities of the life of the school must be linked with the outside life. The school curriculum should consist of simplified, purified and balanced activities of society. The school should become the centre of community life.

Correlation of Subjects with the Craft and Industry—The Zakir Hussain Committee report lays down, "The elements of curriculum which we have recommended are closely correlated with one another, because we have made an attempt to relate them integrally to the life and the environment of the child. Hence the centre of correlation is a craft chosen according to the needs of the environment". Gandhiji said, "The scheme I wish to place before you today is not a teaching of some handicraft side by side with the so-called liberal education. I want that the whole education should be imparted through some handicraft and industry."

Correlation of Different Subjects among themselves—The teaching of different subjects should be done in such a way as one subject constantly helps instruction in the other subject. While teaching history, the history teacher will stress that India had to face foreign invasions because of its economic prosperity. Many social and economic events are the outcome of historical and geographical influences and vice versa. Similarly, in the teaching of physical sciences, attempts should be made to correlate various subjects.

Correlation within the Contents of a Subject—Topics of a subject should be so arranged that one develops as a natural outcome of the other and prepares the way for the succeeding one. It is a well known maxim that the child learns new things in terms of the old. The famous Herbertain steps of preparation, presentation, comparison, generalisation and application are the outcomes of such a way of thinking. The children should be led from the known to the unknown.

Rainfall and climate become the starting point of vegetation in a geography lesson. The natural resources of country may lead to the industrial life of a country in an Economics lesson. The downfall of one empire may lead to the study of the rise of another empire in a lesson of history and so on.

Correlation of Subjects Round a Project—Apart from the correlation of the various subjects like history, geography, economics, langauage, science, drawing, hygiene, civics etc., with the project, there are many opportunities for the development of democratic and social outlook.

Different Types

Multilateral Correlation – In this type of correlation a particular step incident or item is taken and other subjects correlated. The incident of humidity may be taken for teaching subjects like General Science, Mathematics and Social Studies.

Unilateral Correlation – Here we correlate one incident with another.

Collateral Correlation – Knowledge and action are simultaneous. It is learning by doing. The child is counting while winding around the winder.

1. Correlation gives a sort of unity to the curriculum and makes it less cumbersome.
2. It encourages the all round growth and development of the child.
3. It assists in bridging the gulf between school and society.
4. It establishes a close relationship between experience and knowledge.
5. It prevents narrow specialisation.
6. It makes education natural. Various subjects are closely related to each other and are put together.

7. It makes the lesson interesting by bringing various experiences together.
8. 'Learning by doing' takes the place of 'chalk and talk' when we organise projects to correlate different subjects.

The Preconditions

1. Correlation should be spontaneous and natural. Artificial and forced correlation should be avoided.
2. It should be suited to the needs and interests of the students.
3. Correlation should help in making learning easy, interesting and intelligible.
4. In dealing with every topic the teacher should attempt to make use of every bit of associated or allied matter that may be of some help in enabling the child to understand the topic more completely.
5. We require enterprising and imaginative teachers for this art of correlation. We require teachers who are well read, well informed, well equipped with the knowledge of child psychology and who are sufficiently intelligent. Such teachers will be ever ready to correlate their lesson in the proper way and will also inspire and enthuse students.
6. For the successful working of the scheme of the correlation, we require a flexible curriculum. A rigid curriculum will not allow freedom to the teachers to embark upon various projects which give knowledge in a correlated way.
7. Our approach to education should be radically changed. Subject matter of different subjects may have to be reorientated in the light of the activities to be provided in a school.

8. The various subjects of study and the life of the community should be linked together. Knowledge is worth if it leads to appreciation and solution of human problems.
9. Correlation should be based on the nature of the subject and the stage of pupil's mental development.
10. Full freedom of time should be given in proper correlation.

The Limitations

1. One exclusive method cannot be employed in all teaching situations. All subjects and skills cannot be taught through a single method. It is not educationally sound to make one method to the be-all and end-all of teaching in a school. Prof. Naidu remarks, "It is absured to hang all knowledge from the pegs of a single craft."
2. This method cannot be applied with equal efficiency on all occasions by all teachers.
3. The correlated method cannot be used successfully in higher grades when the subjects become distinct and specialised.
4. Cultural subjects cannot be taught through this method. Prof. Naidu writes : "It is impossible to establish any natural association between a craft and the subjects of cultural value which any one system of education should cover through its curriculum".

The Background

Herbart may be said to be the originator of the concept of correlation in teaching-learning. His basis was the 'Doctrine of Mass Appreciation' according to which new knowledge to be effective should be correlated with the previous knowledge of the students.

Herbart's disciple Ziller expanded this principle and introduced the principle of centralisation. This implies that one subject should be made the central subject and other subjects correlated with it. He made 'History' as central point.

Colonel Parker made 'Natural Sciences' as the central point.

Dewery linked education with life activities and called it 'Principle of Integration'.

Gandhiji laid stress on 'craft' as the basis of correlation.

Broader Aspects

Economics deal principally with money, its inward and outward flow which in other words means income and expenditure. However, it will be wrong to assume that Economics deals with this limited role. It has a wider spectrum to cover. Hence, it has rightly been defined as the science dealing with production, distribution and consumption of goods and services.

In Economics we often hear one term, i.e., Gross National Productivity which is taken to be an indicator of national progress. When we talk of national progress it is not confined to people's monetary status but it covers overall status of a person. Modern economics has become a complex subject because it now deals with multifarious socio-economic and financial matters of an individual as well as of society. It studies systematically and methodically the economic network of society including agriculture, business, money and banking, international trade, transportation, planning, growth and development. Because of an intimate relationship with nation's developmental aspects, subjects like chartered accountancy, cost accountancy, operational research, industrial relations, labour relations, social administration, economic administration, business administration, industrial administration, statistics, sociology, public administration, social work and social welfare which cumulatively contribute to the gross national productivity have become an integral part of Economics.

Study of Economies has now assumed great importance as the activities of modern society cannot be comprehended in isolation. It has close links with production, management and distribution of goods and services of a variety of nature not only at national but also international fronts. Economists are constantly engaged in analysing and interpreting a number of economic phenomena occurring at a rapid pace and influencing all aspects of human life. The growth of industries, expansion of business and all-round economic advancement make it essential to take decisions intelligently and fairly quickly. At this critical juncture economists come forward and contribute substantially to arrive at decisions.

Relationship with other Subjects

The Dictionary of Economics (1998) states that the borderlines between Economics and other disciplines like psychology, sociology, accounting and geography are not easily defined and it is, perhaps, not particularly productive to do so. It further states that political economy, an early title for the subject, now sounds old fashioned.

Commerce. Economics and commerce are closely related to each other. Economics provides the base of commerce as a subject of study. The development of commerce is linked with the economic development of the society. Likewise the development of commerce as a discipline is linked with the development of Economics as a discipline. Sometimes commerce is ragarded as a practical application of economic principles.

Arthur Malthy in 'Economics and Commerce' explains the relationship of Economics and Commerce in these words, "Economics is fundamentally concerned with the problems arising from the production of goods and services and the demand for them. Commerce, on the other hand, is essentially invloved with their distribution and the various processes and services which make distribution fully efficient. But while the economist may study the reasons by which one method of distribution can be more advantageous than another, the allied activities of commercial enterprise deal with the way in which distribution is actually achieved. The student of Commerce is more concerned with the 'how' than 'why' of economic activity."

Study of Commerce is based on production and exchange which are economic factors.

The development of special agencies like insurance, banking, agency system, warehousing goes to indicate the close relationship of commerce to economic factors. The fact is that the economic basis of commerce ramains unquestioned.

Examples

1. Development of Indian trade and industry.
2. Indian banking system.
3. Indian business organisation.
4. Indian currency
5. Economic laws and principles.

Political Science. It is of great interest to note that Economics in the past was known as 'Political Economy'. Kautilya's 'Arthshastra' was a manual of statecraft as well as a treatise on Economics. In modern times MacIver and Marx have regarded both the sciences to be closely interrelated. 'Economic Interpretation of History' as discussed by Marx has established beyond doubt that Economics and political science are inseparable. Economic situations have a decisive say in the political life of a country. Economic conditions in Russia brought about a new form of political government. Similarly political set up of various countries has greatly affected the economic conditions and policies. The political domination of the British exercised a tremendous influence on the economic situation in India. Gandhiji was both a political scientist as well as an economist. Every political party is supposed to have its economic programme.

Aristotle described in detail economic problems of the state in his book 'Politics'. Chanakya's 'Arthshastra' as already referred to discuss various political aspects like justice, war, peace and diplomacy side by side with agriculture, commerce, revenue, currency and other economic and financial aspects.

Garner has very rightly observed, "The burning questions of present day politics at the same time are fundamentally questions of Economics, indeed the whole theory of government administration is largely economic." According to Gilchrist, "Political movements are profoundly influenced by economic causes, economic life is conditioned by political institutions and ideas."

There is no doubt that several of the problems of the state are economic ones and the state works for their solution.

Examples

1. Economic and political policies and systems.
2. Colonisation and decolonisation.
3. Monetary systems.
4. Taxation.

Geography. In the present age of science and technology, human activities are influenced and controlled more by economic and geographical forces. It is therefore, in the teaching of Economics, a good deal of attention is paid to geographic conditions which have a great bearing on economic activities. Economic Geography has become an integral part of Economics in some respects. In Economic Geography, various situations are described in which geographical factors play an important role. In other words Economic Geography is the study of man's activities as controlled or influenced by physical environment. Agriculture, minerals, forests, industries and trade are all influenced by geographical or physical environment. So Economics, which is sometimes called the 'science of wealth' cannot be effectively and properly studied without the knowledge of geography. It is the geographical factors which govern the wealth of a country or a nation. Thus geography provides the background to Economics.

The geographical factors determine to a great extent the means of livelihood of the people.

When geographical conditions are favourable, economic activities relating to agriculture, commerce, trade and industry flourish.

Industrial centres come up on account of climatic factors. Coal mines lead to the development of Coal industry in those areas.

Sugar mills are established in the areas which grow sugarcane in abundance.

On account of divergent geographical situations, countries like Japan, Denmark and Switzerland etc. have different economics.

Examples

1. Localisation of industries.
2. Indian trade.
3. Development of industries in India.
4. Sources of energy .
5. Food problem.
6. Development of Indian agriculture.

History. Economic factors have been great determiners of historical events. It is common knowledge that the economic prosperity of India attracted foreign invaders who in due course greatly influenced the history of India. The British domination of India was on account of the economic and commercial activities of the East India Company. With the beginning and end of British rule in India, a new chapter in the history of India is clearly discernible.

History tells us how different countries achieved rapid economic development by adopting particular policies and how these policies could be adopted by underdeveloped countries for the betterment of their economies.

Every economic problem of the present can be properly understood and solved satisfactorily in the light of historical background. The history of past economic events throws valuable light on the present economic policies and guides us in the formulation of various economic laws and theories.

History describes the story of man and Economics describes the activities of man in relation to production, distribution, consumption and exchange. History describes the social nature of all economic activities of man.

Economic revolutions in several countries have radically changed the course of history of these countries.

Industrial Revolution in Europe led to increased production. The need for marketing the produced goods and getting raw materials from other countries led to the 'Colonisation' of several countries. India also became a victim. With the arrival and departure of the British from India, new chapter in its history began.

Examples

1. On account of the close relationships between Economics and History, some scholars tend to call these as 'Twin sisters'.

   The Russian Revolution, the French Revolution and the War of American Independence were the outcome of economic considerations. Economic considerations by and large led to the First World War and Second World War.

2. Japan established its supremacy over China for a considerable period on account of economic considerations. This changed the course of history

Mathematics. Recently, the relationship of Economics with mathematics and statistics have become very closer. Statistical data have become an important instrument in propounding several theories of Economics.

Statistical data in Economics provide concreteness and vividness to various economic situations.

In the words of Marshall, "Statistics are the straw out of which I like every other economist, have to make bricks."

As observed by R. D. G. Alters, "The economist gets nowhere without statistical guidance; the statistician has a few stock answers but needs more instructions from an Economics than he is usually given."

Drawing of curves, diagrams, graphs, sketches and tables in Economics depends on the knowledge of Mathematics and Statistics.

Mathematical symbols in Economics serve a number of purposes in Economics.

Almost all theories and practices in Economics derive their reliability when tested on the touchstone of calculation and principles of Mathematics and Statistics.

There is no doubt that Statistics has become an integral part of Economics. Without statistics, Economics is incomplete.

Curriculum in Economics formulated by the NCERT and CBSE assigns an important place to Statistics.

Examples

1. Malthus theory of population.
2. Quantity theory of money.
3. Keynes theory of interest.
4. Business knowledge.
5. Law of production.
6. Law of demand and supply.
7. Elasticity of demand.
8. Consumer's surplus.
9. Mathematical curves, diagrams, graphs, and tables etc.

Education. Recently the economists and educational planners have begun to take a keen interest in the relationship of economic development and educational development. A detailed discussion on this aspect is provided in a chapter entitled 'Economics of

Education : Relationship of Economics and Education'. Here only some select opinions on this relationship are given.

According to B. G. Tilak who has done very useful work in this area in India, the relationship between educational growth and economic growth is a two-way process – one of a reciprocal nature of mutual contribution.

John Veizey, in his book, 'The Economics of Education' has humorously but rightly described the relationship between economic growth and educational growth like a 'chicken and egg'.

Harbison and Myers are of the view that "Education is both the seed and flower of economic development."

The system of economy or the economic order or the economic philosophy and the system of education are interdependent. Each influences the other.

The system of education in the following systems of economy greatly differs in several aspects, i.e., aims, contents, methodology, discipline and organisation etc.

1. Agarian economic order.
2. Trade economy.
3. Industrial Economy.
4. Capitalist Economy.
5. Mixed Economy.
6. Socialist Economy.

Sociology. Till recently Economics and Sociology did not form separate disciplines. They were considered as one. Economics and Sociology have a great bearing on each other. Economic and social conditions of a society are interrelated.

The economic policy and programmes can be comprehended properly when we are fully acquainted with the social structure of a society. Economic situations and conditions are greatly influenced by the social structure which include family structure, position of women etc.

Economic conditions also exercise a tremendous influence on the social structure. They determine the way of living of different sections of the society, their status in the society and their food habits also. The structure of a capitalist society will largely differ from a socialist society.

QUESTIONS

Essay Type Questions

1. Explain the meaning of correlation. State its merits and limitations.
2. Explain how would you correlate the teaching of Economics with other subjects.
3. Illustrate correlation as a method of teaching Economics.
4. Discuss the relationship of Economics with Commerce, Geography, Political Science and History.

Short Answer and Objective Type Questions

5. Write notes on :
   (i) Association of ideas and correlation.
   (ii) Gestalt point of view and correlation.
6. Write two examples to show the relationship of Economics and History.
7. Write 'Yes' or 'No' against the correct statement :
   (i) Economics is closely related it with Hindi literature. ( )
   (ii) Economics has no relation with the discipline of Agriculture. ( )
   (iii) Economics is a branch of Commerce. Therefore, there is close relationship. ( )
   (iv) Economics and Political Science are closely related. ( )

14

Preparation of Curriculum

Curriculum in Economics derives its objectives and contents from the objectives of education. For realising the objectives of education curriculum is an important instrument. It includes a number of disciplines (subjects), learning experiences, methods to achieve the learning outcomes and evaluation of the learning outcomes. There are some broad principles and considerations for the formulation of the curriculum. Economics being a constituent of the curriculum, its curriculum is also guided by all these elements. Accordingly, the meaning, definition, principles and considerations in the formulation of the curriculum in Economics follow the overall concerns of curriculum.

Essential Factors

Curriculum is a tool in the hands of the artist (the teacher) in his studios (school) to mould his materials (learners) to achieve ends (objectives). It is, therefore, very essential that the teacher must understand the objectives of curriculum as without the adequate knowledge of the objectives, the teacher is likely to grope in the dark. The tool, i.e., the curriculum is liable to be misused if its objectives are not fully comprehended. Like the axe, the tool of the carpenter which can be used for beneficial as well as harmful purposes, the curriculum, i.e., the tool of the teacher can be used as well as misused.

Syllabus and Books

Curriculum is the base on which the subjects, activities and experiences of the students are planned. It is more than the text-book, move than the subject matter or course of studies. It is the totality of all the learning to which students are exposed during their stay in the school; in the class-room, in the laboratory, in the library and the playground. Syllabus is just a part of the curriculum. It is generally concerned with the subject matter of various subjects. It is divided term-wise, month-wise or week-wise. It indicates the specific tasks pertaining to the contents of various subjects the portions to be taught during a particular period and the activities related to the subject-matter. The most important point about the syllabus is that it must be finished within the time.

The Perceptions

The term 'Curriculum' is defined in many ways by educators. Some use the term in very limited and specific context while others attach very broad and general meanings. Some define it in descriptive term, i.e., what curriculum is and others in prescribed terms, ie., what curriculum ought to be. Again curriculum is defined in terms of subjects, activities and experiences.

Following are some of the important definitions of the curriculum :

1. F. Bobbit in the Curriculum (1918) has observed that "Curriculum is that series of things which children and youth must do and experience by way of developing abilities to do things well that make up the affairs of adult life; and to be in all respects what adults should do."

2. Alberty A. and Alberty E: (1959) define "Curriculum as the sum total of student activities which the school sponsors for the purpose of achieving its objectives."
3. In the words of H. Robert Beck and W. Walter Cook, "Curriculum is the sum of the educational experiences that children have in school."
4. "A curriculum is a structured series of intended learning outcomes" (Johnson, 1967). This definition emphasises that learning outcomes and not learning experiences constitute the curriculum. These outcomes are linked with objectives.
5. Blond's Encyclopaedia (1969) of Education defines "Curriculum as all the experiences a pupil has under the guidance of the school."
6. "A curriculum is an attempt to communicate the essential principles and features of an educational concept in such a form that it is open to critical scrutiny and ca pable of effective translation into practice." (Lawrence Stenhoue, 1975) This definition views curriculum as an attempt, an activity aimed at communication.
7. "A curriculum is the formulation and implementation of an educational proposal, to be taught and learnt within school or other institutions and for which that institution accepts responsibility at three levels : its rationale, its actual implementation and its effects." (Jenkin and Shipman, 1975)
8. "A curriculum is an organised set of formal educational and/or training intentions." (David Pratt, 1980)
9. Derek Rowntree in A Dictionary of Education (1981) defines curriculum in these words, "Curriculum can refer to total structure of ideas and activities, developed by an educational institution to meet the needs of students and to achieve desired educational aims."

10. R. Doll, in Curriculum Improvement: Decision Making (1982) has stated : "Curriculum embodies all the experiences which are offered to learners under the auspices or direction of the school."
11. A curriculum is all of the experiences that individual learners have in a programme of education whose purpose is to achieve broad goals and related specific objectives, which is planned in terms of a framework of theory and research or past and present professional practice (Glen Hass, 1987).

The first definition gives importance to 'adult activities'. The second definition lays emphasis on the word "sponsors" and the third definition tends to give importance to spontaneous as well as 'sponsored'. The fourth definition stresses the word structured series. The fifth lays stress on 'guidance' in providing experiences. Definitions at serial numbers 9 and 11 seem to be quite comprehensive and are in conformity with the objectives of education.

The Conditions

Principle of Self-sufficiency or Allaround Development – This is the foremost principle. After going through the course or content, the learner should develop self-reliance and self-confi-dence.

The Conservative Principle – It has been stated that 'nations live in the present, on the past and for the future'. This means that the present, the past and the future needs of the community should be taken into consideration. The past is a great guide for the present as it help us to decide what has been useful to those who have gone before and what will be useful to those who are going through now.

This principle will be of help only when we carefully select as to what things of the past are likely to help us in the present. All the things of the past may not suit us. It is, therefore, essential that we should select only those subjects and activities which are required by the present generation.

The Forward-Looking Principle—Children of today are the future citizens of tomorrow. Therefore, their education should be such as it enables them to be progressive-minded persons.

The Creative Principle—In the curriculum that content should be included which enables the child to exercise his creative and constructive powers. The objective of education is to discover and to develop his special interests, tests and aptitudes.

The Activity Principle—The content must ensure the activity of body and mind. It should be the centre of the curriculum. All modern methods of teaching, i.e.. Kindergarten, Montessori, Project, Basic etc., are based on this principle of activity.

Principle of Preparation for Life—We have to prepare the child in such a way as he is capable of facing the various challenges of the complex problems of the future.

Child-centred Content or Interest-centred Content—It is true that the child is to be prepared for life. But this does not mean that his immediate interest should be sacrificed for the sake of the future which is indefinite. As Ryburn puts, "'The best preparation for life that we can give a child is to help him to live fully and richly his life at that stage at which he is."

Principle of Maturity—Content should be adapted to the Stage of the pupils and to their stage of mental physical development.

Principle of Individual Differences or Principles of Flexibility—Individuals differ in taste, temperament, skill, experience, aptitude, innate ability and in sex. Therefore, the content should be adapted to individual differences. It should not be rigid.

Vertical and Horizontal Articulation—On the one hand each year's course should be built on what has been done in previous years and at the same time should serve as basis for subsequent work. It is absolutely essential that the entire content should be co-ordinated.

Principle of Linking with Life or Principle of Utility—The community needs and characteristics should be kept in view while selecting the contents.

Principle of Comprehensiveness and Balance—The content should be selected in such a way as every aspect of life, i.e., economic relationship, social activities, occupations and spiritual life, is given due emphasis.

Principle of Loyalties—The content should be selected in such a manner that it teaches a true sense of loyalty to the family, the school, the community, the town, the province, the country and the world at large. It should enable the child to understand that there is unity in diversity.

Principle of Significance—Content should take into consideration the special needs and circumstances of the pupils and the community. Curriculum of the girls may not always be identical with that of boys. The special needs of both the sexes should be given their due consideration.

In general the content of the village and the urban school will be the same but there might be variation according to the specific needs of the locality.

Principle of Core or Common Subjects—There are certain broad areas of knowledge, skill and appreciation with which all the children must be made conversant and these should find a place in the curriculum. This is more important at higher secondary stage where there are diversified courses. These subjects are to be common to all groups. They are known as core subjects. Mother tongue or regional languages, social studies (general course), general science including mathematics and one craft are expected to be the core subjects.

Principle of Feasibility—It should be possible to translate into action the content in the light of existing resources.

Principle of Authenticity—The content should enable the implementers of curriculum to realize the objectives set.

State of Affairs

The Secondary Education Commission 1952-53 which went into all aspects of secondary education made important observations on school curriculum also. Regarding curriculum at the secondary stage (IX to XI) it suggested seven groups of subjects like Humanities, Sciences etc. Students could select three subjects from one of the seven groups.

Group 1 (Humanities), among other subjects, included Elements of Economics and Civics. In other words, Economics was not treated as a separate subject.

In Group 4 (Commercial) it included commercial geography or elements of Economics and Civics. Here too it did not recognise Economics as a separate subject.

The Education Commission (1964-66), popularly known as the Kothari Commission which considered all aspects of education at all stages of education, did not provide for the teaching of Economics in class IX and X—common curriculum at this stage.

At the higher secondary stage (classes XI and XII) no grouping of subjects was done. Students could select three elective subjects out of a given list. Economics was given the status of a separate subject.

In the wake of the introduction of the 10+2 pattern, the NCERT prepared a curriculum for Ten-year School—A Framework in 1975. In this Economics did not find place in class IX and X.

The Ishwarbhai Committee (1977) accepted the claim of Economics as a separate subject at the high school stage.

The NCERT in its publication 'National Curriculum for Elementary and Secondary Education' (1988) did not accept Economics as a separate discipline at the secondary stage (IX and X) and included it as one of the constituents of social sciences. It was not assigned the same position regarding weightage to marks as given to History and Geography. At the senior secondary stage (XI-XII) it was treated as an elective subject. The CBSE also assigned the same position to Economics.

NCERT in its curriculum framed in 2001, included Economics as one of the parts of the social studies in class X.

At the higher secondary stage, Economics is an elective subjects.

Functional Significance

The NCERT in its publication entitled 'Guidelines and Syllabus for Secondary Stage' (2001) has envisaged that the proposed curriculum in Economics will enable the students

(i) to discuss different types of economies.

(ii) to explain the main features of Indian economy.

(iii) to understand the relationship between allocation of resources and decision making.

(iv) to identify the factors influencing shifts in the role of the state.

(v) to understand sectoral changes in the economy due to globalisation.

(vi) to understand the impact of the price rise on different sections of society.

(vii) to identify anti-social practices leading to price rise.

(viii) to apprise the rights and responsibilities of the consumers.

(ix) to appreciate efforts of consumer organisations and the state to protect consumers against exploitation.

(x) to realise the interrelationship among population, poverty and unemployment..

(xi) to understand the magnitude of the problems of poverty.

(xii) to appreciate government efforts to reduce poverty.

(xiii) to understand the gravity of the problem of unemployment.

CBSE Curriculum

The restructuring of the course in Economics for the senior school has been done with the object of providing the students with an overview of the changing profile of the Indian economy since the British period and to introduce them to economic theory and statistical techniques to enable them to comprehend and analyse the basic economic phenomena.

Typical Motives

The following are the specific objectives of teaching Economics :

(i) To help the students understand the existing economic institutions in India in their historical perspective;

(ii) To help the students understand the structure of our economy and the changes it is undergoing;

(iii) To help the students acquaint with principles, laws and concepts of Economics;

(iv) To help the students understand the concept of national income and methods used in calculating national income;

(v) To help the students appreciate efforts for economic reconstruction.

Class XI

One Paper **100 marks**

Unitwise Weightage

Unit	**Marks**
Evolution of the Indian Economy	
1. Indian Economy at the time of Independence	5
2. Economic Development since Independence	30
3. Industrial Policy and Balance of Payments	10
4. New Economic Policy	5

Elementary Statistics

5. Statistics in Economic Analysis	5
6. Collection and Organisation of Data	8
7. Presentation of Data	12
8. Condensation of Data	20
9. Index Numbers	5

Evolution of the Indian Economy

Unit 1 : Indian Economy at the time of Independence. **5 Pds.**

Unit 2 : Economic Development since Independence. **55 Pds.**

- Development plans : objectives and strategy of development.
- Economic growth and structural changes.
- Growth of investment and saving.
- Price rise : causes, consequences and remedies.
- Population growth and Human resource development.
- Unemployment, poverty and inequality.
- Achievements and Shortcomings.

Unit 3 : Industrial Policy and Balance of Payments. **44 Pds.**

- Industrial Policy Resolution of 1956, Role of Public Sector, Licensing Policy.
- Balance of Trade : meaning of balance of payments, problem of deficit in Indian balance of payments, measures to correct the deficit : import substitution and export promotion.

Unit 4 : New Economic Policy **5 Pds.**

- Need
- Broad features Elementary Statistics

Unit 5 : Statistics in Economic Analysis **4 Pds.**

– Need for empirical and quantitative analysis.

Unit 6 : Collection and Organisation of Data **16 Pds.**

– Statistical data : primary and secondary data.

– Methods of collecting data : census and sample methods.

Unit 7 : Presentation of data. **30 Pds.**

– Tables

– Diagrams : bar diagrams, pie diagrams, frequency curves and graphs.

Unit 8 : Condensation of Data **64 Pds.**

– Measures of central tendency : mean, mode and median.

– Partition values : quartiles.

– Measures of variability : range, mean deviation, standard deviation and coefficient of variation. Measures of Correlation (two variables and ungrouped only).

Unit 9 : Index Numbers **12 Pds.**

– Meaning and significance of wholesale price index, consumer price index and index of industrial production.

Class XII

One Paper **100 marks**

Unitwise Weightage

National Income Accounting

1.	Production Process	4
2.	Goods and Services produced and value added	8
3.	Generation of Income	8

4. Measurement of National Income 15
5. Estimation of national income and related aggregates in India. 10
6. National Income and welfare. 5

Introductory Economic Theory

7. Introduction 5
8. Demand, Supply and Price 25
9. Distribution 5
10. Macro-Economic Theory 10
11. Budget and the Economy 5

Accounting of National Income

Unit 1 : Production Process 10 Pds.

– Basic Concepts.

– Production, expenditure and income flows.

– Production of goods and services for self consumption and for exchange.

– Categories of producers: government, Corporate and Household enterprises.

Unit 2 : Goods and Services Produced and Value Added 12 Pds.

– Categories of goods and services produced.

– Economic and Non-economic goods and services.

– Consumer and producer goods and services.

– Intermediate and Final goods and services.

– Value of output and value added.

Unit 3 : Generation of Income 20 Pds.

– Domestic factor incomes :

(a) Compensation of employees

(b) Operating surplus

(c) Mixed Income.

Unit 4 : Measurement of national income **44 Pds.**

– Methods of measuring National Income :

(a) Value added method.

(b) Income method.

(c) Expenditure method.

– Estimation of Final -Expenditures in India :

(a) Final Consumption expenditure :

– General Government

– Private

(b) Gross capital formation

(c) Net exports of goods and services.

Unit 5 : Estimation of National Income and Related Aggregates in India

– Industrial classification, methodology of national income originating in selected sectors:

– Agriculture, unregistered manufacturing and construction sectors.

– National disposable income, private income, personal income and personal disposable income.

– Note—The students may be familiarized with the National Accounts

– Statistics published by the CSO. However no question will be set on this.

Unit 6 : National Income and Welfare **10 Pds.**

– Adequacy of national income as index of welfare; quality of life index and human development index.

Introductory Economic Theory

Unit 7 : Introduction **10 Pds.**

- The Economic Problem : Meaning, Central Problems of an economy.

Unit 8 : Demand, Supply and Price **60 Pds.**

- Law of demand, shift in demand, price elasticity of demand
- Revenue : total, average and marginal.
- Production : Total, average and marginal product; returns to a factor and returns to scale.
- Cost : total, average and marginal
- Law of supply, shifts in supply, price elasticity of supply
- Perfect Competition : Features, market equilibrium of industry.
- Effects of shift in demand and supply.
- Other market forms : Concept and features of monopoly and monopolistic competition.

Unit 9 : Distribution

- Determination of price of a factor of production with specific reference to wages and rent under competitive conditions.

Unit 10 : Macro Economic Theory **28 Pds.**

- Aggregate demand and aggregate supply and their components.
- Propensity to consume and propensity to save. Marginal efficiency of investment.
- Concepts of multiplier, involuntary unemployment and full employment.
- Problems of excess and deficient demand.
- Measures to correct excess demand

- reduced budget deficit.
- restricted availability of credit.

– Measures to correct deficit demand

- step-up investment
- increased availability of credit.

Unit 11: Government Budget and Economy 10 Pds.

– Components of government revenue and expenditure, Meaning and implications of budgetary deficit, revenue deficit and fiscal deficit.

NCERT Curriculum at Secondary Stage : The NCERT has formulated the following Economics Curriculum :

Economic Development

– ***Economic Development :*** An Overview; Economy : Types of Economics: Features and Sectors of Indian Economy; Factors Determining Allocation of Resources and Decision Making by Individuals; The Market and the State; Process of Liberalisation and Globalisation; WTO; Their Impact on the Indian Economy; Sustainable Economic Development.

– ***Economic Issues and Challenges :*** Price Rise : Causes of Price Rise including Black Marketing, Hoarding, Smuggling, State Initiatives for Controlling Price Rise : Consumer Awareness : Factors Leading to Consumer Exploitation, Awareness of Consumer Rights and Duties, Legislations Ensuring Consumer Rights, Improving Public Distribution System, Standardisation of Products; Poverty : Causes of Poverty, Incidence of Poverty, Poverty Alleviation Programmes : Unemployment : Types of Unemployment, Population Growth and Unemployment, Strategies to Reduce Unemployment, World Labour Market and International Migration, Skill Development and Entrepreneurship Development.

NCERT Curriculum at Senior Higher Secondary Stage

Objectives/Purposes to be Achieved

Class XI

Semester I

Introduction to Statistics

Semester II

Indian Economic Development

Class XII

Semester III

Introductory Micro-Economic Theory

Semester IV

Introductory Macro Economics

Note—There will be four textbooks, one for each semester.

The Assessment

Semesterisation is recommended for this course. 40 per cent of the marks for each semester would be for continuous assessment and 60 per cent of marks will be allotted for the final examination. In case there is no semesterisation, there will still be continuous and comprehensive evaluation of the students. 60 per cent of the marks will be allotted for the continuous evaluation and the rest 40 percent of the marks will be for final examination.

Class XI

Semester I

Introduction to Statistics **(Periods 104)**

Unit I : Introduction

- Meaning Scope and Importance of Statistics in Economics.

Unit II : Collection and Organisation of Data

(Periods 10)

- Collection of data – census and sampling methods; sources of data – primary and secondary.
- Organisation of data – frequency array and frequency distribution.

Unit III : Presentation of Data **(Periods 15)**

- Tables
- Diagrams – Geometric forms (bar-diagrams, pie-diagrams), Frequency diagrams (histogram, polygon and ogive). Arithmetic line graphs (time series graph).

Unit IV : Condensation of Data **(Periods 64)**

- Measures of Central Tendency – mean (simple arithmetic mean), median, quartile, mode.
- Measures of Dispersion – absolute dispersion (range, quartile deviation, mean deviation, standard deviation): relative dispersion (co-efficient of quartile-deviation, co-efficient of mean deviation, co-efficient of variation).
- Correlation – meaning, scatter diagram.
- Measures of correlation – Karl Pearson's method (two variables ungrouped data) Spearman's rank correlation.
- Introduction to Index Numbers – meaning, types – wholesale price index, consumer price index and index of industrial production, uses of index numbers. Unit V: Project for Application of Statistics in Economics (Periods 10)
- Preparation of a Project Report on – consumer awareness amongst households through collection of primary data by designing a questionnaire.

Or

Productivity awareness amongst enterprises through use of statistical data from statistical tables from Newspapers/Economic Surveys/RBI Bulletin/Government Budget of the State/the Nation/Census Reports/NSS Reports etc.

Semester II

Indian Economic Development **(Periods 104)**

Unit I: Economic Growth and Development **(Periods 14)**

- Concepts of Economic Growth, Economic Development, Sustainable Development and Quality of Life
- Indicators of Development: Per Capita Income; Quality-of-Life Index; Human Development Index.

Unit II: Structural Changes in the Indian Economy Since Independence **(Periods 45)**

- Structure of the Indian Economy at the time of independence – Occupational Structure, Relative Contribution of Sectors (Agriculture, Industries and Service Sector) to National Income, Infrastructure – Economic (energy, transport and communication) and Social (education, health and housing).
- Development Strategies till 1991 : economic planning – meaning, main objectives; main features of economic policies; main achievements and failures.
- Economic Reforms since 1991 : need and main features – liberalisation, globalisation, privatisation. Unit III: Current Challenges Facing Indian Economy (Periods 45)
- Population – size, rate of growth and its implications for development; main measures taken to check the high rate of growth.
- Poverty – absolute, and relative (inequalities); main programmes for poverty alleviation.
- Unemployment – types.
- Infrastructure – Energy, Transport and Communication, Health, Education.
- Other emerging issues – Environment, Gender and Migration (internal and international).

Class XII

Semester III

Intoductory Micro Economic Theory (Periods 104)

Unit I : Introduction (Periods 10)

- What Economics is all about ?
- Central problems of an economy, production possibility curve, and opportunity cost
- Micro Economics – meaning.

Unit II: Consumer Behaviour and Demand (Periods 25)

- Consumer's equilibrium – meaning
- Demand, market demand, determinants of demand, demand schedule, demand curve, movement along and shifts in demand curve, concepts of price elasticity of demand, measurement of price elasticity of demand – percentage, total expenditure and geometric methods.

Unit III: Producer Behaviour and Supply (Periods 24)

- Producer's equilibrium – meaning
- Supply, market supply, determinants of supply, supply schedule, supply curve, movement along and shifts in supply curve, price elasticity of supply, measurement of price elasticity of supply – percentage and geometric method.
- Cost and Revenue : concepts of costs, short-run costs (fixed and variable costs; total, average and marginal costs); concepts of revenue, total, average and marginal revenue and their relationship.

Unit IV : Forms of Market and Price Determination (Periods 30)

- Forms of market – Perfect competition, Monopoly, Monopolistic competition – their meaning and features.
- Price determination under perfect competition – Equilibrium price, effects of shifts in demand and supply.

Unit V : Factor Price Determination **(Periods 15)**

- Demand for a factor – meaning, supply of a factor – meaning, determination of price of a factor under perfect competition
- Differences in absolute and relative factor prices – meaning and effects on internal and international specialisation.

Semester IV

Introductory Macro Economics **(Periods 104)**

Unit I : Introduction **(Periods 4)**

- Macro Economics – meaning, difference between Micro and Macro Economics

Unit II : National Income and Related Aggregates : Basic Concepts and Measurement.

(Periods 30)

- Circular flow of income, concepts of GDP, GNP, NDP, NNP (at market price and factor cost), National Disposable Income (gross and net).
- Measurement of National Income – Value added method. Income method and expenditrue method.

Unit III: Determination of Income and Employment

(Periods 25)

- Aggregate demand, aggregate supply and their components.
- Propensity to consume and propensity to save (average and marginal).
- Meaning of involuntary unemployment and full employment.
- Determination of income and employment.
- Concept of investment multiplier and its working.
- Problems of excess and deficient demand.

- Measures to correct excess and deficient demand—availability of credit, change in Government spending.

Unit IV : Money and Banking **(Periods 20)**

- Money—meaning and functions.
- Money supply—meaning.
- Commercial banks—meaning and functions.
- Central bank—meaning and functions.

Unit V : Government Budget and the Economy

(Periods 15)

- Government budget—meaning and its components
- Classification of receipts—revenue and capital; classification of expenditure—revenue and capital, plan and non-plan, and developmental and non- developmental.
- Balanced budget, surplus budget and deficit budget—revenue deficit, fiscal deficit and primary deficit—meaning and implications.

Unit VI : Balance of Payments **(Periods 10)**

- Foreign exchange rate—meaning and determination.
- Balance of payments account—its meaning and components.

Model Curriculum

While discussing curriculum in Economics it must be borne in mind that its presentation and implementation must receive its due attention. Even ideal contents of the curriculum may lose their significance in case they are not presented effectively.

Presentation of the subject matter of Economics must be guided by the following principles:

1. Principle of simplicity.
2. Principle of individual differences of children.
3. Principle of psychological treatment to the subject matter.

4. Principle of linking with life situation and economic activities of the society.
5. Principle of maturity of the students.
6. Principle of conformity with national economic and social policies.
7. Principle of the use of dynamic and progressive methods of teaching.
8. Principle of conformity with expected outcomes of the study of Economics.
9. Principle of continuous and comprehensive evaluation.
10. Principle of career development.
11. Principle of vocational efficiency.
12. Principle of optimum utilisation of resources both human and material.

Evaluation of the Existing Curriculum : Main considerations and points to be kept in view while evaluating curriculum are :

1. There is no ideal curriculum which would be welcomed by all sections of the society.
2. Like the proverbial elephant and the five blind men, everybody, i.e., an academician, an artisan, a biologist, a household, a merchant, an educator, a moralist, a priest, a philosopher, a politician, a psychologist, a statesman, a student, a teacher seems to have his own concept of curriculum which is influenced by his own outlook on life and his past experiences in a limited field. Hence a lot of diametrically opposed expectations from the Economics Curriculum.
3. Vested interests of those who had learnt Economics the traditional way tend to oppose reforms.
4. The armed-chair academicians are in the habit of finding fault whatever exists.

5. Curriculum renewal is an on-going process. It needs constant revision.

6. Presentation and implementation of the curriculum is equally rather more important than the contents of the curriculum.

7. Curriculum is a very broad concept. It is more than its contents. It includes methodology of teaching and evaluation. It includes several types of learning experiences related to daily economic activities.

A review of the NCERT curriculum in Economics which has by and large been accepted by the CBSE would indicate the following :

1. The curriculum is forward looking.
2. The curriculum takes note of the challenges posed by the Information Technology (IT) in various fields including economic activities.
3. The curriculum is prepared after taking into considerations the following national concerns :
   - (i) Integrating India's indigenous knowledge.
   - (ii) Including India's contribution to mankind in various fields.
   - (iii) Impact of globalisation on economic policies and programmes.
   - (iv) Impact of the New World Economic Order.
   - (v) Impact of privatisation on economic activities.
   - (vi) Linking Economics with life situation.
   - (vii) Needs for establishing of an egalitarian society.
   - (viii) Need for raising productivity.
   - (ix) Requirements of a welfare society as envisaged in the constitution.
   - (x) Rule of economic development in human development.

(xi) Importance of dynamic and progressive methods of teaching Economics.

(xii) Appropriate evaluation mechanism in Economics.

As already observed, proper implementation of the curriculum is more important than its contents. Suitable conditions and environment will have to be created for converting contents into concrete and tangible outcomes.

Objectives of Curriculum

About the rationale of the introduction of Economics at the secondary stage, the NCERT (2001) observes :

Economics, as a discipline, is introduced at the higher secondary stage in the form of an elective subject. At the secondary stage of school education, the study of economics, as a component of social science, has been dealt with in a very general manner avoiding the rigours of economic theory. But, at the higher secondary stage, the students are in a position to develop their own perception, exercise the power of thinking, and are also in a position to comprehend, and appreciate the basic concepts and theories of economics. It is, therefore, an appropriate stage when the students are initiated into studying economics separately as a discipline. At this stage, the students could be exposed to the issues involving the study of the structure of the economy, the market forces, the strategy of achieving higher levels of economic growth and development, structural and institutional changes, the planning process, the new challenges before the Indian economy, including globalisation and liberalisation. Besides, the course aims at equipping them with statistical tools that will help them understand, interpret and explain statistical information or data, and draw meaningful conclusions. The course designed for the students at this stage, thus, intends to provide them an opportunity to acquaint and familiarise themselves with the recent developments in the discipline as well as with the functioning of various economic, financial and other institutions.

Some project activities in the syllabus are also introduced in order to enable the students to develop better insight. This would provide the students an opportunity to have, not only a better understanding of the subject, but also to apply the skills that they have acquired. The syllabus is so structured as to help the students to use computers, wherever applicable, for analysis of data and preparation and presentation of report.

Teaching Aims

The course in Economics will help learners to

1. Familiarise themselves with some basic economic theories and concepts such as demand, supply, consumption, production distribution;
2. Understand the implications of market forces determining the choice and allocation of resources;
3. Get acquainted with the basic concepts of national income aggregates, theories of income and employment, money and functions of banks;
4. Familiarise themselves with the structure of the Indian economy and the economic development of India since independence;
5. Enhance their awareness of issues and problems confronting the Indian economy and the concepts of sustainable development;
6. Equip themselves with the various statistical tools to analyse, interpret and explain data and information;
7. To help the students to understand the existing economic institutions in India in their historical perspective;
8. To help the students understand the structure of our economy and changes it is undergoing;
9. To help the students acquaint with principles, laws and concepts of Economics;

10. To help the students understand the concept of national income and methods used in calculating national income;
11. To help the students appreciate the need for economic reconstruction.

Other Motives

The curriculum and syllabi in Economics would enable the student to :

1. understand the existing structure of the Indian economy and the economic development since Independence.
2. enhance awareness of issues and problems confronting the Indian economy and the concept of sustainable development.
3. understand the role of Planning Commission in India's economic and human development.
4. understand theories and concepts such as demand, supply, consumption, production and distribution.
5. understand the implications for market forces determining the choice and allocation of resources.
6. get acquainted with the basic concepts of national income aggregates, theories of income and employment, money and functions of the banks.
7. appreciate the need for economic reconstruction of the country.
8. equip with the various statistical tools to analyse, interpret and explain data and information.
9. discuss different types of economics.
10. understand the relationship between allocation of resources and decision-making.
11. identify the factors influencing shifts in the role of state.
12. understand sectoral changes in the economy due to globalisation.

13. understand impact of price rise on different sections of society.
14. identify anti-social practices leading to price rise.
15. apprise the rights and responsibilities of consumers.
16. appreciate efforts of consumer organisations and the state to protect consumers against exploitation.
17. realise the inter-relationship among population, poverty and unemployment.
18. understand the magnitude of the problem of poverty.
19. appreciate the Governmental efforts to reduce poverty.
20. understand the gravity of the problem of unemployment.

Professional Aspects

High philosophies apart, the full education for an individual must be both for 'making a living' and 'making for life'. Thus viewed, the full education of an individual involves both 'vocational education' and 'cultural or liberal education'. The individual must be able to earn a living for leading a civilised life. In such a perspective, business education is to be looked upon as just one phase of education, not inferior or superior to any other phase or branch. Gandhiji has observed, "True education ought to be for them (boys and girls) a kind of insurance against unemployment". The vocational education can train individuals to become socially efficient. Therefore, they will neither be drags nor parasites on the society. They will contribute to increase production and national wealth. The advocates of the vocational aim of teaching Economics argue that all the knowledge a pupil gains in an educational institution, all the culture he requires will be of no use, if he is not able to make both ends meet when he enters life.

It is true that an individual does not live by bread alone. It is also equally true that without bread an individual cannot live. The 'bread and butter aim' does not mean that an individual will not be trained for higher values of life.

Jawaharlal Nehru has very rightly pointed out, "Education has mainly two aspects, the cultural aspect which makes a person grow, and the productive aspect which makes a person do things. Both are essential. Everybody should be a producer as well as a good citizen and not a sponge on another person even though the other person may be one's own husband or wife."

While favouring the vocational aim of education, it must be home in mind that it is not restricted to 'money making'. If it happens, education would be deprived of its elevating and inspiring influence which leads to fuller and richer life.

The words of wisdom said by the University Education Commission 1948-49 must also be remembered by all those who advocate vocational aim so that this aim does not remain one-sided and narrow. "If we wish to bring about a savage up-heaval in our society, a 'Rakshak Raj', all that we need is to give vocational and technical education to starve the spirit. We will have a number of scientists without conscience, technicians without taste, who find a void within themselves, a moral vacuum and a desperate need to substitute something, anything for their lost endeavour and purpose." The fact is that we neither can starve the body, nor the mind and nor the spirit. A harmonious blend of the three is needed.

"There is" as the great philosopher Whitehead puts it, "only one subject matter of education and that is life in all its manifestations." Trade, commerce and industry constitute a vital part of our life activities. These aspects of our life's experiences are extremely important and if we despise them, all our educational efforts will prove fruitless.

QUESTIONS

Essay Type Questions

1. Explain the meaning, need and principles of curriculum construction.

2. What is the significance of the Economics curriculum? What consideration and principles should be kept in view while formulating the curriculum?
3. "Curriculum is more important than the syllabus." Explain this statement and bring out the importance of Economics curriculum.
4. What are the basis of the construction of the Economics curriculum ? Explain.
5. Evaluate the present curriculum of Economics as prescribed at the school stage. Do you think it meets the present requirement of the society ? Support your answer with arguments.
6. What are the objectives and functions of Economics curriculum at the school stage ? To what extent are these served ?
7. What considerations should be kept in view while presenting the curriculum of Economics at the School stage?
8. Teach Economics in schools ?
9. What are the factors determining aims and objectives of teaching Economics in India? Explain these aims and objectives.
10. What did she be the main objectives of teaching Economics at the high/higher secondary stage in Indian schools?
11. Discuss the vocational aim of teaching Economics.
12. What is the rationale of including Economics in the school curriculum ?

Short Answer and Objective Type Questions

13. Some statements are given below. Write 'yes' if the statement is true and 'No' if it is false :
    (i) Curriculum includes syllabus. ( )
    (ii) Implementation of the curriculum is as important if not more as its formulation. ( )

(iii) Economics curriculum should reflect the economic scenario of the country. ( )

(iv) Curriculum in Economics is formed by the Board of High School/ Higher Secondary/Intermediate Examination. ( )

(v) In the implementation of Economics curriculum, projects and survey occupy an important position. ( )

14. Some statements are given below. Write 'yes' against the statement in case it is correct and 'no' in case it is incorrect.

(i) The aims and objectives of teaching Economics derive their inspiration from the broad aims and objectives of education. ( )

(ii) Aims and objectives of teaching of Economics should be graded at the school stage and college stage. ( )

(iii) Knowledge of statistics is not required in the teaching of Economics. ( )

(iv) Teaching of Economics is helpful in developing consumer-effciency. ( )

(v) Teaching of Economics is helpful in choosing a vocation. ( )

(vi) Teaching of Economics is only concerned with the laws of Economics. ( )

(vii) Teaching of Economics has no relevance in Indian schools. ( )

15. Write a short note on the vocational aims of Economics.

15

Planning the Lesson

The Importance

To be effective, every intelligent person plans out his work before undertaking its implementation. A surgeon diagnoses the case, prepares his surgical instruments before he puts the patient on the operation table; a lawyer makes attempts to anticipate and prepares for every move in the court, and engineer prepares his blue print before he actually starts the construction work of a bridge or a building the house mistress plans the details of the daily meals; the sales manager gives careful attention to every step in a proposed selling campaign. So must a teacher plans and prepares his teaching lesson.

R.L. Stevenson has very aptly emphasised the importance of lesson planning in these words "To every teacher I would say, 'Always plan out your lesson before-hand but do not be slave to it." Begley has put it thus, "However, able and experienced the teacher, he could do never without his preliminary preparation."

I. K. Davis is perfectly right when he says, "Lesson must be prepared for there is nothing so fatal to a teacher's progress as unpreparedness."

The Perceptions

A lesson plan is the blue print of the teaching-learning programme of the teacher which he is expected to follow in his classroom teaching in his daily work. It is prepared by him and indicates the aims to be realised by teaching a lesson, the methods to be employed and the activities to be undertaken in the class so that it is kept engaged for the realisation of the aim. A lesson plan is actually a plan of action. It indicates :

(i) The working philosophy of the teacher.

(ii) His information and understanding of his pupils.

(iii) His comprehension of the objectives of education.

(iv) His knowledge of the material to be taught.

(v) His ability to use effective methods of education.

Following definitions deserve careful attention for understanding the broad meaning of a lesson plan.

Bining and Bining—Daily lesson planning involves defining the objectives, selecting and arranging the subject matter and determining the method and procedure.

Lester B. Stands—A lesson plan is actually a plan of action. It, therefore, includes the working philosophy of the teacher, his knowledge of philosophy, his information about and understanding of his pupils, his comprehension of the objective of education, his knowledge of the materials to be taught, and his ability to utilize effective methods.

N.L. Bossing—"Lesson plan is the title given to a statement of the achievements to be realized and the specific means by which these are to be attained as a result of the activities engaged in day-to-day under the guidance of the teacher." This definition tends to focus the teacher's attention upon :

1. Outcomes or results in terms of the pupil.
2. Definite processes and procedures with a recognition of activity as the basis of learning.
3. The pupil in the foreground and the teacher in the background as guide and director only of the learning activity.

The Concept

According to Bossing, "Lesson planning is essentially an experience in anticipatory teaching. It is living through in advance, mentally and emotionally, the classroom experience as the teacher visualizes it. The eager faces, the questions that will arise, the difficulties the pupils will encounter, the way these difficulties are to be met—all these the teacher will experience in imagination. This is the first essential of good planning. It is here that the teacher can bring into play to subtle power of well-developed imagination. The more vivid, the better, so long as it is fully tinged with realism'.

Working Aspects

Planning is essential not only in teaching but In all aspects of human activity. Probably, there is no type of work where the results of poor planning are so devastating as in teaching. R.L. Stevenson said, "To every teacher I would' say, 'Always plan out your lesson before-hand but do not be slave to if." Bagley has put it thus, "However, able and experienced the teacher, he could do never without his preliminary preparation." To be effective, every intelligent worker plans out his work. A surgeon diagnoses the case, prepares his surgical instruments before he puts the patient on the operation table; a lawyer, makes attempts to anticipate and prepare for every move in the court, an engineer prepares his blue print before he actually starts the construction work of a bridge or a building; thc house mistress plans the details of the daily meals; the sales manager gives careful attention to every step in a proposed selling campaign. So must a teacher plan and prepare his work.

A lesson plan indicates the aims to be realised by teaching a lesson, the methods to be employed and the activities to be undertaken in the class so that it is kept engaged for the realisation of the aim.

The lesson plan affects the teacher's skill, intelligence, ability and his personality. Following are the chief functions of planning:

1. It delimits the field of work of the teacher as well as of the students and provides a definite objective for each day's work.
2. As the goal is determined, the teacher gets impetus to realise his goal.
3. It tends to prevent wandering from the subject and going off the way. It serves as a check on the possible wastage of time and energy of the teachers and students. It makes teaching systematic, orderly and economical.
4. Planning helps the teacher to organise the systematise the learning process. The activities in the lesson are well-knit, inter-connected and associated. The continuity of the educative process is ensured.
5. Planning helps in avoiding needless repetition.
6. Planning helps the beginning teacher to overcome the feeling of nervousness and insecurity. It gives him confidence to face the class.
7. Lesson planning gives opportunities to the teacher to think out new ways and means of making the lesson interesting and to introduce thought-provoking questions.
8. Lesson planning ensures a definite assignment for class and availablility of adequate materials for the lesson.

Four Types of Planning—These are given as under :

(a) Planning of the work of the year in a definite manner and in units.

(b) Planning of each unit.

(c) Daily lesson planning.

(d) Planning shared with pupils.

The modern emphasis is on providing learning experiences. We have repeat-edly emphasised that good and effective teaching is 'causing students to learn'. It must stimulate the child to think and motivate him to learn further. The teacher is there to create learning situations and organise them in such a way that the child feels the inner urge to know, to think and to do. Therefore, the modern education makes the work of planning all the more important. Planning is not so elaborate and difficult in the traditional system of education which simply glorifies the subject-matter and fails to develop desirable habits, attitudes and skills. The present stress is on development of the abilities of the students, their attitudes, their experience and capacities. It is, therefore, inevitable for the modern teacher to plan his lessons very skilfully and carefully.

Development of confidence in the Teacher—The prepa-ration of the lesson plan arouses self-confidence in the teacher as he is able to forecast problems and their probable solutions.

Delimitation of the Subject-matter—The teacher is well aware of the definite subject-matter that he is going to cover in the allotted period.

Systematic Management of Teaching-learning—Lesson planning brings about system in the teaching-learning process. The teacher is able to present the proper material at the proper time and in the proper manner.

Suitable Environment—Objectives are fixed. Teaching techniques and devices are decided before hand. Teaching aids are also predetermined. All these elements help the teacher to create a suitable environment in the class.

Linking Previous Knowledge—The teacher presents the subject-matter on the basis of the previous knowledge of the students. This cements the new knowledge.

Pre-determination of Learning Experiences and Activities—Pre-determination of learning experiences to be provided to the students in the class enables the teacher to make the lesson effective.

Orderliness in the Teaching—Planning ensures clear-cut programmes and activities in the class-room.

Procurement of Teaching Aids—The teacher prepares/collects the teaching aids to be used in the class.

Scientific Management of Teaching-learning—It tends to prevent wandering from the subject and going off the way. It serves as a check on the possible wage of time and energy of the teachers and students. It makes teaching system orderly and economical.

Thought-provoking Questions—Lesson planning provides opportunities to the teacher to think of new ways and means of making the lesson interesting and to introduce thought provoking questions.

Selection of Material—Lesson planning enables the teacher to prepare a suitable scheme of selection and organisation of subject-matter, materials and activities.

Avoidance of Repetition—It enables the teacher to avoid repetition of activities, aids and devices.

Well-Knit Lesson—Planning helps the teacher to organise the activities in the lesson into a well-knit unit. Activities are also inter-related.

Individual Differences of the Students—Lesson planning enables the teacher to prepare a variety of material suitable to different needs of the students.

Suitable Use of the Blackboard—A planned lesson enables the teacher to think of way and means of making the best use of the blackboard.

Suitable Recapitulation—The teacher prepares recapitulatory questions before hand.

Appropriate Summary—The teacher prepares before hand an appropriate summary.

Characteristics of a Lesson Plan

R. Schorling in Student Teaching suggests the following principles and steps in planning a good lesson plan :

1. Select the most-appropriate aims.
2. Provide the illustrative materials available.
3. Include crucial questions.
4. Consider the level of the ability and interests of the pupil.
5. Consult course of study and grade requirement.
6. Select the best procedures.
7. Tie the lesson with previous ones.
8. Take into consideration the knowledge already possessed by pupils.
9. Include an appropriate assignment.
10. Consider supplementary materials in making the assignment.
11. Emphasise the main points of interest.
12. Give a logical order to activities that would lead towards a realization of the aim of the lesson.
13. Provide for adequate summaries.
14. Make the plan flexible enough to allow teacher to leave it temporarily and follow pupil interests.
15. Budget the time devoted to phases of the lesson.
16. Provide a means for evaluating the results of the lesson and the teaching.

The Fundamentals

Generally speaking the following are the important characteristics of a good lesson plan:

Clear Aims—The lesson plan should clearly state the objectives, general and specific to be achieved.

Linked with the Previous Knowledge—The plan should not let the lesson remain as isloated one. It should have its basis on the background of the class. It should grow out of what the pupils have already learnt.

Techniques of Teaching—It should state clearly indicate the various steps that the teacher is going to take, and also various questions that he will ask.

Written Form—A lesson plan preferably be written and should not remain at the oral or mental stage. Panton writes, "The teacher is strongly advised, at least in the early stages, to make a written note of his preparation. Memory sometimes proves a treacherous servant, especially when his attention is divided." It is advisable however, not to teach from notes. Excessive reliance upon these may undermine the teacher's confidence so that he can never do without them. If, however, the teacher has occasion while teaching to refer to his notes, it is better for him to do so openly than to take a suspicious look at them. He loses nothing in the eye of the children by the former method whereas by the second he is likely to be misjudged by his pupils. Writing helps in clarifying thoughts with concentration.

Suitable Subject-matter—The materials of instruction or subject matter should be carefully selected or organised.

Divided into Suitable Sections or Units—The plan should be divided into units, but care should be taken to see that the lesson remains an integrated whole and every unit develops from the previous and submerges into the next one.

Provisions for Activity—The children must be given enough scope to be active. It should not make them mere passive listeners.

Individual Differences—The plan should be prepared in such a way as it does full justice to all the students of varied abilities.

Certain Routine Things—The plan should indicate the duration of the period, the period itself, average age of the students, subject and the class.

Illustrative Aids—The illustrative aids to be used should be shown in the lesson plan.

Flexible—The plan is a means and not an end. It is wrong to follow it slavishly. It is an instrument and should be used as such. The teacher should be prepared to change his teaching methods from those as referred to in the plan, if need be.

Reference Materials—The plan becomes more useful if it refers to other reading materials. This will motivate the bright students to do extra reading. Care should be taken to suggest only that material which is available in the school library.

Assignments for Students—A good lesson plan cannot be thought of without appropriate assignments for the students. Assignments can take different forms.

Self-evaluation—A good lesson plan must have a suitable plan for self-criticism. The teacher should put some questions to himself and find out the answer and thereby judge the effectiveness of the lesson or otherwise.

Summary—The lesson plan should include the summary of the whole lesson which is to be developed on the blackboard with the help of students.

Different Angles

Following are the main approaches to lesson planning :

1. The Herbartian Approach or Five Steps Approach.
2. Gloverian Approach.
3. The Evaluation Approach.
4. Unit Approach or Morrisonian Approach.
5. Project Approach.
6. RCEM Approach.

Herbartian Approach

J.F. Herbart (1776-1841) and his followers developed the Five Steps Approach to lesson planning. To a great extent these steps are being followed with some modifications even today. Herbart propounded four steps : (1) Clearness, (2) Association, (3) System, (4) Method.

These names were changed by his disciples as given below :

1. Clearness to Preparation
2. Association to Presentation
3. System to Abstract (Comparison and generalisation)
4. Method to Application. These were further modified as:
    (i) Preparation
    (ii) Presentation
    (iii) Association and Comparison
    (iv) Generalisation
    (v) Application.

The Preparation

This step is concerned with the preparation of the mind of the students so that they may receive new knowledge. This is very essential both for the teachers as well as the children. The teachers must know what the children have already learnt and assimilated. He must have an accurate idea of what the children already know. The children must be made to realize what they do not know so that they may have a desire to know more. Preparation is just like 'preparing the ground before sowing the seed in it.' Nothing is to be imparted in vacuum. The 'Apperceptive masses' must be brought to the forefront. J. Welton writes, "Let the teacher then -- as briefly and concisely as possible, pick up the thread of knowledge and get the pupils into the line of thought which leads from their present requirement to the new end. The better the teacher knows his class, the more accurately and quickly can he do this. This starting point must be known before the planning of the lesson can be profitably begun. It is this determination of the starting-point, this power of putting oneself in the mental place and attitude of the pupils, that marks off the true artist in teaching from the mere mechanical grinder of facts and formulae. To know where the pupils are and where they should try to be are the two essentials of good teaching."

This step of preparation is also known as introduction.

Preparation means preparation on the part of the teacher as well as on the part of the students.

In preparation the 'will to learn' is aroused to some extent, whereas in motivation it is reinforced to a high degree.

Main Features

1. It should contain no new knowledge.
2. It should stimulate curiosity.
3. It should be as brief as possible.
4. Much time should not be devoted to this step.

How to Start a Lesson?

(a) The teacher may start his lesson with the help of two or three interesting questions.

(b) The teacher may start with the help of some aids, i.e., pictures, charts or models.

(c) He may put some questions, on the subject-matter previously taught.

(d) He may start with the help of a situation. For examples in some topics he may take the situation of a co-operative store for profit and loss.

(e) He may start with the help of a relevant story.

Statement of the Aim

Announcement of the statement of the aim of the lesson in a clear, concise and specific form is very essential. It is necessary both for the teacher and pupil to know the general and specific aims of the lesson.

The form of the statement of the aim may be a brief question or a statement like this : "Today we shall study the role of the Reserve Bank of India."

Presentation or Development

It is here that the actual lesson is commenced. This step should involve a good deal of activity on the part of the students. The teacher will take the aid of various devices, e.g., questions, illustrations, explanation, expositions, demonstration and sensory aid etc. Information and knowledge may be given, explained, revealed or suggested.

The teacher should bear in mind the following principles at the presentation stage :

Principle of Selection and Division—The material to be presented should be wisely and judiciously selected. It should be divided into different sections. The teacher should also decides as to how much he is to tell and how much the pupils has to find out for themselves.

Principle of Successive Sequence—The different sections should be well connected and should maintain a proper sequence. The teacher should ensure that the succeeding as well as the preceding knowledge is dear to the students.

Principle of Absorption and Integration—In the end separation of parts must be followed by the combination of the understanding of the whole.

Sometimes the word development is used in place of presentation as the term presentation smells of passivity. The term development of the lesson indicates the facts that there is pupil-teacher activity.

Association and Comparison

This step is related to the task of strengthening the acquisition of new material. New knowledge is to be presented to the children in such a way as it becomes associated with their previous knowledge or facts. The students are persented with new knowledge and are asked to observe it very carefully and to compare it with another set of facts and knowledge they already know. This helps to associate it with the old and thus to turn it into something new.

Generalisation

This step is concerned with the systematising of the knowledge learnt. Comparison and contrast lead to generalisation. In the Inductive type of lessons the students are often required to establish some generalisations, rules or formulae. As far as possible, the teacher should see that the students draw out the conclusion themselves. If the generalisation is not the product of the student's own thinking, reflection or experience, it is of little value to them. The teacher should remain in the background. In the words of Ryburn, "It is bad teaching to give children ready-made general conclusions, concepts as we call them in psychology, which are founded on experience of the child himself, on his own precepts...... The child, with the teacher's help and guidance must be led to make his generalisations for himself."

Application

Knowledge is power only when it is used and tested. T. Raymont writes, "The mere acquisition of rules, precepts, principles, definitions and laws makes directly for pedantry rather than for healthy mental development." The fundamental law of psychology regarding learning is that the consolidation of knowledge takes place only when the knowledge learnt is applied to similar situations. Knowledge when it is put to use and verified becomes clear and a part and parcel of the mental make-up.

The application also serves the purpose of revision and recapitulation of the principles learnt.

There is a difference between application and recapitulation. Recapitulation merely denotes revision or repetition of the knowledge learnt in the lesson whereas application requires a good deal of mental activity to think and apply the principles learnt to new situations.

Forms of Application

Following are the important forms of application :

1. Solving problems.
2. Drawing maps, charts or models.
3. Writing an essay.
4. Doing some practical work.
5. Setting New Type Tests.

Evaluation of the Concept of Herbartian Steps

1. It assists in making teaching systematic. The teacher proceeds on well thought-out and definite lines.'
2. It helps in avoiding unnecessary repetition in teaching.
3. It is useful in achieving the congnitive objective of teaching.
4. It makes use of the previous knowledge of the students for imparting new knowledge.
5. It employs the deductive and inductive methods of teaching.
6. It provides a useful framework confidence and self-reliance by following these steps and thus makes teaching effective.

The Limitations

1. The scheme being very much intellectual in character is suited to knowledge lesson only. The scheme is not so useful in the case of skill and appreciation lessons.
2. There is more stress on teaching rather than learning.

3. The term preparation has been used in a vague manner. Preparation may be concerned with both teachers as well as learners.
4. Generalisation is not so simple a process as is envisaged by Herbart. It is not possible to have this step in many cases.
5. The plan is rigid, stereotyped and mechanical in nature. This scheme does not provide for much thinking on the part of the students.
6. The term presentation has also been criticized as it speaks of inactivity on the part of the pupils.
7. Herbart was wrong to think that association was a distinct phase of the learning process. The fact is that this process of association and comparison is present from the very start of presentation.

After considering both pros and cons of the Herbartian steps, one tends to conclude that there is no doubt that the steps as suggested by Herbart are of great value. They present us an attempt to point out the need of an orderly and systematic arrangement of instruction based on sound psychological laws. Steps or preparation and application have been recognized as universally valid. Regarding the value of general rules relating to the teaching process, T. Raymont writes, "The young teacher cannot be too earnestly warned that for him the great thing is to appreciate the 'spirit' of the formal steps and how much does this mean. It means that, though all the steps are not necessarily gone through in the treatment of any one section or unit of teaching, yet the 'order' in which steps occur cannot be departed from without disadvantage. That the acquisition of knowledge or of skill is a process of assimilation of new matter in the context of the old, that the relevant parts of the pupil's previously acquired stock of ideas should, therefore, first be recalled, that there should be a progress from the concrete and particular to the abstract and general, that ideas must be possessed before they can be applied, and that application in its turn makes for effective and permanent possession—these are truths as sure as the law of gravitation because they embody the plain facts of the working of a child's mind."

At another place Raymont writes, "Like the rules of any other art however, the rules of the teaching art will not always be overtly employed. As soon as the teacher has thoroughly imbibed their spirit he may be left quite free to dispense with a formal array of preparation, presentation and the rest. Though the steps may no longer be explicitly stated or even thought of, they will always remain implicit in his best efforts, and he will be wise enough not to despise them because he has learnt to practise his art without conscious need of their help."

Gloverian Approach

A.H.T. Glover in his book New Teaching for a New Age criticised Herbartian steps on the ground that these are stereotyped, gives less scope for pupil activity and fail to motivate students. If of all suitable, the Herbartian pattern is suitable in the case of 'academic subjects' and the 'verbal child'.

Glover's scheme is based on four points :

(a) Questioning.
(b) Discussion.
(c) Investigation.
(d) Pupil-activity.

Questioning—By a conscious process of good questioning, an intelligent teacher can lead his pupils through unfamiliar regions to a desired destination. The teacher should ask questions at different stages of the lesson. He should also encourage students to ask questions.

Discussion—The next step is discussion. For this purpose it is better to divide the class into groups. The discussions should be directed in such a way as students are encouraged to express their ideas freely. Discussion should help the students to remove their difficulties.

Investigation – Investigation may be individual or group investigation. The students are required to investigate on the topics selected.

Pupil-Expression – This will be the last step. This should be in the form of practical activities. Glover classifies these as :

1. *Passive* – Here emphasis is on observing and listening.
2. *Active* – Activities may take the form of handwork, craftwork, gardening, drawing etc.
3. *Artistic or Recreative* – This includes activities like dancing, music and acting.
4. *Organisational* – This aspect may be present in the above activities.

Morrison's Approach or Unit Approach

This approach is associated with the name of Professor H. C. Morrison (1871-1945) of the University of Chicago. Morrison has explained the Unit Method in detail in his book 'The Practice of Teaching in Secondary Schools' (1926). The unit method is very popular and frequently used in the U.S.A. The unit approach is based on the growing acceptance of the Gestalt-Organismic-Field Theories of learning which emphasise the 'wholeness' nature of learning. This approach is contrary to the older atomistic conception of learning according to which learning was a matter of adding one small item of knowledge to another bit by bit. The new approach is based upon the assumption that effective learning takes place in an environment in which the goals are clearly perceived and every phase of the operational procedure is viewed as a relational part of the total learner situation. The underlying assumption is that the learner reacts to the situation as a whole and not to parts in isolation.

A unit may be defined "as a means of organising materials for instructional purposes which utilises significant subject matter content, involves pupils in learning activities through active participation intellectually and physically and modifies the pupil's behaviour to the extent that he is able to cope with new problems and situations more competently."

Major Elements/Steps of Unit Approach

A good teaching unit has nine elements but the sequence of those elements is not fixed. Following sequeneces is generally followed :

Overview—This implies the consideration of the needs of the students while formulating the objectives of teaching unit.

Inventory or Background or Exploration—This element is concerned with exploring the entering behaviour of the students. The teacher is required to establish the behaviour repertoire by linking the new knowledge with the previous knowledge of the students.

Presentation—This element is concerned with providing new experiences to the learners. It includes an analysis and presentation of the elements of teaching units in a logical sequence so that they are helpful to the students. With a view to encourage students' participation in teaching, question-answer strategy is employed.

Motivation—This element of the teaching unit is concerned with the creation of motivational situations to facilitate learning.

Summarization—This element of the unit is concerned with providing a summary of the unit.

Drill—This element provides an opportunity to the students for drill or practice which enables them to retain longer what is learnt.

Review—This implies giving the salient features of the unit orally.

Organisation—This element involves giving assignments to the students to organise their learning experiences of their own.

Evaluation—This element of teaching unit consists of ascertaining how far the teacher has been successful in achieving the objectives of the lesson, i.e., to what extent students have grasped the content and developed meaningful behaviour.

The Merits

1. It is based of Gestalt Psychology which emphasises the 'Wholeness' nature of learning.
2. Since the subject matter is divided into small units, it leads to easy comprehension.
3. In the unit approach, learning does not remain just 'memorisation'. It develops understanding.
4. On account of the delimitation of the learning contents and specification of the unit objectives, teaching and learning becomes more objective.
5. Division of the learning material into small units and sub-units makes the task of teaching-learning easy, interesting and simple.
6. All the steps in the unit approach are directed to achieve the desired mastery.
7. This approach encourages the habit of independent and self-study among the students.
8. By providing adequate opportunities to the students to remain active, this approach leads to healthy interaction between the students and teachers.
9. Learning process becomes organised, systematic and sequenced.

The Limitations

1. Unit approach is time consuming.
2. This approach is more suitable in the case of intelligent students.
3. This approach puts heavy demands upon teachers.

4. The present day syllabus is very heavy and with this approach it is very difficult to complete the entire syllabus in time.

Limitations of Bloom's Evaluation Approach

The task of integration among behavioural objectives, learning experiences and evaluation devices puts heavy demands on teachers and the students.

This approach does not take into account the mental processes or mental abilities for writing out the educational objectives.

This is a highly structured approach and dominated by the role of the teacher in the teaching learning process.

This approach makes the task of lesson planning quite rigid and mechanical.

Project Approach to Lesson Planning

This approach developed by John Dewey and W. H. Kilpatrick stresses self-activity, social activities and real life activities.

RCEM Approach

This approach to lesson planning has been developed at the Regional College of Education, Mysore and accordingly it is known as RECM Approach.

This approach makes use of the concept of system approach to education. The three main steps involved in this approach are Input, Process and Output. The three aspects are as under :

Expected Behaviour Outcomes – EBOs

Communication Strategy – CS

Real Learning Outcomes – RLOs

Input step is concerned with the identification and specification of the educational objectives. It also includes the identification of the entering behaviour of the students. The objectives are written in behaviour terms. Input step resembles the 'introduction' step.

Process resembles the 'presentation' step of Herbartian approach. It represents the interaction process of the classroom. It includes activities of the teachers as well as students and teaching strategies.

Output is concerned with the evaluation phase of the lesson.

The Merits

1. It is more suitable to Indian schools as it has been developed in this country.
2. Objectives are stated in terms of measurable abilities and mental process.
3. Teaching-learning situations, strategies, aids and materials are properly stated.
4. Evaluation aspect is properly taken care of.

The Limitations

1. It is very tedious to write lesson plan of this type.
2. It is time consuming.
3. Very little literature is available on this approach.

Eclectic Approach

Herbartian approach is limited to the realization of the congnitive objective and is hardly feasible in skill and appreciation lesson. Evaluation approach has a wider scope. Both approaches are highly structured, and teacher-dominated.

Evaluation approach is based upon sound psychological principles of learning but it is very difficult to follow in the normal classroom set-up. It needs more expertise on the part of the teachers. Herbartian approach on the other hand, is simple and can be easily followed.

We should be practical in our approach and try to pick-up the good points of every approach and apply them suiting our classroom environment. We need a harmonious blending of all the approaches, as far as possible. The crucial point is that we follow an approach process and makes it effective and meaningful.

Summary

Steps in Daily Lesson Plan and their Significance

Steps	*Significance*
1. Title of the topic	For taking up the lesson in a definite framework.
2. Objectives of the lesson	For pin-pointing the learning outcomes so that these could be measured after teaching the lesson.
3. Teaching aids	For making teaching-learning more effective and at the same time making enjoyable.
4. Previous knowledge	For serving as abase for the lesson.
5. Statement of the aim	For preparing students for new learning and focusing their attention on a specific aim.
6. Presentation	For teaching the topic and giving new knowledge and understanding. It is in act the heart of the lesson.
7. Application	For providing opportunities to apply, the newly acquired knowledge and understanding.
8. Recapitulation	For finding out whether learning has taken place or not. This is also necessary for feedback.
9. Blackboard summary	For focussing attention on fundamentals of the lesson.
10. Home assignment	For reinforcement, practice and evaluation.

Notes

1. Student-teachers are advised to follow the guidelines and the format of the lesson plan recommended by their supervisors and teachers.
2. In very rare circumstances, to meet the extraordinary situation in the class, the pupil-teacher may make a total departure from the lesson plan.
3. A lesson plan based on instructional behavioural objectives will be quite different.

4. A revision lesson will have a different lesson plan.
5. As far as possible, at the presentation or development stage of the lesson, it should be avoided to ask questions from the students from the subject-matter which is yet to be taught.

Devices for Lesson Planning

The data collected in Economics are always in an unorganised and varied forms in schedules or questionnaires etc. On account of the limitation of human mind to understand such a complex, unorganised and varied data, it is necessary to make them available for comparison, analysis, interpretation and appreciation by making proper and suitable arrangement in condensed form. Also there is a great need to present data through diagrams and graphs etc.

Classification of Data: According to Professor Cannor, "Classification is the process of arranging things in the groups according to their resemblances and affinities and give expression to the unity of attributes that may subsist amongst a diversity of individuals."

According to this definition, the chief features of classification are :

1. The facts are classified into homogenous graphs.
2. All the units having similar characteristics are placed in one class or one graph.
3. Classification may be either actual or notional.
4. Classification is according to the identity, similarity or resemblance of the data.

Objectives of Classification

1. To present the facts in a simple form.
2. To bring out clearly points of similarity and dissimilarity.

3. To facilitate comparison.
4. To bring out relationship.
5. To present a mental picture.
6. To prepare the basis for tabulation.

Representation of Data

Pictorial aids in the form of diagrams and graphs are very affective in attracting attention.

Diagrammatic Presentation	*Graphic Presentation*
1. One dimensional diagrams	**1. Graph of frequency distribution**
(i) Simple bar diagram	(i) Line frequency graph
(ii) Sub divided bar graph	(ii) Histogram
(iii) Multiple bar diagram	(iii) Frequency polygon
(iv) Percentage bar diagram	(iv) Smoothed frequency curve (frequency curve)
(v) Deviation bars	(v) Ogive or Cumulative frequency curve
(vi) Broken bars	(vi) Percentile curve
2. Two dimensional diagrams	**2. Graphs of time series**
(i) Rectangles	(i) One variable Graph
(ii) Squares	(ii) Two or more than two variable graph
(iii) Circles	(iii) Graphs of different units.
(iv) Pie-diagrams	
3. Three Dimensional Diagrams	
(a) Cubes	
(b) Cylinders	
(c) Blocks etc.	
4. Pictograms	
5. Cartograms or maps	

Diagrams and Graphs: In the words of M. J. Moroney, "Just as maps give us a bird's eyeview of the wide stretch of a country, so diagrams help us to visualize the whole meaning of numerical complex at a single glance."

Importance and Uses of Graphs and Diagrams

Interesting, Attractive and Impressive : Graphic representation enables us to study the trend of the statistical values as they are very interesting, attractive and impressive. Even a layman gets the message from graphic representation of data and figures etc.

Simple Method of Presenting Data : As graphs make the data simple, they do not put any mental strain.

Making Comparisons Easier : Graphic representation is very helpful in comparing one period to another or from one section of society to another etc.

Having Universal Utility : Since facts and figures are presented in an attractive manner, they are popularly used in board meetings, exhibitions, fairs and newspapers etc.

Finding Positional Values : Special type of graphs are used for finding positional values like median, mode, quartile etc.

General Guidelines for Constructing Diagrams : The diagrammatic representation of statistical data can be more advantageous if following general rules are observed :

1. A diagram should be appealing to the eye.
2. It should be attractive, neat and accurate.
3. It should be easy and simple to understand.
4. A suitable heading on the top of the diagram should be provided.
5. A proper scale should be selected to suit the size of paper.
6. A diagram should be drawn with the help of geometric instruments.

7. Footnotes may be given just below the diagram to clarify certain points.
8. All Index must be given for identification of different shades or colours used to make the diagram more attractive.

The Limitations

1. Diagrams cannot show a large number of facts at a time as their capacity to provide information is limited.
2. Diagrams can show only approximate values.
3. Diagrams as a means of drawing conclusions can be misused for propaganda purposes. When not supported by tables etc., they can misrepresent facts.
4. Diagrammatic representation is very useful for the layman but not for the expert.

Simple Bar Diagrams. They are very simple to present but only one type of variable can be presented. A simple bar diagram can be drawn either on horizontal or vertical base, but bars on horizontal base (showing vertical bars) are more common. It is used to represent one variable, e.g., students, prices, production, population, sales etc. This diagram can present any type of information of one category either in years, months, weeks etc., or relating to different places, sections or groups. All the bars can be beautified by a single colour or shading to make them more attractive.

Sub-divided Bar Diagrams. These diagrams show the total of values and its break up into parts. The bar is sub-divided into various parts in proportion to the values given in the data and a bar as such represents the total. These diagrams are also called Component Bar Diagrams. We can use different colours like black, green, red or different shades of colour to distinguish sub-divisions of a bar. One should always remember that the various components should be kept in the same order in each bar.

Multiple Bar Diagrams. These diagrams are used when a comparison is to be made between two or more variables. The multiple bar-diagram represents two or more sets of inter-related data. We can call such diagrams Component Bar Diagrams also. Separate bars are drawn for each value. We can compare one variable over different years and different variables at the same time using different colours or shades to these variables. It is advisable to arrange the categorical information as far as possible either in ascending or descending order to facilitate comparisons.

Percentage Bar Diagrams. It is sub-divided bar diagram drawn on percentage basis. All the values are changed into percentage as a result the length of the bars is equal to 100. Divisions of bar are beautified by using different colours for different components.

Broken Bars. Sometimes we may get a series in which some values may be very small and other are very large. In this situation the longest bar or bars may be broken to get space.

Deviation Bars. This diagram is used to show plus and minus values when net profit and loss are given. Net quantities can be calculated in plus and minus values to plot them on the diagram.

Two-Dimensional Diagrams: We take only the length into account in the case of one dimensional diagrams and the width is just for beautification. But in the case of two-dimensional diagrams, we consider length as well as breadth. Such diagrams are also called surface diagrams or area diagrams. The most important types of such diagrams are :

(a) Rectangles, (b) Squares, (c) Circles or pie-diagrams.

Rectangles. Such diagrams are used for representing relative magnitude of two or more variables. The area of rectangle represents the proportion of values. Rectangles are kept side by side for comparison. This is popular form of statistical presentation of data. We can present the same data, even on percentage basis; where all the values are converted into percentages.

Squares. When the values of items have wide range, it is inconvenient to use rectangles for diagrammatic presentation. We can have the choice of squares in that case.

Circles or Pie-Diagrams. The circle diagram is an alternative to the square diagram. Pie-diagrams are very useful in emphasising areas and are comparatively easier to draw. Circle areas represent various values. Square-roots of the values are calculated as we did in the case of square-diagrams. Here, the square-roots are used to determine the radius of the circles.

Pictograms : Pictograms are the means of presenting statistical data through pictorial symbols. As pictograms are more attractive therefore, they invite more attention of the common man.

In a pictogram a symbol represents a certain values.

The pictogram method is also known as the Vienna Method for it was developed by Dr. Otto Neurath, a resident of Vienna.

Graphs : Graphs are flat pictures which employ dots, lines or pictures to visualise numerical and statistical data to show relationship or statistics.

Graphs are of several types :

Line Graphs. In a line graph data is presented with the help of simple lines horizontally or vertically drawn. For increasing the interest and readability concepts, pictorial Illustration and cartoon are occasionally used on the line graph.

Bar Graph. A bar graph consists of bars arranged horizontally or vertically from a 'zero' base. The colour, length and size of the bars represents different values.

Circle Graph. Data may be presented in a circle graph. (Sometimes the concepts graphs and diagrams are used synonymously. It may, however be remembered that graphs are covered under diagrams.)

Important Uses of Graphs in Economics. Graphs occupy an important place in the presentation of different kinds of data in the teaching of Economics. They are very helpful in presenting in an attractive manner the statistical data and several types of economic situations. Certain theories and laws of economics can be illustrated effectively through graphs. Laws of diminishing utility and the rise and decline of the utility and the like phenomena can be shown through graphs. Like-wise population data, food production data, wholesale price index etc. can be depicted through graphs.

Proper Preparation and Presentation of Graphs : Following guidelines may be kept in view while preparing and presenting graph:

1. The measurement and scale of the graph should be accurate, simple and easily intelligible to students.
2. Pencil or ink used should be of good quality.
3. Graphs should be properly explained.
4. The teacher should be well-versed in the technique of explaining the construction of graphs to the students.
5. Wherever possible, graphs may be drawn on the blackboard in the classroom.
6. Students should be given training in the preparation of graphs.
7. Students should be trained to read and interpret graphs.
8. Different types of graphs should be used.
9. Graphs should drawn in a neat and clean manner.
10. Graphs should be very accurate.

Tables: A statistical table is a represen-tation of quantitative data in vertical columns and horizontal rows. Tabulation is the process of arranging data in tables. It is a scientific process of presentation of classified data in a proper order to facilitate comparison. In Economics, tables are frequently used to present data.

The Definition—"A statistical table is a systematic organisation of data in columns and rows."

—Neiswanger

"Tables are a means of recording in permanent form the analy-sis that is made through classification and of placing juxtaposition things that are similar and should be compared."

—H. Secrist

"A statistical table is the logical listing of related quantitative data in vertical columns and horizontal rows of numbers, with sufficient explanatory and qualifying words, phrases and statement in the form of titles, headings and notes to make clear and full meaning of the data and their origin."

Uses and Advantages of Tables—1. They simplify complex data and the data presented are easily understood. 2. They facilitate comparison on account of proper systematic arrangement of statistical data in different columns. 3. They leave a lasting impression without any confusion. 4. They present facts in minimum space and unnecessary repetition and explanation are provided and required figures can be located more quickly. 5. They facilitate computation of different statistical measures namely average, dispersion, correlation etc. 6. Tabulated data makes easy for summation of various items and errors and omissions can easily be detected. 7. Tabulated data are good for references and they make it easy to present the information on graphs and diagrams.

Essentials of a Good Table

1. A table should be according to the object of statistical investigation.
2. A table should not be overloaded with details.
3. A table should be complete within itself, containing all the explanations necessary to make the meaning to items preferable clear.
4. Units of measurements must be clearly states such as 'price in rupees' or 'weight in kilograms'.
5. The size of the table should be neither too big nor too small.

6. A table should have suitable title, proper captions and stubs, source, foot-notes etc.
7. Columns and rows should be numbered when it is desired to facilitate reference to specific parts of a table.
8. Certain figures which are to be emphasized should be in distinctive type, or in a 'circle', or a 'box', or between thick lines.
9. A table should have miscellaneous column for the data which cannot be grouped in the classification made.
10. A table should be attractive and well balanced.
11. Care should be taken in deciding the size of a table as well as proportion of columns and rows.

Parts of Table

1. Table number.
2. Title.
3. Captions and stubs. (Column and row headings)
4. Body of the Table.
5. Prefatory Note or Head Note.
6. Footnotes.
7. Source.

QUESTIONS

Essay Type Questions

1. What is the meaning of the lesson plan ? State its importance to the Economics teacher.
2. Can an Economics teacher do without a lesson plan ? Explain this.
3. "However able and experienced the teacher, he could do never without his preliminary lesson planning." Elucidate this statement.

4. Why should a teacher prepare his lesson plan ? State the main points that he should consider in this regard.

5. State in brief various approaches to lesson planning Which of these approaches do you like most ? Give reasons in support of your answer.

6. "A teacher should not be wedded to the lesson plan." Explain this statement and point out when he can make changes in it.

Short Answer and Objective Type Questions

7. Some statements are given below. Write 'Yes' against the statement if it is correct and 'No' in case it is not correct.

    (i) Lesson planning is a must for every teacher. ( )

    (ii) A lesson plan does not include the methods of teaching the lesson. ( )

    (iii) A lesson plan has no fixed objective. ( )

    (iv) Implementation of a lesson plan is as important as its planning. ( )

8. Under column 'A' are given the names of the type of the lesson plan and under 'B' the author of the type. Match the correct answer with 'A'.

A	B
Unit Plan	Herbart
Evaluation Approach to Lesson Planning	Glover
Five Steps Approach	Regional College of Education Mysore
Four Points Plan	Morrison
RCEM	Bloom

9. Mention three chief characteristics of a good lesson plan.

10. Give three reasons for planning a lesson.

16

Ideal Lesson Plan

Pupils and teachers are expected to follow the guidelines for preparing lesson plans as suggested by their supervisors. A lesson plan based on instructional behavioural objectives will "have a different format from that of a Herbartian plan. A lesson plan based on survey/project or outdoor work will also have a different design. A revision lesson plan will also differ from a normal plan. In very rare circumstances, a pupil-teacher may make a departure from the lesson plan. In such a situation, he should be fully prepared to justify his action. In the lesson plans given here, general objectives of teaching Economics and other routine particulars like period etc. are not mentioned. While preparing questions and teaching aids for lesson plans, teacher may consult the chapters on Examination, Evaluation, Question Bank and Preparing and Using Diagrams etc.

Broader Perspective

To help the students :

1. familiarise themselves with same basic economic theories and concepts such as demand, supply, consumption, production and distribution.
2. understand the implication of market forces determining the choice and allocation of resources.
3. get acquainted with the basic concepts of national income aggregates, theories of income and employment, money and functions of banks.
4. familiarise themselves with the structure of the Indian economy in historical perspective and the economic development of India since independence.
5. enhance their awareness of issues and problems confronting the Indian economy and the concept of sustainable development.
6. equip themselves with the various statistical tools to analyse, interpret and explain data and Information.
7. appreciate efforts being made in India for economic reconstruction.
8. understand national economic issues in the context of globalisation and liberalisation.
9. understand the functioning of the Indian Planning Commission.

Lesson Plan No. 1 : Wants and Their Characteristics

Date :	**Period :**
Class : IX	**Time :** 40 Minutes
Subject : Economics	**Topic :** Wants and their Characteristics

Specific Objectives of the Lesson

Knowledge Objective : The pupil recalls and recognises the following terms and concepts :

(a) Wants
(b) Necessaries
(c) Luxuries
(d) Desires
(e) Consumption
(f) Production

Understanding Objective : The pupil understands :

(i) Man's different wants
(ii) Need for satisfaction of Wants
(iii) Laws of supply and demand

Appreciation Objective : The pupil establishes :

(i) Relationship among wants, necessaries and luxuries.
(ii) Relationship between satisfaction of wants and standard of living and standard of life.
(iii) Relationship between consumption and production.

Attitude Objective : The pupil develops attitudes against luxuries.

Skill Objective : The pupil collects facts and figures about the life of the group of people who are unable to get bare minimum necessaries of life and the group who enjoy luxuries.

Material Aids

A chart showing the classification of wants.

Previous Knowledge

The pupils know that every individual has certain desires which he wants to fulfil. They are also aware that food, clothes and shelter are the primary needs of a human being.

Introduction/Preparation

A poor man desires to have a car? Why can buy the same ?

1. What are the prime things without which a human being cannot live ? Mention three such things.
2. What are the main teaching of Lord Buddha ?

Unit I. The Definition of Wants

Matter	*Instructional/Teaching Devices*
1. A poor man or a miser has no means or capacity to buy a car.	1. Why can't a poor man or a miser buy a car ?
2. A rich person who is willing to spend money can buy a car because he has the desire and capacity to pay for it.	2. Why is a rich person not willing to spend money to buy a car ?
3. A person can buy a thing only if he has the desire to buy, willing to spend and capacity to pay for it.	

Generalisation

We therefore, define want as the desire which is accompanied by the willingness to spend and capacity to pay. In short want is an effective desire.

Recapitulation

1. Why can't a rich miser buy a car ?
2. Who can buy a car ?
3. Should a labourer buy a car ?
4. Who can have an effective desire ?

Unit II

Matter	*Instructional or Teaching Devices*
1. We cannot live without food and drink.	1. Why can't we live without food and drink ?
2. The early man wandered from place to place.	2. Why did the early man wander from place to place ?
3. The early man did not know how to cook.	3. How did the early man get his food?

Contd.

Matter	*Instructional or Teaching Devices*
4. After food and drink, our next need is to protect ourselves from cold or heat.	4. What is our next need after food?
5. We need some shelter—a hut or a house to live in and protect ourselves from rain, heat, cold and wild animals etc.	5. What do we want next when our needs of food and clothes are satisfied?
6. So, food, clothes and shelter are our most essential or necessary wants.	6. The teacher makes a statement.
7. We feel comfortable with a pair of chappals in addition to a pair of shoes.	7. A person has only one pair of shoes. He buys a pair of chappals. How will he feel now?
8. With two pairs of shoes and one pair of chappals, we feel more comfortable.	8. If he purchases another pair of shoes, how will he feel now?
9. If we possess shoes and chappals, more than necessary, we feel all the more comfortable.	9. Teacher's statement. The second type of wants are called comforts.
10. We feel elated with several shoes and chappals.	10. Teacher's statement. Such things become luxuries.

Generalisation

Now we infer that wants are of 'Three' Kinds :

Necessaries, Comforts, Luxuries.

Recapitulation

1. Name any four things which are necessary for a labourer.
2. Name any four things which are necessary for a businessman.
3. Which of the following are comforts and necessaries for a teacher ?
   - (i) A dictionary
   - (ii) Car

(iii) Newspaper

(iv) Five storey house.

4. Is a car comfort or luxury for an industrialist ?

5. Is a motor cycle comfort for a daily wage earner ? Black-Board Summary

Answers of the students of the above questions will form the B. B. summary. Classification is not rigid. It depends upon the needs of the individual.

Application

Prepare a list of some necessaries, comforts and luxuries for a teacher earning drawing Rs. 10,000 per month.

Lesson Plan No. 2 : Problem of Poverty and Inequality

Specific Objectives of the Lesson

Knowledge Objective : The pupil recalls and recognises the following terms and concepts :

(a) Absolute and relative poverty.

(b) Poverty Line.

(c) Economic Inequality.

Understanding Objective : The pupil understands :

(i) Dynamic and structural causes of poverty.

(ii) Consequences of poverty.

(iii) Consequences of inequality of income.

(iv) Structure of poverty.

(v) Structure of inequality.

(vi) Measures to eradicate poverty.

(vii) Measures to minimise inequality.

(viii) Comparative views of Indian situation with some developing and developed countries.

Appreciation Objective : The pupil:

(a) Establishes cause-effect relationship of poverty – vicious circle of poverty.

(b) Draws conclusion that more investment, hard work and skilled manpower are needed to increase wealth.

(c) Draws conclusion that several measures should be taken by the Government to minimise inequality.

Attitude Objective : The pupil develops attitude against luxurious consumption, receptions, dowry etc.

Skill Objective : Collects facts and figures about the extent of poverty and inequality from reports, journals and books etc.

Instructional Aids

1. Charts of comparative studies of poverty.
2. Graphs showing poverty in rural and urban areas.
3. Comparative data on poverty in respect of a few developed and developing countries.
4. Charts/graphs showing concentration of wealth in a few hands.
5. Figure showing vicious circle of poverty.
6. Slides of pictures of slum areas.

Teaching Hints

1. Teacher may show slides or pictures of slum areas or he may show some charts/graphs etc. on poverty and inequality of income. On this, he may ask different types of questions regarding their health, education and income etc.
2. Following types of activities may be arranged :
   (i) Survey of the locality or mohalla etc.
   (ii) Visits to different types of areas, i.e., slums, posh colonies etc.

(iii) Self Study.

(iv) Comparative studies to find out the structure of poverty in India and comparison with some countries.

(v) Debates, lectures etc.

(vi) Preparation of charts, diagrams etc.

Assignment/Evaluation

Objective Type Questions : Fill in the blanks :

(i) About...................per cent of India's population lives below poverty line.

(ii) Main cause of increase in poverty in India is ....

(iii) Poverty is...............prevalent in...............areas than ....areas.

(iv) ....capita income is an indicator of poverty.

Short Answer Questions

(1) Write any two causes of poverty in India.

(2) Mention any two consequences of poverty in India ?

(3) Define poverty line.

(4) Explain vicious circle of poverty.

(5) Define economic inequality.

(6) Mention two measures for minimising inequality of income.

Essay Type Questions

(1) Discuss the extent of poverty in India. Enumerate its causes and effects. What steps should be taken to eradicate poverty in India ?

(2) Suggest the measures for reducing inequalities in income.

Practical Work

(1) Poverty leads to poverty. Draw a diagram.

(2) Prepare graphs of at least two estimates made regarding poverty in India.

(3) Prepare a table showing extent of poverty in India, three developing countries and three developed countries.

Lesson Plan No. 3 : Human Resources and Economic Development

Specific Objectives

Knowledge Objective : The pupil acquires knowledge of the following terms and concepts :

(a) Human Resources

(b) Human Capital

(c) Quality of Life

(d) Investment in Human Capital

(e) Manpower Planning

Understanding Objectives : The pupil understands the following major ideas

(a) Impact of human resources on the economy.

(b) Measures need to improve the quality of life.

(c) Approaches to manpower planning.

Application Objective : The pupil appreciates the role of human capital in economic development.

Attitude Development Objective : The pupil develops socially desirable attitude towards the size of the family and quality of life.

Skills Development Objective : The pupil collects relevant facts and figures and presents them with the help of charts, diagrams, graphs and tables etc.

Teaching Aids

1. Map of India showing physical features.
2. Map of India indicating various resources.
3. Map of India showing density of population.
4. Charts showing growth of population through ages.
5. Chart showing effects of over population on the economy and the quality of life.
6. Diagram showing relationship of income and investment. Low Income Less Investment
7. Graphs showing increase in population and increase in food production and their relationship.

Teaching Hints

The teacher may introduce and develop the lesson with the help of the following type of questions :

1. What are the resources of a family ?
2. What are the resources of a farmer ?
3. What are the resources of an industrialist ?
4. Which resource is not important for the farmer ?
5. Which resource is most important for industry ?
6. Why land and capital are not of much use without labour?
7. What is the importance of skilled labour in increasing production ?
8. How can we develop efficient human resources ?

The impact of higher investment in education leads to better living standards and improvement in the quality of life may be illustrated as follows :

Higher Investment in Human Capital

Higher Skills and Rational Social Attitudes

Higher Productivity of Labour or Educated Personnel

Higher Economic Development

Improvement in Quality of Life

Lower Death and Lower Birth Rate

Stabilisation of Population

Low Pressure on Economic Resources

Enrichment of the teaching learning process. The teacher may plan following types of activities suiting local needs

Community Survey. Before taking up the lesson, the students may be encouraged to contact farmers and find out availability of land for cultivation. They may also acquaint themselves with their standard of living.

Self-Study. Student may be asked to study the relevant literature. Organisation of debates, panel discussion etc.

Preparation of visual aids. Students may be encouraged to prepare charts, diagrams etc.

Note : Lesson may be introduced and developed on the basis of experiences of students in these programmes.

Assignments or Evaluation. (Some of these questions can also be used while developing the lesson.)

Short Answer Questions

(1) Explain the following terms briefly :

(a) Human Capital

(b) Capital Formation

(c) Investment in Human Capital

(d) Human Resources.

(2) What is meant by manpower planning ?

(3) How do health and nutrition affect the efficiency of the workers ?

(4) What is the role of education in manpower development?

(5) Distinguish between human capital and physical capital ?

Essay Type Questions

(1) Write an essay on human resources and economic development?

(2) Suggest measures to develop human resources ?

Objectives Type Questions

(1) Population of India increased by............percent during 1991-2001.

(2) Density of population in India is............ .

(3) Manpower in India is not............ . Therefore there is less productivity.

Lesson Plan No. 4 : Planning in India

Specific Objectives of the Lesson

Knowledge Objective : The pupil :

(i) recalls the unplanned colonial economy in India.

(ii) understands the era of planning.

(iii) familiarises himself with the planned method of development.

Understanding Objective : The pupil:

(i) distinguishes between planned and unplanned development.

(ii) distinguishes between socialistic and democratic planning.

(iii) distinguishes between Five Year Plans and Annual Plans.

(iv) distinguishes between the national income and per capita income.

(v) understands the problems of unemployment and underemployment.

Application Objective : The pupil analyses :

(i) the condition of Indian economy.

(ii) achievements and limitations of the Five Year Plans.

Development of Skills Objective : The pupil acquires the skills of:

(i) drawing various types of charts, graphs etc.

(ii) interpreting data given in various tables.

(iii) drawing conclusions from the data.

Attitude Development Objective : The pupil develops the attitude of:

(i) of taking interest in economic matters.

(ii) of solving economic problems.

Teaching Hints for Various Stages of the Lesson Questions

1. What is the objective of planning in life by an individual?
2. What is the objective of planning a career ?
3. What is the need for planning daily schedule of studies?
4. What happens if we do not plan ?
5. What consideration should be taken into account while planning an activity or programme ?
6. What is the basic idea of planning ?
7. What is needed to plan a factory ?

8. What are the basic needs of a nation ?
9. What is the difference between democratic planning and autocratic planning ?

Teaching Aids

1. Figure showing the planning process.
2. Graphs/charts showing the planning periods.
3. Graphs/tables showing outlays on different programmes.
4. Copies of the planning documents.
5. Documents like Economic Surveys.

Development of the Lesson

The lesson will be developed with the help of the types of questions and aids as mentioned above. It will be ensured that the students participate actively in the lesson.

Recapitulation/Evaluation/Home Assignment

Essay Type Questions

1. What do you mean by planning ? What is its importance?
2. Explain in brief the various types of planning ?
3. State the objectives of planning ?

Short Answer Type Questions

1. Mention any two important objectives of planning ?
2. State the role of the Planning Commission ?
3. What is the difference between an Annual Plan and Five Year Plan ?
4. What is mixed economy ?
5. Why has India followed mixed economy ?

Objective Type Questions Fill In the blanks

(1) The apex body of planning in India is the .... Commission.

(2) The Chairman of the Planning Commission is.............

(3) The First Five year Plan in India was started in.............

(4) The 9th Five year Plan covered the period between ....and............

Write 'Yes' or 'No' against Each Statement

(a) Planning covers only economic sector.

(b) Central Finance Minister is the head of the Planning Commission.

(c) Ninth Five Year Plan covered the period 1997-2002.

(d) Evaluation of implementation of planning is done from time to time.

Practical Work

Prepare a chart indicating the following :

Plan	*Period*	*Outlay*
First Plan		
Second Plan		
Third Plan		
Annual Plans (1994-95, 1995-96 and 1996-97)		
Fourth Plan		
Fifth Plan		
Sixth Plan		
Seventh Plan		
Eighth Plan		
Ninth Plan		
Annual Plans (1995-96 and 1996-97) Tenth Plan		

Lesson Plan No. 5 : Economic Growth and Structural Changes

Specific Objectives of the Lesson

Knowledge Objective : To enable the student to know the meaning of economic growth at the time of India's independence and during the planning period.

Understanding Objective

(i) To enable the students to understand the comparison of the quantum of growth and rate of growth of economy in India with those of other countries.

(ii) To enable the students to calculate it in real terms.

(iii) To enable the students to understand the contribution of primary, secondary and tertiary (service) sectors to G.D.P.

Application Objective : To enable the pupil to :

(i) analyse unfamiliar situations pertaining to an economy passing through a particular stage of economic development.

(ii) to make suggestions for increasing growth rate to expedite structural changes.

(iii) to draw inferences from data relating to Indian economy.

Skill Objective : To enable the pupil :

(i) to draw curves.

(ii) to draw pie charts etc.

(iii) to draw bar diagrams.

Attitude Objective : The pupil:

(i) develops interest to collect data from magazines, newspapers etc. regarding growth of output in various sectors or items of economy.

(ii) develops interest in listening to radio and T.V. on issues of growth rate and structural changes.

(iii) develops interest in discussing issues with friends, class-mates, parents and teachers.

Teaching Hints

Lesson will be developed by :

1. encouraging the students to read some journal or news-paper dealing with economic growth and structural changes.
2. taking the students to agricultural and industrial areas.
3. asking following type of questions :
   (i) What do you understand by economic growth ?
   (ii) What is the significance of economic growth ?
   (iii) What are the factors that may lead to balanced economic growth ?

Evaluation/Home Assignment

1. Explain the term 'Economic growth'.
2. State the indicators of economic growth.
3. What is the relationship between economic growth and occupational structure ?
4. Fill in the blanks :
   (i) Economic growth is measured by changes in the growth of......... (GDP)
   (ii) ....change implies shift in the relative significance of different sectors in the economy. (structural)
   (iii) ....Sector consists of services like banking, insurance, commerce etc. (Tertiary)

Practical Work

Students would be asked to prepare a table indicating the contribution of different sectors to economic growth.

Lesson Plan No. 6 : Fiscal and Monetary System of India

Specific Objectives of the Lesson

Knowledge Objective : The pupil:

(i) acquires the knowledge of the various levels of government.

(ii) knows about the major heads of revenue and expenditure of the government.

(iii) recalls the major trends in the revenue and expenditure of the government.

(iv) gains knowledge of the ways of financing the budgetarygap.

(v) knows various aspects of the centre-state relations.

(vi) recalls the evaluation of the currency system of India.

(vii) knows the various functions money performs in an economy.

Understanding Objective : The pupil understands :

(i) the effect of nationalisation of banks.

(ii) the nature and functions of the institutions providing long term finance for industrial development.

(iii) the distinction between a balanced and unbalanced budget.

(iv) the distinction between developmental and non-developmental expenditure.

(v) the distinction between tax and non-tax revenue.

(vi) the distinction between direct and indirect taxes.

(vii) the distinction between internal and external finances.

(viii) the need for financial assistance from the centre of the states.

Application Objective : The pupil

(i) suggests methods of reducing the budgetarygap.

(ii) establishes relationship between deficit financing and inflation.

(iii) applies the knowledge of the fiscal system in understanding the government budget.

(iv) establishes the relationship between economic development and increase in money supply during Plan periods.

(v) establishes relationship between the expansion in money supply and the inflationary trends in the economy.

(vi) analyses the importance of exchange rate manipulation.

Interests and Attitude Development Objective : The pupil :

(i) appreciates the need of the government for collecting taxes.

(ii) realises that wasteful expenditure both at personal and government level should be avoided.

(iii) develops interest in the reading of newspapers, magazines and journals on the subject.

Teaching Hints

The lesson will be developed with the help of the following type of questions :

1. What are the sources of Income and items of expenditure of a school ?
2. What are the sources of income and items of expenditure of a family ?
3. What are the main sources of Income of the government?
4. What are the main items of expenditure of the government ?
5. How can government balance its budget?
6. On which item does your family pay taxes ?
7. How can government expenditure help in achieving the objectives of social justice?

8. What are the sources of revenue of the Central Government and the State Governments?

Practical work

Organise a debate on the merits and demerits of bank nationalisation.

Lesson Plan No. 7 : India's Balance of Payment

Specific Objectives

Knowledge : The pupil recoils and recognises :

(a) the concept of balance of trade.

(b) the concept of balance of payment.

(c) the composition of India's balance of payment.

(d) the composition of India's foreign trade. (e) the direction of India's balance of payment.

Understanding : The pupil :

(a) distinguishes between balance of payment and balance of trade.

(b) distinguishes between visible and invisible foreign trade.

(c) distinguishes between favourable and unfavourable balance of payment.

(d) understands the effects of economic growth on the composition of exports and imports.

Interests and Attitudes : The pupil :

(i) appreciates the need for export-promotion.

(ii) takes interests in current issues relating to India's foreign trade and balance of payment.

Skills : The pupil :

(i) draws pie diagrams showing the share of different items in India's exports and imports.

(ii) draws pie diagrams or sub-divided bar diagrams showing the percentage distribution of export and import trade with different countries in different years.

(iii) draws diagrams showing India's balance of payment position in different years.

Application : The pupil:

(i) suggests measures for export promotion.

(ii) establishes relationship between advance, balance of payment and dependence on foreign assistance.

Teaching Hints

Reading of Newspapers/Journals : The students may be encouraged to read newspapers and periodicals on the subject. They may also keep cuttings from them.

Talks by Experts : Knowledgeable persons may be invited to give lectures on India's Balance of Payments and drive towards self-reliance.

Group Discussions : The students may be encouraged to discuss measures taken by the Government for the promotion of exports and import substitutions.

Developing, Recapitulatory and Evaluatory Questions

1. What is the need for foreign trade ?
2. State important commodities of exports and imports.
3. Name the countries from which we import on a large scale.
4. Name the countries to which we export on a large scale.
5. Suggest measures for encouraging exports.
6. Suggest measures for curtailing imports.
7. State whether India's balance of payment is favourable or unfavourable. Give reasons in support of your answer.

Practical Work

Students may be asked to prepare the following chart :

Name of the Country	*Item of Export*	*Export Value*
1.		
2.		
3.		
4.		
5. Likewise chart in respect of imports may be prepared..		

Lesson Plan No. 8 : Agricultural Development

Specific Objectives

Knowledge Objective : The pupil:

1. knows the role of agriculture in Indian economy.
2. recognises the position of Indian agriculture before planning from the point of view of:
   (a) agricultural production and productivity.
   (b) area under cultivation.
   (c) contribution to national income.
   (d) percentage of labour employed.
   (e) impact of institutional and technological factors.
3. recalls and recognises the important items and distinctive points under institutional and technological factors.

Understanding Objective : The pupil :

1. identifies the items that can be classified under :
   (a) agricultural output.
   (b) food grains.
2. classifies the growth factors under two-subheads :
   (a) institutional.
   (b) technological.

Application Objective : The pupil:

1. translates the given data relating to agricultural output in general and food in particular into verbal communication.
2. draws inference from given data regarding the growth of agricultural output.
3. establishes relationship between institutional factors and technological factors.

Skill Objective : The pupil prepares different types of charts, graphs and tables relating to agricultural production.

Interest and Attitudes : The pupil takes interest in discussing issues relating to improvement of the life of agriculturists and development of agriculture.

Teaching Hints

Teaching Aids

1. Statistical charts may be used to present statistical data regarding various aspects of agriculture.
2. Pie diagram may be used to show the area under cultivation.
3. Tables showing contribution of three sectors of economy over a period of time should be used.
4. Contribution of agriculture to industry should be identified.
5. Charts, graphs etc. should be used to show food-grains and other agricultural products.

Questions : Illustrative type of questions to be asked during the course of development of, the lesson.

1. What are the different types of agricultural products ?
2. Students may be asked to name the agricultural commodities exported and imported.

3. What are the different types of food grains ?
4. Mention the types of crops grown in India.
5. What are cash crops ?
6. Classify food crops and non-food crops.
7. What are the factors that lead to increase in agricultural production ?

Recapitulation/Evaluation and Home Assignment

Following types of questions may be used :

Tick the Correct Answer

Agriculture's contribution to total national income now is :

A. Between 10% to 20%

B. Between 20% to 30%

C. Between 30% to 40%

D. Above 40%

Fill in the Blanks

(i) India...........foodgrains for a long time to meet its requirements.

(ii) India's food production in 1950-51 was..........m. t

(iii) India's food production at present is........... m. t.

Practical Work

1. Go to a nearby village and find out the types crops of grown.
2. Go to a nearby village and find out the sources of irrigation.
3. Prepare a chart showing the food grain production during the plan period.

4. Prepare charts showing increase in area under cultivation, irrigation since independence.
5. Take two flower plots and use fertilizers in one of the plots and observe the difference. (Teacher may arrange visit to a village.)

Lesson Plan No. 9 : Industrial Development

Specific Objectives of the Lesson

Knowledge Objective : The pupil recognises :

(i) the need for industrial development of the country.

(ii) the significance of policy of 'Mixed Economy'.

(iii) the contribution of industries to national economy.

(iv) the trend in industrial output and growth of specific industries.

(v) the salient feature of industrial policy.

Understanding Objective : The pupil :

(i) distinguishes between large scale, small scale and cottage industries.

(ii) distinguishes between public and private sector industries.

(iii) gives reasons for the rapid growth of public sector.

(iv) understands the recent change in policy regarding public sector industries.

(v) understands the reason for the development of small scale and cottage industries.

Application Objective : The pupil:

(i) establishes the relationship between the growth of large scale industries and small scale industries.

(ii) establishes the relationship between the growth of public sector and private sector industries.

Skills Development Objective : The pupil:

(i) reads graphs and diagrams relating to the growth of industrles.

(ii) prepares charts, graphs, diagrams relating to growth of industries.

(iii) locates important industrial centres.

Interest and Attitude Development Objective : The people :

(i) takes interest in current issues relating to industries.

(ii) reads newspapers and journals to get latest information on the development of industries.

(iii) visits important industrial centres. (iv) studies the manufacturing process of some industry.

Teaching Hints

Use of Visual Aids : Charts and diagrams etc. Process of manufacturing some article.

Introductory Questions

1. Name some large scale industries.
2. Name some industries which usually people run at small premises.
3. Name some industrial centres.
4. Name cities famous for brasswares.

Developmental Process : With the help of above mentioned questions the teacher will explain the classification of different types of industries, their definition and distinction. He will also explain the importance of industrial development. He will acquaint the student with the industrial policy of the government.

Developing, Recapitulatory and Evaluatory Questions : (Teacher may choose according to the stage of the lesson.)

1. State the position of industrial development before independence.
2. Distinguish between :
   (i) Large scale and cottage industry.
   (ii) Mixed economy and socialist economy.
   (iii) Public and Private enterprise.
   (iv) Licensing system of industries and liberalisation.
3. Explain the role of cottage and small scale industries in the economy of country.
4. Give arguments to show the need for following a liberal policy for industrial developments.
5. List a few industries which come under :
   (a) Small industries
   (b) Cottage industries
   (c) Heavy industries
   (d) Public Sector Industries.

Practical Work

1. On the map of India show the places where following industries are located:
   (i) Iron and Steel
   (ii) Fertilizers
   (iii) Hosiery
2. Visit one cottage and one small scale industry and note the following differences :
   (i) Persons employed
   (ii) Output
   (iii) Capital invested
   (iv) Labour welfare.

Lesson Plan No. 10 : Economic Activities

Class : XI **Subject:** Economics **Topic :** Economic Activities

Specific Aim of the Lesson

To enable the students to understand the meaning and types of economic activities.

Previous Knowledge Assumed

The students are aware of the day-to-day activities of the people living in a community.

Teaching Aids

Charts showing different kinds of activities.

Introduction

1. State the main activity of a carpenter.
2. State the main activity of a mother who is not working anywhere.

Statement of the Aim

Well, students today we shall learn about economic activities.

Recapitulation

1. Define an economic activity.
2. State the difference between an economic and non-economic activity.

Blackboard Summary

A chart showing different types of activities into business, profession, and service will be drawn on the blackboard.

Assignment

1. Write down the difference between economic and non-economic activities.
2. Differentiate between a profession and service.

Project Work

1. Prepare a list of 10 economic activities carried on in your locality.
2. List 5 professions.
3. List three activities which can be categorised as economic or non-economic activity depending upon their nature in different situations.

Lesson Plan No. 11 : Trade and Its Classification

Class : XI **Subject :** Economics **Topic :** Trade and its Classification

Previous Knowledge Assumed

Student understand the meaning of economic and business activities.

Instructional Objectives

1. To acquire the knowledge of facts, terms, concepts, conventions, trends, principles, generalisations, assumptions, hypotheses, processes etc. in trade.
2. To develop understanding of facts, terms, concepts, conventions, trends, principles, generalisations, assumptions, hypotheses, processes etc. in trade.
3. To apply the acquired knowledge of trade and its classification and its understanding to familiar situation.
4. To acquire practical skills essential for the study of trade.

5. To develop interest in the subject and problems related to trade and its classification to life of the people of one's country and those of the world
6. To develop desirable positive attitude necessary for developing a broader outlook as a trader and as a citizen.

Specification of Instructional Objectives : The pupil :

1. recalls the meaning of various types of trade.
2. understands the meaning of various types of trade.
3. defines the term various types of trade.
4. lists the feature of various types of trade.
5. analyses the features of various types of trade.
6. illustrates the features of various types of trade compares various types of trade.
8. draws a chart on the characteristics of various types of trade.
9. visits of trade establishments.
10. reads articles or books trades.

Recapitulation

1. State the meaning of trade.
2. What is the difference between home trade and foreign trade ?
3. What are the merits of wholesale trade ?
4. Is foreign trade essential for a country ? Give arguments.

Home Assignment

1. Differentiate between home trade and foreign trade.
2. Differentiate between wholesale and retail trade.

Project/Practical Work

1. Prepare a list of wholesale traders of your locality.

2. Prepare a list of 5 articles that we import from other countries.
3. Find out the government sponsored organisations that deal with some goods of foreign trade.

Lesson Plan No. 12 : Industry and its Classification

Class : XI **Subject:** Economics

Topic : Industry and its Classification

Instructional Objectives

1. To acquire the knowledge of facts, terms, concepts, conventions, trends, principles, generalisations, assumptions, hypotheses, processes etc. of industry.
2. To develop understanding of facts, terms, concepts, conventions, trends, principles, generalisations, assumptions, hypotheses processes etc. of industry.
3. To apply the acquired knowledge of industry and its understanding to familiar situation.
4. To acquire practical skills essential for the study of industry.
5. To develop interest in the subject and problems related to the industrial life of the people of one's country and those of the others.
6. To develop desirable positive attitude necessary for developing a broader outlook as a commerce entrepreneur and as a citizen.

Specification of Instructional Objectives

The pupil :

1. recalls the meaning of an industry
2. understands the meaning of an industry.
3. defines the term an industry.

4. lists the features of an industry.
5. analyses the features of an industry.
6. illustrates the features of an Industry.
7. compares of various industry.
8. draws a chart on the characteristics of an industry.
9. visits an industrial establishment.
10. reads articles or books on various industries

Teaching Aids

Chart showing the classification of industry and prodilcts.

Previous Knowledge Assumed

Students have learn about trade.

Introduction

1. What are business activities ?
2. What do you understand by agriculture ?

Statement of the Aim : Well students, to-day we shall study the various aspects of an industry.

Recapitulation

1. Define an industry.
2. Explain genetic industry with the help of an example.

Black-board Summary

Chart will be drawn on the blackboard illustrating the classification of and industry.

Project/Practical Work

1. Visit any genetic industry or farm house.
2. Collect information on the operations involved in any one industry.

3. Find out towns famous for manufacturing cotton or sugar.

Lesson Plan No. 13 : Transport

Class : XI **Subject:** Economics **Topic :** Transport

Instructional Objectives

1. To acquire the knowledge of facts, terms, concepts, conventions, trends, principles, generalisations, assumptions, hypotheses, processes etc. in transport.
2. To develop understanding of facts, terms, concepts, conventions, trends, principles, generalisations, assumptions, hypotheses, processes etc. in transport.
3. To apply the acquired knowledge of modes of transport and their understanding to familiar situation.
4. To acquire practical skills essential for the study of transport.
5. To develop interest in the subject and problems related to transport in the life of the people of one's country and those of the world.
6. To develop desirable positive attitude necessary for developing a broader outlook as a transporter and as a citizen.

Specification of Instructional Objectives

The pupil :

1. recalls the meaning of transport.
2. understands the meaning of transport.
3. defines the term transport.
4. lists the feature of transport.
5. analyses the features of transport.

6. Illustrates the features of transport.
7. compares different modes of transport.
8. draws a chart on the characteristics of different modes of transport.
9. visits a transport agency or airport etc.
10. reads articles or books on different modes of transport.

Teaching Aids

Model showing modes of transport.

Previous Knowledge Assumed

Student are aware of the modes of transport.

Introduction

1. What are the aids to trade?
2. How do they help in carrying out trade ?

Recapitulation

1. What is transport ?
2. State any three functions of transport ?

Black-board Summary

Teacher will draw a chart on the blackboard showing the comparative use of modes of transport.

Home Assignment

"Transport is essential for carrying out trade ?" Do you agree? Give arguments in support of your answer.

Project/Practical Work

1. Collect some articles on any mode of transport.

2. Find out the name of the nearest airport.
3. Find out the route of any highway.

Lesson Plan No. 14 : Insurance

Class : XI **Subject :** Economics **Topic :** Insurance

Instructional Objectives

1. To acquire the knowledge of facts, terms, concepts, conventions, trends, principles, generalisations, assumptions, hypotheses, processes etc. in insurance.
2. To develop understanding of facts, terms, concepts, conventions, trends, principles, generalisations, assumptions, hypotheses, processes etc. in insurance.
3. To apply the acquired knowledge of insurance and its understanding to familiar situations.
4. To acquire practical skills essential for the study of insurance.
5. To develop interest in the subject and problems related to insurance in the life of the people of one's country and those of the world.
6. To develop desirable positive attitude necessary for developing a broader outlook as a commerce entrepreneur and as a citizen.

Specification of Instructional Objectives

The pupil :

1. recalls the meaning of insurance.
2. understands the meaning of insurance.
3. defines the term insurance.
4. lists the feature of insurance.
5. illustrates the term insurance.

6. analyses various aspects of insurance of different types.
7. compares different types of insurance.
8. draws a chart on the characteristics of insurance.
9. visits an insurance agent or company.
10. reads articles or books on insurance.

Teaching Aids

Pamphlets and forms on insurance.

Previous Knowledge Assumed

Students are acquainted with different types of aids to trade and the term business risk.

Statement of the Aim

Well students, you shall learn how business risks can be minimised through insurance.

Meaning of the Term Insurance. Protection provided against different categories of risks to individual as well as business on payment of a nominal sum called premium to recover the loss, if any, arising out of risks. It is an agreement between two parties whereby one of them called insurer agrees to protect the other called insured against an unexpected loss.

Recapitulation

1. Define the term insurance.
2. Explain the difference between life insurance and fire insurance.

Black-board Summary

Teacher will draw a chart showing miscellaneous types of insurance.

Home Assignment

Write an essay on various kinds of insurance and different kinds of policies.

Project/Practical Work

1. Prepare a chart showing different types of insurance policies.
2. Meet an insurance agent and find out the process of taking out an insurance policy.

Lesson Plan No. 15 : Bank and its Functions

Class : XI **Subject:** Economics **Topic :** Bank and its Functions

Instructional Objectives

1. To acquire the knowledge of facts, terms, concepts, conventions, trends, principles, generalisations, assumptions, hypotheses, processes etc. in banking.
2. To develop understanding of facts, terms, concepts, conventions, trends, principles, generalisations, assumptions, hypotheses, processes etc. in banking.
3. To apply the acquired knowledge of banking and its understanding to familiar situation.
4. To acquire practical skills essential for the study of banking.
5. To develop interest in the subject and problems related to banking in the life of the people of one's country and those of the world.
6. To develop desirable positive attitude necessary for developing a broader outlook as a commerce entrepreneur and as a citizen.

Specification of Instructional Objectives

The pupil:

1. recalls the meaning of a bank.
2. understands the meaning of a bank.
3. defines the term bank.
4. lists the features of banking.
5. illustrates the term bank and banking.
6. analyses banking transactions.
7. compares commercial transactions and non-commercial transactions.
8. draws a chart on the characteristics of banking.
9. visits a bank.
10. reads articles or books on banks.

Need and Definition of a Bank. A bank may be defined as an institution which is engaged in accepting deposits, making loans, and providing other services to its customers and the general public.

Banking refers to the business of accepting deposits and lending money.

Function of a Bank

I. Accepting deposits Types of deposits (i) Fixed deposits (ii) Recurring (ili) Saving account (iv) Current account

II. Granting loans (i) Overdraft (ii) Cash credit (iii)Term loans

III. Discounting Bills of Exchange

IV. Miscellaneous services

   (a) Locker facilities

   (b) Payment of school fees

   (c) Electricity bill payment

(d) Traveller's cheque

(e) Credit cards

Method

1. You save some money out of your pocket money. Where do you keep that money ?
2. State the services and facilities which are necessary for business activity.
3. A person wants to take up some business. He has not enough capital. From where can he arrange this ?
4. What are the sources of finance of business ?
5. What are the services rendered by a bank?

   (Teacher will show different kinds of cheques, passbooks and withdrawal receipts)
6. Can a bank advance loans to a businessman without any surety ? If not what types of sureties it accepts ?
7. How do you pay your school fee ?
8. You are going out of station. You do not want to take cash with you. How can you make purchases in such a situation ?

Recapitulation

1. What is banking ?
2. What are the functions of a bank ?
3. Why does a businessman need the services of a bank ?

Black-board Summary

The teacher will illustrate the function of a bank by drawing a chart on the blackboard.

Home Assignment

Define a bank and state its functions.

Project/Practical Work

Visit a bank and watch the activities and functions of various employees.

Lesson Plan No. 16 : Planning

Topic : Planning **Class :** XI

Subject : Economics

Instructional Objectives

1. To acquire the knowledge of facts, terms, concepts, conventions, trends, principles, generalisations, assumptions, hypotheses, processes etc. in planning.
2. To develop understanding of facts, terms, concepts, conventions, trends, principles, generalisations, assumptions, hypotheses, processes etc. in planning.
3. To apply the acquired knowledge of planning and its understanding to familiar situation.
4. To acquire practical skills essential for the study of planning.
5. To develop interest in the subject and problems related to planning in the life of the people of one's country and those of the world.

Specification of Instructional Objectives

The pupil :

1. recalls the meaning of planning.
2. understands the meaning of planning.
3. defines the term planning.
4. lists the feature of planning.
5. illustrates the term planning.
6. analyses planning process.

7. compares planning and non-planning.
8. draws a chart on the characteristics of planning.
9. visits an organisation.
10. reads articles or books on planning.

Teaching Aid

Chart illustrating characteristics of planning.

Introduction

1. Why do you plan your work ?
2. What points do you consider while planning your schedule of studies ?

Statement of the Aim

Today we take up the need and other aspects of planning a business. Development of the Lesson.

Meaning and Objectives of Planning. Planning means determining a course of action to achieve some desired result. It is deciding in advance what to do, how to do, when to do, and who is to do. It indicates our destination – where we are and where we want to go.

Definitions of Planning. A few definitions of planning – for example of the following authors will be taken up.

(1) Alderson
(2) Alien
(3) Brown
(4) Erwing
(5) Fayol
(6) Robert

Reference to the Planning Commission will be made.

Characteristics of Planning

1. Planning is an intellectual process.
2. Planning is goal-oriented.
3. Planning is the primary function of management.
4. Planning involves a choice between alternative courses of action.
5. Planning pervades all management activity.
6. Planning is an interdependent and a consistent process?
7. Planning leads towards efficiency.
8. Planning is based on forecasting.
9. Planning enables us to face risks.
10. Planning is flexible.

Method : The lesson will be developed with the help of the following questions :

1. What do you intend to take up after completing your studies ?
2. What preparation would you make to achieve your aim?
3. Why is school year divided into different terms ?
4. How do you plan to secure good marks in the Board's examination ?
5. Who makes plans for your school ?
6. How will you organise your school games ?
7. What steps have been taken by the Government of India to remove unemployment.
8. Is planning a physical exercise ?
9. If not, what is required in planning ?
10. What is the objective of planning ?
11. Who plans or plan your school programmes ?

12. Who are the persons associated with the planning of your school programme ?
13. Is planning of school programmes confined to the head?

Recapitulation

1. Explain the term planning ?
2. State the main features of planning ?

Black-board Summary

A chart showing the main features of planning will be drawn on the black-board.

Home Assignments

Explain the meaning of planning by giving some definitions of planning. What is the purpose of planning ? List its important features.

Project/Practical Work

List the various steps and factors that you consider important in planning your career.

Lesson Plan No. 18 : Indian Economy during the British Period

Instructional/Specific Objectives of the Lesson

1. To provide the students the historical background of Indian economy during the rule of the East India Company.
2. To develop their understanding of the economic consequences of the British rule.
3. To give them a bird's eye view of the Indian economy on the eve of independence.

Teaching Hints

Introductory questions :

(i) Why was the East India Company formed ?

(ii) What was the political condition of India in the 18th century ?

(iii) Why did the East India Company interfere in the political affairs of India ?

Development of the Lesson

Following types of activities depending upon the mental level of the students may be undertaken :

1. Students may be taken to visits to a cotton textile mill or some other mill.
2. Students may be asked to survey the village crafts.
3. Debates may be arranged on the following topics :
   (i) Commercialisation of agriculture during the British rule was in the interest of England.
   (ii) India would have grown industrially faster had there been no British rule in India.
   (iii) Development of railways was in the interest of the British Company.
4. Students may be asked to prepare charts for showing development of some industries like the Jute Mill Industry.
5. Knowledgeable persons may be invited to give lectures on important aspects of economy of mid 18th century in India.
6. Narration and explanation where needed.

Material Aids

1. Map of India showing location of British factories in India.

2. Map of India showing political condition of India in the 18th century.
3. Copy of the 'Farman' issued by the rulers.
4. Map of India showing 'Buxer' etc. places of major battles.
5. Map of India showing a few industrial places where mills were first set up in India.

Evaluation

Multipurpose Choice Type : Some statements are given below. Mark the statement which you consider to be the best from the point of view of the British rulers. Britishers converted India into:

(a) Agricultural hinterland of Great Britain.

(b) Importers of agricultural goods from Great Britain.

(c) Supplier of manufactured goods to Great Britain.

(d) Manufacturer of manufactured goods for Great Britain.

Matching Type Question : Match the content of column 'A' with those of column 'B'

Column A	*Column B*
1. Laissez faire	First Cotton mill in India
2. Industrial Revolution	Protection granted to the sugar industry in India
3. Village artisan	First Jute Spinning mill in India
4. Swadeshi Movement	Fundamental changes in the techniques of industry
5. 1932	An important segment of Indian economy
6. 1854	Free trade
7. 1838	Boycott of foreign goods and use of Indian goods

Short Answer Type Questions

(1) State the forms of economic exploitation during the British rule.

(2) What were the characteristics of market economy during the British period.

(3) What was the meaning of 'drain' on Indian economy ?

(4) State the three adverse effects of British rule on Indian economy ?

(5) What were the main consequences of commercialisation of agriculture in India ?

(6) What were the main characteristics of modern industries in India during the British rule ?

(7) What were the main causes of poverty in India during the British rule ?

(8) What were the forms of 'Economic Drain' during British rule in India ?

(9) State the causes of decay of the old towns in India during the British rule.

(10) What were the adverse consequences of introduction of railways in India ?

Essay Type Questions

1. Discuss the chief features of colonial exploitation of India during the British rule in India.
2. What were the causes of the disintegration of India's old village economy in the early British period ?
3. Briefly describe the new land revenue system introduced by the British and indicate its consequences.
4. In what respect did the Indian economy become dependent on British economy ?

17

The Measurement

Evaluation in education implies a checking or assessment of what goes on in an educational institution for the many sided development of the student. This is done so that actual facts of a situation may be ascertained and remedial action taken where necessary. Since a detailed analysis helps to isolate the factors which may contribute to the malfunctioning of the whole educational system, evaluation can perform a vital diagnostic role by suggesting corrective action at every stage of preparation, instead of having the system with all its errors proceed blindly to its final end. Evaluation used specifically for this purpose of correcting an ongoing process, rather than only for final product assessment, is one of the most important contributions of systems thinking to programmes in education. Formative or continuous evaluation (providing feedback which enables adjustment of the programme to meet intermediate objectives), results in a better chance for the programme to achieve its final objectives.

Economics is not merely concerned with imparting information of economic issues to the students but is also concerned with the development of several attitudes, skills and values needed in life to become a useful member of a democratic society. Evaluation, therefore, assumes great importance in Economics

The following definitions throw a lot of light on the various dimensions of evaluation and their significance.

According to Wiles, "Evaluation is a process of making judgements that are to be used as a basis for planning. It consists of establishing goals, collecting evidence concerning growth or lack of growth toward goals, making judgement about the evidence, and revising procedures and goals in the light of the judgements. It is a procedure for improving the product, the process, and even the goals themselves."

Chester T. McNemly observes, "The purpose of any programme of evaluation is to discover the needs of the individuals being evaluated and then to design learning experiences that will solve these needs..... Evaluation is an important and delicate process not onty from the standpoint of determining the needs and growth or programmes of individuals but also from the standpoint of what it does to the individuals being evaluated..... An evaluation cannot adequately be made by using a single check list, an isolated anecdotal record, or a battery of examinations; a complete evaluation will require the use of many techniques."

Thomas H. Briggs and Joseph Justman write that evaluation is "a process by which the values of an enterprise are ascertained."

Shane and McSwain conceive evaluation, "as a process of inquiry based upon criteria cooperatively prepared and concerned with the study, interpretation, and guidance of socially desirable changes in the developmental behaviour of children.... It is a process within the child as a result of which he responds to the psychological interpretation he makes of his school-community environment."

One of the best definitions of evaluation is given by Clara M. Brown, "Evaluation is essential in the never-ending cycle of formulating goals, measuring progress towards them and determining the new goals which merge as a result of new warnings. Evaluation involves measurement which means objective quantitative evidence. But it is broader than measurement and implies that considerations have been given to certain values, standards and that interpretation of the evidence has been made in the light of the particular situation."

Broad Objectives

Overall purposes of evaluation are as under :

1. Evaluation appraises the status of and changes in pupil behaviour.
2. Evaluation discloses pupil's needs and possibilities.
3. Evaluation aids pupil-teacher planning.
4. Evaluation expands the concepts of worthwhile goals beyond pure achievement.
5. Evaluation serves as means of improving school-community relation.
6. Evaluation familiarizes the teacher with the nature of pupil learning, development and progress.
7. Evaluation relates measurement to the goals of the instructional programme.
8. Evaluation facilitates the selection and improvement of measuring instruments.
9. Evaluation appraises the teacher's competence.
10. Evaluation appraises the supervisor's competence.
11. Evaluation serves as method a self-improvement.
12. Evaluation serves as a guiding principle for the selection of supervisory techniques.

Different Angles

Schemically the concept of educational evaluation may be presented by showing the relationship among objectives, content (subject-matter), learning activities and evaluative procedures (testing).

The inter-relationships of these four aspects of evaluation clearly indicates that the process of evaluation is a continuous one and involves continual appraisal of objective of the teaching-learning process and of the testing procedures used by the classroom teacher.

1. Identifying and defining general objectives.
2. Identifying and defining specific objectives.
3. Selecting teaching points.
4. Planning and implementing of suitable learning programmes and activities.
5. Appraising and assessing the achievements.
6. Using the results as feedback.

New Trends

Fairly exhaustive techniques have been designed by educationists to evaluate the various aspects of a child's growth. Following are the commonly used techniques :

1. Achievements tests.
2. Aptitude tests.
3. Intelligence tests.
4. Personality tests.
5. Tests of attitude and behaviour.
6. Rating scales.
7. Questionnaires and check lists.
8. Interview.
9. Anecdotal records.
10. Autobiographical method.
11. Pupil's diary.
12. Case history.
13. Sociometric techniques.
14. Projective techniques.

Hierarchy of Instructional Objectives and Mental Processes or Abilities in Evaluation of Various Subjects (Knowledge Domain)

Objective	*Mental Process or Ability*
1. Knowledge	1. Recall
	2. Recognise
2. Comprehension	1. See relationship
	2. Cite example
	3. Discriminate
	4. Classify
	5. Interest
	6. Verify
	7. Recognise
3. Application	1. Reason
	2. Formulate
	3. Establish
	4. Infer
	5. Predict
4. Analysis	1. Analyse
	2. Identify
5. Synthesis	1. Combine
	2. Discuss
6. Evaluate	1. Judge
	2. Defend Identify

Normative and Summative Assessment

Evaluation in Economics is classified into the following two categories on the basis of their roles :

1. Formative evaluation
2. Summative evaluation

Formative Evaluation—Formative evaluation is described as evaluation used for the on-going improvement of a process. It is designed to enhance the effectiveness of the teaching-learning process. It aims at discovering the strengths and weaknesses of the students in various subjects so that remedial steps may be taken by the teacher to remove their deficiencies. It is not done for 'pass' or 'fail' purposes.

Formative evaluation may be done during the course of a daily teaching lesson.

Formative evaluation is done by informal, periodical teacher conducted class-room tests.

Teacher teaching the same subject and same students conducts the formative evaluation.

School promotional examinations and public examinations or tests conducted by external agencies fall under the category of summative evaluation.

Summative Evaluation—The summative level of evaluation is described as evaluation of finished products which have been refined by the use of formative evaluation.

Summative evaluation is concerned with making final judgement about the progress of students.

Formative evaluation is a means and summative evaluation is an end. Most of the criticism relating to evaluation is with regard to its summative nature and summative functions.

Latest Attitudes

1. Question papers usually consists of four types of questions : (i) long essay type; (ii) short essay type; (iii) very short essay type and (iv) objective type.
2. Roughly, the division of marks in percentage is as : essay type 60, short answer type 20, very short answer type 10 and objective type 10 marks. Of course, there is no watertight compartment in the allocation of marks to different types of questions.
3. Generally there are no overall options in the paper.
4. Alternative questions are given.

5. The Central Board of Secondary Education, Delhi has introduced multiple set of question papers, of course of the same standard. The main objective of this approach is to minimise copying in the examination.
6. For the guidance of the teachers to use suitable questions, question banks have been established at various places.
7. The Association of Indian Universities, New Delhi has published question banks in different areas at the college level. Several universities have also established examinations reform units.
8. The NCERT and various School, Boards have published a good deal of literature on examination and evaluation.
9. There has been a trend to provide assessment in the scheme of examinations.
10. Sessional marks are taken into consideration in the determination of final results in the internal examinations of institutions.
11. Some progressive institutions take into account the home assignments also.
12. Credit is given to project work in various institutions,
13. The system of grading has been introduced at various places instead of awarding marks at various places. Grades at various places are given separately for internal assessment, external assessment and aggregate assessement.
14. Students are now permitted to improve their grades.
15. Re-evaluation of answer scripts is also allowed at various places. Thus we find that attempts are being made to reduce the subjectivity and vagaries of examinations.

Different Kinds of Tests

Survey—comprehensive examinations used to determine general, academic standing.

Subject — examination in specific fields — for example. Economics, Commerce, English, Mathematics.

Diagnostic — cover a wide range of academic skills (in reading or arithmetic, for example) and are designed to reveal specific weaknesses and strength.

Diagnostic and Prognostic Tests

The main purpose of a diagnostic test is to analyse the nature of the difficulties experienced by the students in the learning of economics and thereafter taking remedial steps for improvement in learning. A diagnostic test can also be used as an inventory test to find out 'how much'. The students know about a particular area of the subject matter. A diagnostic test can be a standardised test as well as a non-standardised test.

While constructing a standardised diagnostic test, the teacher has to consider the individual difficulties experienced by students in solving problems. The test items should also give due consideration to the varying abilities of students in solving different types of problems. The age-norm, and the group-norm etc. should also be given their due consideration. Before constructing such a test, a pilot study should be conducted over a given area or unit and its results analysed before finalising the test.

The reliability of co-efficient of the test has to be calculated and then a diagnostic test deemed to be considered fit for administration over a large sample.

Formative type of evaluation is primarily meant for diagnostic purposes. A unit test can be administered for this purpose. We can think of a unit test in production, a unit test in income and expenditure and a unit test in banking etc., depending upon the prescribed syllabi.

A study of wrong answers given by the students is very helpful for purpose of diagnosis. The teacher's informal test in the class is generally meant for the purpose of finding out difficulties of the students. Teacher made diagnostic tests usually fall under the category of non-stadardised tests. Diagnosis is necessarily to be followed up by remedial measures.

A prognostic test is aimed at finding out the future prospects of success of a student is a particular area. This test is very helpful in providing guidance in choosing a career or a vocation.

Aptitude tests help us to measure the probability of success in a subject or an activity.

Tests of aptitudes for specific subjects have been developed in several countries.

An achievement test is used to measure the learning acquired by a student.

The Procedure

For the development of an effective evaluation programme, the teacher must be acquainted with :

(i) the objectives of teaching Economics in respect of the subject as a whole and of specific units.

(ii) the relationship between objectives of instruction and evaluation.

(iii) the varied purposes of evaluation, i.e., diagnosis, guidance, grading, classification etc.

(iv) the elementary theory and practice of measurement.

(v) the techniques and tools of evaluation—their preparation and uses.

(vi) the follow-up procedure to utilize the 'feedback' in the classroom.

The above discussion leads us to conclude that formulation of the objectives of teaching Economics at a particular stage of education is the foremost task. Everything that a teacher does must be based upon the kind of behaviour he wishes to result from his teaching.

Some Examples

1. Explain four major changes introduced in India's Economic Policies since Independence. (Recall)
2. Explain four major changes introduced in India's Industrial Policies since Independence. (Recall)
3. Compare economic advantages of 'individual fanning' and 'cooperative farming'. (Comparison)
4. Compare economic advantages of 'small scale industries and large scale industries'. (Comparison)
5. Why did India adopt/ mixed economy for economic development ? (Comparison)
6. Which, in your views, is better for economic development of India – planned or unplanned economy ? (Decision)
7. How do you account for the effectiveness of planned development during the last five decades cause and effect ? (Comparison)
8. Summarise the economic advantages and limitations of the nationalisation of banks in India. (Summary)
9. Summarise the economic advantages and limitations of cooperative farming in India. (Summary)
10. Why are Indian agriculturists not enthusiastic of cooperative farming ? (Analysis)
11. Examine some problems relating to cottage industries that require further study. (Formulation of question)
12. Suggest a plan for providing the truth or falsity of the contention that establishment of Super Bazars is a good policy to control prices of customer articles. (New method or procedure)
13. Give five practical suggestions to improve the functioning of Super Bazar. (Organisation)

14. Differentiate between production-oriented and consumption-oriented activities. Which of them in your opinion is more important for a developing economy like India ? (Application of knowledge to new situation)
15. How are production, consumption and investment related ? (Explanation)
16. Do you think that India erred in placing too much emphasis on the Public Sector ? Discuss. (Evaluation)
17. On the basis of the following hypothetical data, show whether the real national income has gone up or not.

Year	*National Income*	*Price Index*
1980-81	40,000 crores	100
1981-82	9,76,000 crores	160

(Interpretation)

Short Answer Questions

1. Give three reasons for according priority to the Public Sector in Indian Plans. (Discrimination)
2. List three criteria for evaluating achievement of the five year plans in India. (Recall)
3. How does decision-making in a controlled economy differ from that in a free market economy ? (Comparison)
4. How will GNP be affected if Indians buy shares of foreign emphasis on a large scale ? (Cause and effect)
5. Distinguish between an open economy and a closed economy. (Discrimination)
6. Why has the government of India adopted the price support policy for agriculture ? (Explanation)
7. Give two examples each of invisible exports and imports. (Classification)

8. If our trade relations with Japan breaks off, name two important industries which will be adversely affected. (Evaluation)
9. Name three factors which brought about 'Green Revolution' in the Indian economy. (Recall)
10. Name two economists who have been awarded the 'Nobel Prize'. (Recall)
11. Name the first economist who gave a General Theory of Employment. (Recall)
12. Give those factors which determine a household's demand for a commodity (Recall)
13. Why does the supply curve of labour sometimes slop backwards ? (Recognition of data)
14. Suggest two fiscal measures for reducing inequality of income. (Suggestion)

Unit Test

Meaning of a Unit in Economics : A unit may be described as a block of closely related subject matter in Economics as it can conveniently be overviewed by the learner. For instance, major industries of India in Economics syllabi may be a unit of study at the lower secondary stage spread over three or four periods, but at the higher secondary stage 'Iron Industry' may constitute a unit of study by itself, spread over almost the same instructional span. Likewise means of transport may be a unit of study at the lower secondary stage but at the higher secondary stage 'Railways' may constitute a unit of study by itself.

The size of the unit will vary from stage to stage depending upon the mental maturity of the learners and the depth at which a particular study is proposed to be undertaken.

Central Idea of the Unit—The central idea around which a unit of study is commonly woven may either come from the content of a specific discipline or broad field content or even learner's own interest or experience. Commonly, the salient themes or topics drawn from a subject area or prescribed syllabi become the basis of the constitution of a unit of study.

A number of units of study thus constitute a course of study.

Examples of Units in Economics

1. Comparative Economic Systems
2. Stages of Economic Development.
3. Consumption and Human Wants.
4. Capital.
5. Production.
6. Money.
7. Income and Expenditure.
8. Our Resources.
9. National Income.
10. Agriculture in India.
11. Industries in India.
12. Monetary Institutions in India.
13. India's foreign Trade.
14. Labour as a Factor of Production.
15. Economic Planning in India.

Meaning of a Unit Test—A unit test is basically a 'miniature test'. It differs from a full test mainly in regard to the limited content area on which it is based. Otherwise, it has all the characteristics of a full test.

Specific Characteristics of a Unit Test—A unit test has the following characteristics :

1. It is based on a small block of content that is cohesive and well integrated.
2. It is administered immediately after the conclusion of a teaching-learning programme without any formal time for preparation or a formal schedule for administration.

3. It is primarily confined to the unit under study.
4. There is greater flexibility regarding testing devices to be employed than in the case of a course test.
5. The evidence obtained through the unit test is used immediately for feedback for the purpose of improvement of learning, modification of teaching strategies, remedial work etc.
6. A unit test is basically an informal test, but can be used as a formal device also after taking proper precautions.

Planning of a Unit Test—The planning, preparation and administration of unit test involves almost all those points that are used in setting an improved type of question paper.

(i) Drawing up a design—weightage to objectives, content (sub-topics) form of question etc.

(ii) Developing a blue print—the three dimensional chart—taking care of objectives etc.

(iii) Framing of question items.

(iv) Assembling, arranging used editing the test.

(v) Preparing a scoring key (objective type items and marking scheme).

(vi) Undertaking question wise analysis.

Uses of a Unit Test—Following are the main uses of a unit test:

1. Ascertaining the effectiveness of teaching-learning.
2. Finding out the weakness and strengths of individual teacher.
3. Assessing the progress of learning.
4. Guiding the teacher in planning his instruction.
5. Motivating the learner.
6. Developing steady study habits in pupils.

7. Using as self-evaluating device for students since the test contains a key and a marketing scheme.
8. Using a unit test as home assignments
9. Using for remedial work.

Unit Test and a Formal Summative Test (Quarterly, Half yearly or Monthly Test) - A formal summative test is organised at the end of a course of study or some part thereto to ascertain the degree and kind of progress made by the pupils. The basic idea of this type of test is to grade the pupils and certify their achievements. In between these terminal and semi-terminal points lie the various stages at which different units of study are completed. It is necessary to test the progress of learning at the end of each unit primarily with a view to finding out the extent of pupil achievement in respect of that unit for providing the pupils necessary remedial instruction. It also helps to find out whether a certain place of learning has really gone into before embanking upon the next unit. It thus requires a sort of informal testing, a kind of mastery test.

Teacher Education

The effectiveness of testing programme depends greatly upon the competence of the teacher in the use of various tests. The high level of competence depends upon the following factors :

(a) The Economics teacher should attend several courses in the field of psychological measurements and statistical techniques.

(b) The teacher should be well-versed with different types of tests.

(c) The teacher should know where to find detailed information on specific tests.

(d) The teacher should know how to supplement the test data.

(e) The teacher should be acquainted with the elementary statistical measurement.

(f) The teacher should keep himself in touch with the latest methods of the use of tests.

(g) The teacher should bear in mind that tests are one of the several kinds of techniques that are devised to facilitate understanding of the individuals.

Administration and Recording of Aptitude and Other Tests : Following considerations may be kept in view while planning, administering and recording tests.

1. Tests should be given under standardised conditions that permit each teste to perform at his best, i.e., physical environment, emotional environment etc.
2. The testers should prepare themselves in advance.
3. The testers should give clear instructions to the testers.
4. The testers should follow verbatim the test instructions contained in the manual.
5. Orientation talks on the usefulness of testing may be given to the students so that they are motivated to take tests and are convinced that tests are genuinely important.
6. Records should be kept systematically so that they are made use of conveniently by the appropriate agency. Of course, results should be kept confidential.

A Word of Caution—A word of caution may be said in the use of tests. Tests are tools and should be used as such. It would be a great error to use tests as the sole basis for evaluating pupil needs and abililities. Ross writes, "Guidance is always more than the giving of tests, no matter how extensively or carefully done."

Tests, when correctly used, yield more accurate and speedy information than the subjective techniques, such as the interview, observation and questionnaire. However, these have their own limitations. They fail to provide comprehensive measurement. There are factors like cultural and social background, emotional stability, etc. which play their own role and these tests fail to measure them.

QUESTIONS

Essay Type Questions

1. Explain the meaning of evaluation ? In which respect does this concept differ from examination ? What is its scope in Economics ?
2. What is evaluation ? What are its purposes ? Prepare a scheme of complete evaluation in Economics.
3. What are the difficulties of the Economics teacher in carrying out the complete scheme of evaluation in Economics ?

Short Answer and Objective Type Questions

4. Write notes on :
   (i) Achievement tests in Economics.
   (ii) Prognostic tests in Economics.
   (iii) Diagnostic tests in Economics.
   (iv) Unit test in Economics.
5. Give three examples each of objective based essay types questions and short answer questions.

18

Methods of Assessment

Examinations have been existant from time immemorial. Their significance has been highlighted by Sir Michal Sadler, the Chairman of the Sadler Commission (1917) in these words, "To close down examinations would be to give the signal for educational saturnalia." Similarly J. C. Mathur (1959) emphasised the value of examination as, "Even in the idealised picture of society portrayed by H. G. Well's Utopia, examinations find an important place."

The Secondary Education Commission (1952-53) has also observed, "Nevertheless examinations and especially external examinations have a proper place in any scheme of education. External examinations have stimulating effect both on the pupils and on the teachers by providing well defined goals and objective standard of evaluation. To the pupil the examination give a goal towards which he should strive and a stimulus urging him to attain that goal in a given time thereby demanding steady and constant effort. This makes the purpose clear and the method of approach definite. He is judged by external and objective tests on which both he and others Interested in him can depend. And, finally, it gives him a hallmark recognised by all."

Working Aspects

1. To evaluate the achievements of the students.
2. To help in diagnosis.
3. To help in prognosis.
4. To act as motivators to students.
5. To measure the efficiency of the teachers and of the educational institution.
6. To give uniformity to standards of instruction.
7. To measure fitness of students for admission to higher courses.
8. To help in selection of candidates by competition.
9. To help in guidance to students, teachers and guidance counsellors.
10. To acquaint the parents with the progress of their wards.
11. To measure personality of the students.

The Epithets

1. A bane of educational system.
2. A begetter of rivalry and strife.
3. A blood sucker.
4. A dead hand of education.
5. A glorification of memory.
6. A growing tyranny.
7. A necessary evil.
8. A presumptuous attempt to gauge the depth of human ignorance.
9. An enemy of true education.

10. An incubus.
11. An obstacle to learning.

The Demerits

1. Examinations lack definite aim.
2. There is a major element of chance.
3. Examinations lower educational standard as the entire energy of students and teachers is spent in preparing for the examination. Stress is laid on spoon feeding and not on understanding.
4. Examinations tempt the students to adopt unfair means to gain success.
5. Subjective attitudes of examiners influence marking.
6. Examinations put heavy strain upon the students who burn the mid-night oil near the examination days.
7. Failure in examination leads to frustration and even to suicide in some cases.
8. Examinations ignore the development of personality of the students.

Various Type of Tests

Essay tests have a long history that dates back to more than four thousand years. W.E. Coffman in an article entitled 'Essay Examinations', published in a book Educational Measurement (1971), edited by R. L. Thomdike observes that essay tests were in use earlier than 2300 B. C. Until the turn of the 20th century, they were almost the only form of written examination.

Very few attempts have been made to define and clarify the concept of essay tests. They have been used so widely that it is assumed, that everybody understands their meaning.

Robert L. Ebel and David A. Frishbie in their book Essentials of Educational Measurement (1986) writes, "An essay test presents one or more questions or other tasks that require extended written responses from the persons being tested."

Gilbert Sax in Principles of Educational and Psychological Measurement and Evaluation (1989) states, "Essay test is a test containing questions requiring the student to respond in writing. Essay tests emphasise recall rather than recognition of the correct alternative. Essay tests may require relatively brief responses or extended responses."

William Wiersma and Stephen G. Jurs in their book Educational Measurement and Testing (1990) writes, "Essay item is an item that requires the student to structure a rather long written response upto several paragraphs."

It is very difficult to give an exact and perfect definition of an essay test. Usually an essay test refers to any written test that requires an examinee to write several paragraphs or passages. However, answer may constitute even a sentence or a paragraph also in some cases. Weidemann (1933), observes that an essay type question may use the following eleven words, signifying the simple to higher mental processes :

(a) What, Who, When, Which and Where.

(b) List

(c) Outline

(d) Describe

(e) Contrast

(f) Compare

(g) Explain

(h) Discuss

(i) Develop

(j) Summarise and

(k) Evaluate.

According to Norman E. Godman (1985) essay questions may be subdivided into two broad types—extended response and restricted response.

In extended response question, no restriction is placed on the student as to the points he will discuss and the type of organisation he will use. An extended response type of essay question permits a student to demonstrate his ability to

(i) recall factual knowledge.

(ii) evaluate his factual knowledge.

(iii) organise his ideas.

(iv) present his ideas in a coherent and logical way.

An example of an extended response question : Describe at length the state of economic affairs during the British period in India.

Restricted Response—In restricted response, the student is restricted as to the form and scope of his answer because he is specifically told the context in which his answer is to be made. For example : Describe in not more than 100 words the state of agriculture during British period in India.

Restricted response questions tend to be more objective while the extended type questions tend to be more subjective.

The restricted response questions are more useful in measuring more specific learning outcomes but they cannot measure learning outcomes which stress integration. The extended response questions are more useful in measuring complex behaviours which cannot be done by other types of tools but how accurately they do so in controversial.

W. S. Monroe and R. E. Carter (1993) list the following types of questions :

1. Analysis.
2. Application of laws, principles and rules to new situations.
3. Cause or effect.
4. Classification.
5. Comparison of two ideas or things in general.
6. Comparison of two things on a single basis.
7. Criticism as to the adequacy, correctness or relevance of a statement.
8. Decisions for and against.

9. Explanation of the use or exact meaning of some word, phrase or statement.
10. Evaluation recall-basis given.
11. Formulation of new questions—problems and discussions raised.
12. Illustration of examples.
13. Inferential thinking.
14. New methods of procedure.
15. Outline.
16. Reorganisation of facts.
17. Selective recall—basis given.
18. Statement of an author's purpose in the selection or organisation of material.
19. Statement of relationships.
20. Summary of some unit of the textbook or of some article.

The Merits

1. Abilities like logical thinking, critical reasoning and systematic presentation, etc. can be best evaluated by the essay type of tests.
2. They provide an opportunity to the students to show their originality of thought as they are permitted freedom of response.
3. They help to develop good study habits such as preparing outlines and summaries, organising arguments for and against a topic.
4. They provide opportunities to students to develop abilities such as to organise ideas effectively, to criticise or justify a statement and to interpret, etc.
5. They can be successfully employed for evaluating the performance of students in all the school subjects.

6. It is relatively easier to prepare an essay type test than to prepare an objective type test.
7. It is relatively easier to administer an essay type test.
8. It takes relatively lesser time to mark an essay type test.
9. Guessing is eliminated to some extent.
10. The students cannot guess the answer because they have to supply it.
11. They give examinees freedom to respond within broad limits.
12. They can measure divergent thinking.
13. They require less time for typing, duplicating or printing. They can be written on the blackboard also if the number of questions and students is not very large.
14. It is more economical to use essay type tests than objective tests.
15. They can measure complex learning outcomes which cannot be measured by other means.
16. They stress integration and application of thinking and problem solving skills.
17. They can be used as an instrument for measuring and improving expression skills and language of the examinees.
18. They are more helpful in evaluating the quality of the teaching process.
19. Students focus on learning broad concept and articulating relationships, comparing and contrasting.
20. They set better standards of professional ethics for teachers because they require more time in assessing and scoring.
21. They provide less scope for the use of unfair means.

The Demerits

1. They generally stress the lengthy enumeration of memorised facts.
2. They have limited content validity because only a sample of questions can be asked in an essay type test.
3. They are difficult to score objectively because the examinees have wide freedom of expression.
4. There is the lack of consistency in judgements even among competent examiners.
5. They have 'halo' affect which implies that the examiner's judgement in evaluating one characteristic is influenced by another characteristic. A well behaved student on account of his behaviour may get more marks.
6. They have 'question to question carry effect'. A student who gives the best answer in the beginning of the answer book is likely to get more marks in the subsequent question and vice-versa.
7. They have 'examinee to examinee to carry effect' which means that a particular student may get marks not only on the basis of what he has written but also on the basis of the answer of the previous student.
8. The examiners may be influenced by the language of the examinees. The quality of handwriting of the examinees may also influence the examiner. The length of the answer rather than the depth of the content may also influence marking.
9. Some examiners are too liberal in marking and some too strict.
10. Sometimes it is said that the 'mood' of the examiner also influences marking. Immediate happy events in the family or the job may motivate the examiner to be more generous. A quarrel in the family may lead to the award of low marks.

11. Essay type of tests may not provide a true picture of the comprehension level of the examinee. Some students cram answers and write the same in the examination and get good marks.
12. They are time consuming both for the examiner and the examinee.
13. The speed of writing may influence the performance of the students. Students who are slow in writing may not be able to provide answers to all the questions in the limited time table allotted for the paper. This results in low scores although the students may be knowing the correct answers of all questions.

Suggesting for Constructing a Good Essay Type Test

(i) The test constructor or the paper setter as he is commonly called should prepare ideal answers to all the questions given in the essay type test. It becomes all the more essential when different examiners are required to examine the answer books. This step is needed to ensure two things :
   (a) The approximate time required to complete the paper and
   (b) To provide uniformity to marking by different examiners.

(ii) The expected length of the answer of each question should be indicated on the paper.

(iii) While preparing questions, it should be kept in mind that the maximum subject matter content is covered.

(iv) There should be no overall choice in the question paper. Choice should be given of each question or it should be sectionwise.

(v) Questions should be such as they require the examinees to show a reasonable command over the essential knowledge of the subject matter being evaluated.

(vi) Questions should be so worded that all the examinees interpret them in the same manner as the examiner wants.

(vii) It is sometimes advocated that questions requiring opinion should not be asked as in case of different opinion by an examinee from that of the examiner, an examinee may suffer.

(viii) Questions should be very explicit so that the examinee may know the intention of the examiner in asking the question and accordingly he may give the answer.

(ix) The examiner should clearly indicate the weight of each part of the question so that the examinees may determine the time to be devoted to each part of the question.

(x) The number of questions may be large and expected answers within reasonable limits.

(xi) The use of essay type questions should be restricted to those learning outcomes which cannot be measured by objective type items so satisfactorily.

(xii) Reasonable amount of time should be allowed to ensure that the essay type test does not become a test of speed in writing. It should be a power test rather than a speed test.

(xiii) It should be a balanced paper in the sense that it includes different types of questions : essay type, short answer and very short answer type.

(xiv) It should include a variety of questions to assess abilities like knowledge, understanding, analysis, synthesis and applications.

(xv) The questions should not be too general, vague and comprehensive. They should define the task for the candidate and indicate clearly the scope of the answer.

(xvi) A large number of short and more specific questions requiring short or limited answer should find a prominent place in the paper and be preferred to a few long and general questions.

(xvii) The time allowed for the examination should be carefully considered in relation to the amount of writing required on the part of the students. The examinations should be so timed that the students are usefully engaged for the whole duration.

(xviii) The questions may be arranged in order of difficulty, i.e., from the easier to the more difficult.

(xix) Clear instructions to the students regarding the number of questions to be attempted, marks given to each question, or part thereof, and marks reserved for any special purpose, such as diagrams, neatness, etc. may be given in the beginning of the question paper.

(xx) As far as possible, equal marks may be allotted to each question.

(xxi) Question paper may be reviewed before it is handed over to the person concerned. Quite a few points may strike the paper setter on this second reading. A paper setter should safeguard his reputation as a setter by taking all the care that is possible at the beginning.

Illustrative Essay Type Questions

1. Does an increase in population help or hinder the process of economic development ? Explain.
2. What measures would you recommend for solving the problem of educated unemployment in India ?
3. With the help of a diagram show the relationship between total returns, marginal returns and average returns.
4. Briefly describe one of the measures included in the Ninth Five Year Plan to help the small farmers.

5. Does a rise in the GNP necessarily imply the growth of the economy and consequent rise in per capita income ? Explain.
6. How does India mobilise resources for financing development programmes ?
7. What is an economic policy ? State its main objectives with Indian examples ?
8. Illustrate with examples the significance of natural resources in the economic development of a country.
9. Indicate the role of the Public Sector in the process of economic development of India.
10. State the various types of business enterprise. Explain the general characteristics of a public enterprise.
11. Explain the types and functions of commercial banks.
12. How is a company formed ? Distinguish between articles of association and memorandum of association.
13. Explain the import and export procedure.
14. Give the main characteristics of commerce. How does it differ from trade?
15. Why people formulate cooperative societies ? Explain the characteristics and working of any type of cooperative society.

Short-Answer Type Questions

Meaning—In a simple language it may be stated that a short-answer type test is between an essay type test and an objective test. Here we mention a few definitions given by experts to have a comprehensive view.

K. D. Hoppkins, J. C. Stanley and B. R. Hopkins in their book. Educational and Psychological Measurement and Evaluation (1990) write, "The short-answer test is an objective test in which each item is in the form of a direct question, a stimulus word or phrase, a specific direction, a specific problem or an incomplete statement or question. The response must be supplied by the examinee rather than merely identified from a list of suggested answers supplied by the teacher."

William Wierma and Stephen G. Jurs in their book, Educational Measurement and Testing (1996) provide this definition, "Short-answer items are considered objective items in that the correct response can be secured objectively. That is preferably there is a single correct answer so that equally important scores would agree on the correctness of a response."

The Merits

1. It is easy to construct them as they measure only simple learning outcomes.
2. They are very useful for the recall of simple memorised facts and figures.
3. They are useful to test the lowest level of cognitive taxonomy, i.e., knowledge of terminology, classification etc.
4. A large area of subject matter can be covered by the inclusion of a large number of short-answer questions.
5. Marking is relatively objective as compared with essay type of questions.
6. There is very little scope for the influence of handwriting and spelling etc. on marking.

The Limitations

1. They are not suitable for measuring complex learning outcomes.
2. They are not suitable for judging the power of analysing and reasoning of the students.

Suggestions for Improving Short-Answer Tests

1. The intended answer should be thought first and then an appropriate question formed.
2. Questions should not be picked up exactly from the textbook.
3. Sufficient number of short answer questions should be asked to cover the content.
4. A direct question is more desirable than an incomplete sentence.
5. Language of the question should be simple.
6. A scoring key should be prepared.
7. The number of words the answer should contain must be specified.

Illustration of Short-Answer Questions

1. Distinguish between national income at current prices and at constant prices.
2. Why do we compute national income at constant prices?
3. What is meant by process based and product based division of labour ?
4. Should production of goods for self consumption be included in production ? Give reasons.
5. Distinguish between goods and services.
6. Write a note on the concept of production country.
7. How does consumption of fixed capital or depreciation differ from capital loss?
8. Explain the concept of compensation of employers.
9. Distinguish between national income and domestic income.
10. Distinguish between gross national product at market price and gross national product at factor ?

Very Short Answers Questions

1. State any two functions which all economic systems perform.
2. Give one unique characteristics each of
   (a) a mixed economy
   (b) a capitalist economy
3. Suggest two such characteristics of a capitalistic economy which distinguish it from a socialist economy.
4. The phenomenon which characterises socialism is
   (a) Nationalisation of means of production.
   (b) Institution of private property.
   (c) Co-existence of public and private sector.
   (d) Freedom of contract. E. Consumer's sovereignty.
5. Statements relating to Economic Systems are given below. Write 'S' if it pertains to socialism, 'C' for capitalism and 'M' for mixed economy :
   (a) Consumer's sovereignty is maintained. ( )
   (b) Govt. controls and regulates private sector. ( )
   (c) Equality of opportunity is ensured. ( )
   (d) Class struggle continues. ( )
   (e) Classless society is aimed at. ( )
   (f) Laissez faire policy prevails. ( )
6. Give four agruments in favour of economic planning in India.
7. Why rice is grown in West Bengal and Bajra in Rajasthan? Give two reasons.
8. Give two reasons to induce the Indian farmer to grow more food.
9. When does the desire become want in Economics ?

10. Give two examples of each of the 'form utility' and 'service utility' in production.
11. Define the term national income.
12. Define production.
13. Give three examples of economic goods.
14. List two items of immediate consumption of a textile mill.
15. What do you mean by factor income?
16. Why are transfer payments not included in national income?
17. Mention three main components of domestic factor income.
18. When would GDP of a country be smaller than its GNP?
19. Explain the meaning of net acquisition of financial assets.
20. Why are imports not included in the estimation of national income?

QUESTIONS

Essay Type Questions

1. "To close down examinations would be to give the signal for educational saturation." Comment on the statement.
2. State the significance, merits and limitations of essay type examinations. Suggest measures for their improvement. Illustrate essay type questions in Economics.
3. What is the place of short answer questions in Economics ? Give some illustrations of such questions.
4. Give suggestions for the improvement of examination in Economics ? What type of questions should be included ?

Short Answer and Objective Type Questions

5. Mention three merits of essay questions.
6. Give three merits of very short questions.
7. Give two demerits of essay type and short answer type questions.
8. Some statements are given below. Write 'T' if it is true and 'F' if it is false :
   (i) Essay type questions have been in existence from time immemorial. ( )
   (ii) Essay type questions should be supplemented by other type of questions. ( )
   (iii) B. Ed. examination should include only short and very short question. ( )
   (iv) An ideal question paper should include all type of questions. ( )
   (v) Examinations can be abolished altogether in the present system of education. ( )

19

Resultant Factors

The Tradition

Aims are based on philosophical considerations and values on reality. Values are the outcomes of results achieved after teaching according to the aims. Aims are ideals which are not based on experiments. Values on the other hand spring as a result of experimentation or after them into practices.

Classification of Values in Economics

(1)	(2)	(3)	(4)
Cultural Values	Disciplinary Values	Practical Values	Social Values

Cultural Values of Teaching Economics—Economic activity, one of the most important domains of Economics is an important aspect of a nation as well as of an individual. It explains the nature of the society and its special aspect of national prosperity. Economics attempts to relate production with consumption. Appropriate national economic policy, fair dealings in economic activities and pleasant manners—all go to make up the good cultural tracts of the individual in the commercial field. Several philanthrophists in India from the business community have set up a large number of cultural and educational institutions in the country.

Disciplinary Values—The word 'discipline' has a special connotation in an economic activity. It is not in terms of 'order' and 'authority'. It is to be interpreted in terms of intellectual traits only. A study of Economics helps to develop the powers of knowing, understanding and application. It also develops certain skills—how to write good business letters and how to spend etc.

Practical Values—Practical values relate more to the needs of various occupations at different levels in the hierarchy of employment—from clerical to management level.

Social Values—The study of Economics should enable an individual to appreciate that man is a social being and he must play an important role in bringing about social progress. Bad economic dealings, corrupt methods, smuggling and tax evasions are examples of anti-social values which should be avoided as outcomes of a study of Economics. Profit motive should not be the end and-be-all of all business enterprises.

Capability Development

The fulfilment of the objectives of teaching Economics to students who pass out the senior secondary school lies in the development of the following competencies in them :

1. Competency of earning and consuming.
2. Competency to understand the use of knowledge of Economics in day-to-day personal life.
3. Competency in undertaking one's own economic enterprise.

4. Competency of occupational/vocational change.
5. Competency to pursue more than one economic activity.
6. Competency to pursue a specialized vocation.
7. Competency to understand the economic issues facing the nation.
8. Competency to take up responsibility as an active, constructive, cooperative and creative member of the society.
9. Competency in participating in economic and business life of the society.
10. Competency in participating intelligently and rationally in political and social life of the society.
11. Competency in pursuing higher education.

Expected Results

The anticipated outcomes of the teaching of Economics are in terms of the following :

1. Development of understandings in the students.
2. Development of desirable attitudes in the students.
3. Development of essential skills in the students.

Development of Understandings in the Students. The subject of Economics abounds in facts. It is, therefore, very necessary to highlight or draw attention to the more significant facts, generalizations and principles, commonly known as 'understandings'. For instance, 'A child that practises good manners and habits, is loved by all, both at home and school', or 'Man has to depend upon communities far away for satisfying his daily needs', are the understandings that one has to develop through the lessons on good manners, or national and international trade, respectively.

If our teaching is not to result in mere transmission of unrelated and isolated facts, it is an important task of the teacher to help the child to receive various facts in their proper perspective or in their relative importance. It should be the endeavour of the teacher to help the children in developing important concepts of understandings by providing them enough experiences in and outside the class. It has been a common experience that properly developed concepts and understandings are retained longer in our minds, than the host of unrelated and unorganised facts that are memorized for the purpose of examinations.

Understandings include the following :

1. Making the child understand his environment so as to enable him to adjust better with his social and cultural environment.
2. Enabling the child understand social concepts to family, community, state and nation.
3. Enabling the child understand the world around him.
4. Enabling the child develop an appreciation of social change.
5. Enabling the child know the progress of society from primitive to the advanced stage.
6. Acquainting the child about man's ways of living, his significant achievements and the problems that he faces today.
7. Acquainting the child with social institutions.
8. Helping the child understand how far economic conditions influence in moulding the growth of society in different parts of the world.
9. Helping the child learn about vocational activities and opportunities.

Behavioural Development

An attitude is a feeling, developed towards an object, or person or group or anything else. These attitudes last through a life time. The facts that a child learns in the class may be forgotten. But these attitudes linger, and mould his behaviour-pattern for all that is to follow. The child may forget the facts, he learnt about the duties of a policeman or the postman. But the feeling of friendliness he gained, for these public officials will remain for life.

The development of desirable attitudes and appreciation is an important aspect of any good education. The attitudes, appreciations and habits are an inseparable part of the personality of an individual. All agree that it is the attitudes that matter, more than anything else in the behaviour of a person. The development of the attitudes is, however, not to be attempted as a separate item by lecturing or preaching. It should be the natural outcome of all the discussions and activities carried on by the class. They are developed unknowingly. It is often said that attitudes are caught and not taught. The teacher should, therefore, be conscious of this aspect and reflect proper attitudes, through his disposition and behaviour, so that they are rightly adopted by the children under his charge.

Desirable Attitudes Imply

(i) Developing attitudes to assume economic, social and civic responsibility and thus making the child an active participant and an enlightened individual.

(ii) Developing attitudes to act in accordance with democratic principles and values.

(iii) Developing attitudes of personal responsibility, civic and world mindedness, emotional maturity, intellectual integrity, aesthetic appreciation and suspended judgement.

(iv) Developing attitudes of patriotism, cooperation and tolerance.

(v) Developing attitudes to appreciate the viewpoints of others and making one's own contribution.

Teaching Skills

Importance of Skills in the Teaching of Economics—The importance of acquiring skills in a subject is gradually being recognised. L.P. Jacs has stressed this aspect in these words, "The human body is naturally skill-hungry and until that hunger is satisfied, it will be ill-at-ease, craving for something it has not got and seeking its satisfaction in external excitements which exhausts its vitality and diminish its capacity for joy. Short of skill, the perfect health, even of body, is impossible."

James High of the University of California states that a skill is the wherewithal to gain an end.

Meaning of a Skill – According to Webster's New Dictionary, skill is "the ability to use one's knowledge effectively and readily in execution of performance, technical expertness; a power or habit of doing any particular thing completely."

It is wrong to think that learning is entirely a mental process. All learning is influenced by physiological factors both within and outside the individual who is learning. At the same time all learning is accompanied by these physiological factors. However, when the physical responses of the individual become more important and prominent, we call it skill development.

Social and Academic Qualities

Prof. Charles A. Beard has analysed these skills as under :

1. Skill in methods of obtaining access to information (a) use of libraries and institutions, (b) use of encyclopaedias, handbooks, documents, sources, authorities, statistical collections, etc.

2. Skill in the sifting the materials and the discovery and determination of authentic evidence in the use of primary sources.
3. Skill in the observation and description of contemporary occurrences in the school and community.
4. Skill in methods of handling information (a) in analysis—breaking down large themes or masses of data into manageable units and penetrating to irreducible elements, (b) in synthesis—combining elements, drawing inferences and conclusions and comparing with previous conclusions and inference—logical and systematic organisation, (c) in map and chart making and graphic presentation.
5. Skill in memorising results of study with consciousness of application to new situations by exact reference and analogy.
6. Skill in scientific method—inquiring spirit, patience, weighing evidence, tentative and precise conclusions.

Mastery of Skills

Mastery of a skill is said to be achieved when the skill can be performed even if something else was also in the mind of an individual. L.V. Douglass, J. T. Blanford and R.I. Anderson (1965) give the following example of mastery of skill. "A teacher once had in class a girl who was unusually expert in taking dictation on the stenotype. She quite often was hired to record discussions and proceedings at conventions and important broad meetings. She had the reputation of never missing a word in her recording. Yet, while she was recording, she habitually also was reading a book or magazine at the same time. She had developed her skill so highly that it was completely automatized; her angers reached instantly when the sound of the voice reached her ears. She had actually found that her records were more accurate when she deliberately kept her mind off her work."

The mastery formula for learning a skill may be expressed in three letters TAS. T stands for techniques, A for accuracy and S for speed. Some teachers prefer to reverse this order and believe in the efficacy of SAT, i.e., speed, accuracy and technique.

Following are the six steps to achieve mastery :

(i) Pre-testing (ii) Teaching (iii) Testing the result (iv) Adopting the procedure (v) Re-teaching and (vi) Retesting and continuing the procedure till the mastery is achieved.

Skill Achievement

Hepen Mccraken Carpenter and Alice W. Spieseke have suggested the following principles:

1. For the acquisition and improvement of skills, the learning activity must focus on skill development. Skill development will not take place by chance.
2. Experience designed to promote growth in skills must be meaningful to the learner. A certain skill must be accepted as important.
3. Experience used in skill development must be geared to the maturation level of the learner. Just as a five-year-old child cannot usually master the flowing script with a fountain pen, neither can a junior high school student be expected to achieve the same degree of skill in synthetic thought as a college professor.
4. For the successful learning and retention of skills, repetitive practice is necessary. Reinforcement of learning is essential.
5. Skills should be developed in connection with on-going activities and not in isolation. Every skill is in the end an integral part of the life of equipment of this citizen.
6. Development of different skills should go on simultaneously. There is a gradual and steady growth of all of the parts in the process of education.

7. Evidence of skill development must be sought to changes in behaviour. The whole purpose of education is to induce an improved behaviour pattern.
8. Provision for the systematic development of skills must be made through the school programme. This is merely to re-emphasise the idea that skills begin with mastery of simple uncomplicated stpes and proceed to more complex and various patterns of activity. This principle is a summary of all the other seven.

Skill and Psychology

Mort and Vincent of the Columbia University have developed and compiled the following 30 psychological rules for building skills :

1. One learns when one feels some urge to learn.
2. What a person learns is influenced directly by his surroundings.
3. A person learns quickly and lastingly what has meaning for him.
4. When an oraganism is ready to act, it is painful for it not to act; and when an organism is not ready to act, it is painful for it to act.
5. Individuals differ in all sorts of ways.
6. Security and success are the soil and climate for growth.
7. All learning occurs through attempts to satisfy needs.
8. Emotional tension decreases efficiency in learning.
9. Physical defects lower efficiency in learning.
10. Interest is an indicator of growth.
11. Interest is a source of power in motivating learning.
12. What gives satisfaction tends to be repeated; what is annoying tends to be avoided.

13. The best way to learn a part in life is to play that part.
14. Learning is more efficient, longer and lasting when the conditions for it a real and life-like.
15. Piece-meal learning is not efficient.
16. You cannot train the mind like a muscle.
17. A person learns by his own activity.
18. Abundant, realistic practice contributes to learning.
19. Participation enhances learning.
20. First-hand experience makes for lasting and more complete learning.
21. General behaviour is controlled by emotions as well as by intellect.
22. Unused talents contribute to personal maladjustment.
23. You start to grow from where you are and not from some artificial starting point.
24. Growth is a steady, continuous process and different individuals grow at different rates.
25. It is impossible to learn one thing at a time.
26. Learning is reinforced when two or more senses are used at the same time.
27. The average pupil is largely a myth.
28. If you want a certain result, teach it directly.
29. Children develop in terms of all the influences which affect them.
30. It has been said that a person learns more in the first three years of his life and all the years afterward.

Important skills relating to Economics :

1. Using reference resources.
2. Using text books.

3. Note taking.
4. Note making.
5. Understanding economic phenomena.
6. Preparing and reading maps, tables, curves, graphs etc.
7. Conducting surveys.
8. Participating in discussions etc.

Participation—The mind of the children should be prepared to learn the new skill. They must be motivated. The students should be made to feel the necessity of acquiring the skill. The preparation or introduction may take different forms.

(i) The students may be taken to markets or banks etc.

(ii) Skill work of some experts may be exhibited.

(iii) A model of some good work may be shown to the students.

Statement of the Aim—The students must know clearly what they are going to learn: otherwise they will be groping in the dark and their co-operation will be half-hearted.

Presentation—The teacher presents the new form of skill. The teacher should give a few instructions to the students so that they may properly watch and observe the demonstration given by him. Sometimes the students may handle the model for close observation. This stage consists largely of observation, listening and seeking on the part of the students. The teacher is doing things and explaining things. The teacher may give the statements of the rules to be observed in practising the skill. But they should be brief and should not be many.

Practice—The students will imitate what the teacher has demonstrated before them. This is the most important step and will also take a longer period. The teacher will not remain passive at this stage. He will supervise and guide the practice of each individual.

Correction—It is a sort of representation. The teacher will point out the defects and show the correct ways of performing the activity. He may restate the rules.

Re-practice—Then again will come practice and the students may practise the skill and acquire improvement. The two steps 'correction' and 'practice' may be repeated a number of times.

Suggestive Ideas

The following guidelines may be considered in teaching and developing skills :

1. The teacher should possess the skill which he proposes to the students to learn.
2. The teacher should identify the factors which determine the pattern of the skill.
3. The teacher should appeal to as many senses as possible in teaching a skill.
4. Each segment of the class period should have a specific objective and each student and the teacher should have proper awareness of it.
5. Repetition is of great value only when it is with conscious direction.
6. In teaching a skill, practice time should be divided into short practice periods.
7. Practices of a skill should be varied before the law of diminishing return applies.
8. Group practices are useful only for establishing the desirable pattern.
9. Attainable goals should be set for each student.
10. A skill should be developed to the level of automatization.
11. The teacher must lay more stress on the technique rather than the speed.

12. The teacher should not overemphasise testing on skill development.
13. The teacher has to promote a skill through proper demonstration. Mistakes can be avoided not by telling but by demtonstrating better ways of working and doing.

QUESTIONS

Essay Type Questions

1. Explain the meaning and significance of developing skills in Economics. What types of skills are needed to be developed in the students studying Economics ?
2. Is it possible to isolate a mental skill from a motor skill ?
3. Prepare a list of skills you would like to develop in the students studying Economics.
4. Select any topic in Economics and prepare a skill lesson.
5. Explain the various steps of a skill lesson.
6. State the principles and guidelines for." developing skills in Economics.

Short Answer and Objective Type Questions

7. Some values are given below. Classify them into cultural, disciplinary, practical and social
   (i) Needs of certain occupation ....
   (ii) Payment of taxes ....
   (iii) Spending money ....
   (iv) Pleasant manners ....
8. Mention any three skills in learning Economics.
9. List any three competencies needed in the students in Economics.

10. Give any two understandings related to the teaching-learning of Economics.
11. List examples of any two attitudes related to the learning of Economics.
12. Write 'yes' against the statement if it is correct and 'No' if it is incorrect.
    (a) Recitation is an important skill in Economics. ( )
    (b) Drawing graph is an important skill in Economics. ( )
    (c) Drawing a political map is an important skill in Economics. ( )
    (d) Tabulating data is an important skill in Economics. ( )
    (e) Conducting a survey is an important skill in Economics. ( )

20

Significance of Education

Relationship with Economy and Polity

The process of development in the country is determined by a harmonious functioning of the triangular of economy, education and polity. Education is conceived as a critical participant of a triangular process which cumulatively leads to change, development and progress in a society in a planned manner.

The economy, education and polity of a country in the modern world are on the one hand, powerful instruments of power with tremendous potential, both positive and negative. On the other hand, they are extremely potent tools for the development of the people provided they are utilised to the maximum. This means that each of the three sides of the triangle, should be themselves, to use. The geometrical terminology on genuine straight lines, i.e., they should be what they are? Supposed to be and each of the three sides should relate itself positively, with the other two to form a triangle of appropriate area.

Role in Economic Growth

Looking at the economic development and educational development together, we notice that countries of the world exhibit a variety of relationships between these two phenomena.

There are numerous indicators which can show the educational development of a particular country or a region. The two most important basic indicators are the literacy rate and enrolment rate.

Economic development includes many aspects such as agricultural or industrial development. Different countries may have different positions on one or the other indicator. Some countries may be agriculturally developed while others may be more advanced industrially. Thus while there is the need for having a common indicator, it is not easy to find any single variable to satisfy all aspects. Quite often, Gross National Product (GNP) and more precisely per capita GNP is used to measure the economic development.

Now coming to the relationship between the two phenomena, i.e., educational development and economic development, it is observed that some of the economically developed countries are also educationally advanced. They have almost cent per cent literacy and all children of school-going age are enrolled in the schools. As opposed to this there are some countries which are not economically much developed but they have registered tremendous educational progress. In this context examples of countries like Sri Lanka, China, Myanmar (Burma) and Philippines may be cited. Further there are countries which are economically well-off but they are educationally backward. The Gulf countries are the obvious example of this type. India is neither economically advanced nor educationally advanced. The overall situation which emerges is that generally the countries having higher levels of income or economically advanced also have higher level of educational attainment. The economically poor countries are likely to remain educationally backward if they do not give importance to education and/or do not allocate more funds to it and ensure optimum utilisation of the available resources.

A Great Asset

1. Though the great founder of modern Economics, Adam Smith, in his Enquiry into the Nature and Causes of the Wealth of Nations published in 1776, placed great stress on education, yet the economics of education and investment remained one of the neglected subjects, in the science of economics. It is only in recent years that a growing number of economists have been making it one of their principal preoccupations, and that the words 'human capital', are coming into widespread use. It is gradually being realised that education has a major role not only in promoting social peace and harmony and self improvement, but also in the process of wealth creation itself.
2. To quote John Vaizey, "Adam Smith, placed education at the centre of his thinking, because it was to its system of national education that Scotland was mainly, 'perhaps, indebted for the superior intelligence, and the providential, orderly habits of her people." This was the basis of good civil government, and it was the basis, too, of economic activity and progress. Ricardo and Malthus felt that education was a potent factor in inculcating habits which would lead to family limitation.

John Vaizey has further observed : "Education has become a major source of skills and trained talent. Indeed, from one point of view, this is education's critical economic role."

He has further stated, "After standardising for race, sex, ability and other characteristics, it can be shown that the higher the level of education a group has, the higher its earning power will be."

3. Alfred Marshall refers to 'education as a national investment' in his Principles of Economics and writes, "There are few practical problems in which the economist has a more direct interest that those relating to the principles on which the expense of the education of children should be divided between the state and the parents. But we must now consider the conditions that determine the power and the will of the parents to bear their share of the expense, whatever it may be." For the working classes and for the middle class, he preferred 'technical education' to the 'narrow range of the old grammar school education'. Regarding the importance of general education, he observed, "It makes him more intelligent, more ready, more trustworthy, in his ordinary work, it raises the tone of his life in working hours and out of working hours, it is thus an important means towards the production of material wealth, at the same time, regarded as an end in itself, it is inferior to none of those which the production of material wealth can be made to subserve." Marshall's view was 'that the most valuable of all capital is that invested in human beings'.
4. In an article entitled, "The Economics of Education', published in Education in World Perspective, Dr. Elba Gomez Del Rey de Kybal, a noted economist from Argentina, observes: "From the standpoint of economic development, three factors are of basic importance—natural resources, physical capital, and human resources. It has been demonstrated that in the present stage of technology natural resources are not the determining factor in economic development; countries like Switzerland, Holland, Denmark, and Norway have achieved a high level of development, despite most meagre endowment in such resources. And experience has proved the investment, though more directly related

to economic development that to natural resources, varies greatly in its effectiveness. Venezuela is a good example of large, investments and lagging development. The problem is not only to bring about an increase in the share of the national product devoted to investment as opposed to consumption; it is also to bring about a more desirable allocation of investment. And to make a full use of capital investment, a qualified, managerial, engineering, and labour force is necessary for selection, operation and maintenance of such investment. Thus, the human element is not only the aim of economic activity, but the most important factor in determining the level and composition of the underlying investment. It follows, then, that education and training are of primary importance, not only from the subjective point of view of the individuals receiving such benefits, but also from the standpoint of accelerating the economic growth of a nation or of a region. No investment is more productive than in education and training."

5. Prof. Theodore Schultz, noted economist of the University of Chicago, writes : "If my hypothesis is correct, it carries radical implications. It implies that fewer steel mills and other big plants should be built in the so-called underdeveloped countries, and more invested in the peoples of those countries."

6. In the words of Prof. John K. Norton of the Columbia University,. "The effects of investment in physical capital depend in a large measure on the intelligence and skill of the people who use this capital."

7. Mrs. Alva Myrdal, a sociologist and educator and at one time Swedish Ambassador in India, in an address at the Central Institute of Education of the Delhi University stated, "Education has, in nations that have advanced

rapidly and firmly, been rather a precursor than a follower in the time-table of progress."

Again she writes in Education in World Perspective, "The paramount role for achieving any kind of development and most definitely any development great enough to be judged beneficial to our whole world of Denmark, Holland, Germany, the U.S.A., the U.K., the U.S.S.R., Japan etc. to the value of education. Further, she writes, "Finally, and most contemporarily there is dramatic indication of the validity of my thesis : the present 'educational race' between the Soviet Union and the United States. The two giant powers of the world have undoubtedly realised that their ultimate strength will depend mainly on their new conquests in science, and on their people, their skills, their ingenuity. Just as the United States in the last century was making possible such enormous forward strides by educating and training its population, so we are seeing the same process at work in this century in the Soviet Union—achieving what must be called, if we recall the status of the pro-revolution Russian people, another miracle of development, chiefly by raising the educational standards and certainly not by an import of capital. When a rigidly planned economy devotes such relatively great sums of education, does this not flash a signal that education is investment and not consumption ?"

8. Don Adams of the Syracuse University observes : "The wisdom distilled from the last two decades of international attention focused on the developing areas of the world suggests that the educational factor is of crucial importance in attaining even modest goals of economic and social development. Although the precise dimensions of the contribution of education to national economic and social goals are a continuing subject for intensive research on the part of today's educators and social scientists, many recent studies demonstrate that economic return from educational investment is real and to some degree measurable."

9. Philip H. Coombs writes in Education and Foreign Aid : "Today it is clear that industrialisation and the whole modernisation process cannot proceed without the development of human resources, and for this a major investment in education is required."

10. Karol W. Bigelow in an article on 'Problems and Prospects of Education in Africa', states : "Good government requires good public administrators. Effective exploitation of natural resources requires good businessmen, good scientists and good technicians. Good education requires good teachers. But 'goodness' in respect to administrative, technological, or teaching performance depends on command of knowledge and skill. And formal education is recognised as the most efficient measure where knowledge and skill can be attained. It follows that the expansion and improvement of formal education are the *sine qua non* of African development. Only through education can the essential supplies of skilled middle, and high level manpower be produced."

11. Prof. Adam Curie in Educationol Strategy for Developing Societies puts his faith in the "country which constantly tackles development as a human problem first and an economic one second, and which bases its approach on the idea that human beings are in themselves of value."

12. The Indian economist, Prof. V.K.R.V. Rao, states : "Let us not think that education is just a consumption or welfare activity, something that can be postponed in preference to investment, to irrigation, power, steel mills or more salaries for government officers who will administer these programmes. The sooner this is recognised by influential persons in this country, the better would be India's chances to achieve the high rate of economic growth which we all desire."

13. H. M. Philips, the Economic Adviser and Director of the Economic Analysis Division, Department of Social Science, UNESCO, describes the impact of the thinking of economists on the educationists : "The sudden recognition by economists of the role of education to economic development caught some educators by surprise. Used to their high calling as custodians and transmitters of human and social values they had not sufficiently realised that they had in their hands one of the most powerful means of wiping out the pathetically low living levels prevailing over most of the globe. Finance ministers were also caught by surprise. Used to regarding education as a purely social expenditure, they suddenly found their economists on the side of the education ministers, and educational budgets as a whole are increasing more than proportionately to total budgets and population growth."
14. Prof. Harold F. Clark, writing about the 'Return on Investment' in the Yearbook of Education, 1956, states : "It is undoubtedly safe to say that on the average the total educational programme in any Western country in the world today has a beneficial effect upon the economy as a whole...... There is every reason to assume, however, that a substantial portion of the difference (between the per capita incomes in the rich countries of the world) is caused by education... the rate of increase will depend very largely upon how drastically the country is willing to change the school system and what price it is willing to pay socially and culturally to bring about the high income. Probably no one would hold that the physical resources, the location of the country and many other items are not important. Such factors are important. Perhaps the best way to state the matter is that all other factors being as they are, there are the strongest reasons for believing that education properly designed can have a powerful effect in increasing the income of any country in the world."

A Countrywise Outlay of Economic Development and National Development Including Education (Around 2000)

	Country	GNP per Capita U.S($)	Infant Mortality Rate under 1 year	Life Expectancy at Birth (Years)	Adult Literacy Rate	Primary School Enrolment ratio (gross)
1.	Afghanistan	250	165	46	32	30
2.	Australia	20,000	05	78	99	101
3.	Austria	26,000	04	77	99	103
4.	Bangladesh	370	58	59	56	97
5.	Bhutan	510	80	62	42	72
6.	Brazil	4,400	34	67	85	128
7.	Canada	19,500	06	79	99	102
8.	China	780	33	70	84	104
9.	Egypt	1,400	41	67	56	100
10.	Ethiopia	100	118	44	33	47
11.	France	23,500	05	78	99	100
12.	Germany	25,300	05	77	99	104
13.	India	450	70	63	58	90
14.	Indonesia	580	38	66	88	114

Contd.

	Country	*GNP per Capita U.S($)*	*Infant Mortality Rate under 1 year*	*Life Expectancy at Birth (Years)*	*Adult Literacy Rate*	*Primary School Enrolment ratio (gross)*
15.	Iran	1,760	37	70	76	107
16.	Iraq	250	104	65	58	107
17.	Italy	19,800	05	78	98	101
18.	Japan	32,000	04	80	99	102
19.	Mexico	4,400	27	73	89	112
20.	Myanmar	250	79	61	83	100
21.	Nepal	220	75	58	45	122
22.	Pakistan	470	84	65	45	84
23.	Russian Federation	2,270	18	67	99	105
24.	Sri Lanka	820	17	74	90	107
25.	Sweden	25,000	03	79	99	103
26.	Switzerland	38,000	03	79	99	103
27.	U.K.	22,600	06	78	99	102
28.	U.S.A.	30,600	07	77	99	103

Source—Data arrived at on the basis of 'The State of Children's World 2001 (UNICEF) and other U. N. Publications.

Note—Drop-out rates at the primary stage are very high in developing countries.

A Selective Statewise Data on Economic and Educational Development in India

	State	*Per Capital state domestic product at current prices (1999-2000) (Rs)*	*Life Expectancy at birth (1993-97)*	*Infant mortality Rate (1994)*	*Literacy Rate (2001)*
1.	Bihar	6,328	59.6	63	47.53
2.	Gujarat	18,600	61.9	63	69.97
3.	Haryana	21,100	64.1	68	68.59
4.	Karnataka	16,300	63.3	58	67.04
5.	Kerala	18,300	73.3	14	90.92
6.	Madhya Pradesh	10.900	55.5	90	64.11
7.	Maharashtra	23,400	65.5	48	77.27
8.	Orissa	9,200	57.2	67	63.61
9.	Punjab	23,000	67.7	53	69.59
10.	Rajasthan	12,600	60.0	81	61.03
11.	Tamil Nadu	19,100	64.1	52	73.47
12.	Uttar Pradesh	9,800	57.6	84	57.36
13.	West Bengal	15,600	62.8	52	69.22
14.	Andhra Pradesh	14,700	62.4	66	61.11
15.	Assam	9,700	59.7	76	64.28

15. In this book 'The Economics of Education' B. G. Tilak has observed that the relationship between education and economic growth is a two-way process—one of a reciprocal nature and other of mutual contribution.
16. John Vaizey has humorously but correctly described the relationship between economic growth and education like a 'chicken and egg'.
17. Harbison and Myers are of the view that "education is both the seed and the flower of economic development."

Observations—Bihar has the lowest literacy rate as well as the least per capita in state, domestic product followed by Uttar Pradesh. Orissa also comes under this category.

Kerala has the highest literacy rate but not the highest per capital in state domestic product.

'Other things remaining the same', there is close relationship between economy and education.

Role in Development of Economics

In recent years there has been a great emphasis on the economics of education because of the following factors :

Rising Cost—The proportion of the national income spent on education has increased in recent years.

Secondary Industries—As individuals become richer, the proportion of their income devoted to food and other basic necessities drops. The amount they spend on health, education etc. rises.

Technological Transformation—The basis of the technological transformation of the world economy can be found in the accumulation of knowledge.

Health and Productivity—The low productivity of many workers in various countries is directly attributable to their poor physical state. This in turn depends to a considerable extent on the type of education that the workers receive.

Shortage of Skills – It is a common belief that shortage of required skills holds back economic growth. An effective educational plan must be based on the needs of skilled manpower of all sorts. An unplanned system of education results in unemployed persons and deprives the nation of their contributions to the growth of national income. Thus the specialised role of manpower forecasting brings the economics of education into prominence.

Demand on Scarce Resources – Education can be made cheap in the developing countries in the sense that there is a super-abundance of 'manpower which can be harnessed very conveniently. Education thus makes limited demands on the scarcest resources of the country. The underdeveloped countries are short of physical and sometimes of natural resources. This implies that the use of the abundant supply of manpower and its endowment with skills is likely to be one of the major objectives of any programme of development.

High Monetary Cost of Education – Education in the developing countries is frequently poorly administered, lacking in planning and co-ordination, and one of the most striking features of many schemes of education reform in the poor countries has been their extra-ordinarily monetary cost.

For the most efficient mobilisation of a country's resources, it is of paramount importance that the plans for the development of economy, and for developing human resources, must be co-ordinated. Education cannot be left out of the general plan. The neglect of education means overlooking the importance of an adequate supply of skilled manpower and the efficient use of resources in education. John Vaizey observes : "Since education makes large demands on public funds – about 20% of government expenditure in recently independent countries – it is an important part of the economic programme, because of its cost alone. But it has also an important positive contribution to make to economic growth."

Planning Strategy

C. B. Padmanabhan suggests that the study of the principles of economics and techniques of economic analysis and an understanding of the process of economic growth will be found useful in educational planning on account of the following reasons:

(a) Planning and economics have something in common – both of them are responses for the challenges arising out of the scarcity of resources and possibility of alternative uses and maximum utilisation of limited resources.

(b) Planning for economic development has become common in almost all the countries of the world.

(c) Educational planning is also part of the overall planning for social and economic development. Objectives of education find a place in the overall planning for social and economic development and plans have to provide for financing educational development for meeting these objectives.

(d) Education is in addition a public service, demand for which is in excess of the supply that any Government is able to make. This is because of the unchanging birth rate, falling death rate and the consequent growth of population in the age group between 5-24 and the rising demand for education.

Significance of Human Power

What is Human Resource Development ? Human resource development is a 'man-centred' approach in which the human being is seen as an end in itself rather than as a means to other developmental ends. The National Seminar organised by National Institute of Educational Planning and Administration on Planning and Management Aspects, held in New Delhi on November 23-25, 1985 explained this concept as "Human resource development seeks to improve the performance abilities of the populace by strengthening their cognitive skills, manual dexterity, and by inculcating appropriate attitudinal values."

The Seminar further observed, "Obviously, such a concept has to be a multi-faceted one. It includes several aspects like nutrition, drinking water, health, housing, education, sports, culture and communications. In this sense, development of human resources is bound in the totality of its environment. However, keeping in view the purpose we are focusing only on educational and education-related aspects of HRD."

Another aspect noted by the Seminar was "The dynamics of human resource development takes explicit cognizance of the positive and negative linkages with environment, and thus provides a basis for intervening in the system as per the consideration of desirability and feasibility."

Resources are not only material ones like natural resources of oil and minerals but also human resources. Manpower is required to put the natural resources to good use, to exploit them to the fullest. Both the types of resources must be attended to simultaneously; for discovering natural resources will not profit the country if it lacks personnel with the required training and skill to put it to good use. On the other hand, training persons in particular skills will take them nowhere if there are no corresponding raw materials to work on and no industries to work in. We are concerned with the second type of resources, there is need for planning the development of manpower human resources.

A country needs educated political leaders, lawyers and judges, engineers, doctors, managers, artists, writers, craftsmen and journalists to spur its development. In an advanced economy the capacities of men are extensively developed; in a primitive country they are for the most part underdeveloped. If a country is unable to develop its human resources, it cannot develop social structure or a sense of national unity, or higher standards of material welfare.

The Second Five Year Plan in the Chapter on Education begins with these remarks : "The system of education has determining influence on the rate at which economic progress is achieved and the benefits which can be derived from it. Economic development naturally makes growing demands on human resources and in a democratic set-up it calls for values and attitudes in the building of which the quality of education is an important element."

Report of Kothari Commission

The Kothari Commission thinks that of the two programmes, i.e.. The Development of Physical Resources and the Development of Human Resources, it is the latter programme the development of which through education is the crucial one. The Commission further observes, "While the development of physical resources is a means to an end, that of human resources is an end in itself; and without it, even the adequate development of physical resources is not possible."

The reason for this is clear. The realisation of the country's aspirations involves changes in the knowledge, skills, interests and values of the people as a whole. This is basic to every programme of social and economic betterment of which India stands in need. For instance, there can be no hope of making the country self-sufficient in food unless the farmer himself is moved out of his age-long conservatism through a science-based education, becomes interested in experimentation, and is ready to adopt techniques that increase yields. The same is true of industry. The skilled manpower needed for the relevant research and its systematic application to agriculture, industry and other sectors of life can only come from a development of scientific and technological education. Similarly economic growth is not merely a matter of physical resources or of training skilled workers; it needs the education of the whole population in new ways of life, thought and work.

Robert Heilbroner describes the journey to economic development undertaken by a traditional society as the 'great ascent' and points out that the essential condition for its success is human "change on a grand scale'. He observes, "The mere lay-in of a core of capital equipment, indispensable as that is for further economic expansion, does not yet catalyse a tradition-bound society into a modern one. For that catalysis to take place, nothing short of a pervasive social transformation will suffice, a wholesale metamorphosis of habits, a wrenching reorientation of values concerning time, status, money, work; and an unweaving and reweaving of the fabric of daily existence itself." These observations are applicable to advances on the social, political and cultural fronts as well.

Dr. V.K.R.V. Rao has listed five elements of the human factor which are responsible for getting the maximum output of goods and services from available facilities and material inputs. These are as under :

1. Technical skills.
2. Motivation.
3. Organisation.
4. Utilisation of underemployed and unemployed manpower.
5. Planning techniques.

It is the business of education to attend to all these elements, since education seeks to develop the human person.

Skill Development

Prof V.K.R.V. Rao has observed, "Utilisation is a crucial factor in determining the extent and pace of economic development. Sometimes planners are so apt to be carried away by the importance of material inputs and physical capital formation that they seem to think that economic development just means the creation of irrigation, power, transport, mining capacity, coal, steel, fertilisers and machine building capacity. Undoubtedly all these are necessary; but by themselves they do not constitute a sufficient condition for economic growth. In the last analysis, it is the human being who has to operate these instruments of production. Unless he is equipped with the necessary skills and is motivated to play his appropriate role in production and organises himself properly for the purpose with due regard to economic considerations, the developmental facilities that are created will not be utilised either economically or at their optimum capacity."

Utility of Human Power

Prof. V.K.R.V. Rao further states, "Technical skills are now universally recognised as the most important aspect of manpower and planning for economic development. A preliminary condition for the building up of technical skills on a massive scale—and one that has been frequently forgotten in many developing economies—is the need for securing 100 percent literacy in the population, especially the adults who constitute the human material engaged in productive activity. Literacy in this context does not merely mean imparting the ability to read and write. For aiding development it must involve functional literacy."

Role of Economics in Educational Planning

In the opinion of the Committee on Education Planning and Administration and Evaluation in the Fourth Five Year Plan presided over by Mr. J.P. Naik, Adviser, Ministry of Education, Government of India, "The first important reform needed was preparation of a comprehensive educational plan which should deal not merely with the allocation of resources provided by the Central and the State Governments to different sectors of education and within a given sector to different types of programmes but also with the present educational situations, educational objectives in view and the programmes proposed to realise these objectives. It should thus cover planned as well as non-planned programmes that involve finance and those that do not and also programmes for better utilisation of existing facilities and economising expenditure. The linkage with programmes of social and economic development should be much closer than at present."

Value of Productivity

The Kothari Commission stresses this point in the context of Indian situation with these words, "India is in transition from a society in which education is a privilege of a small minority to one in which it could be made available to the masses of the people. The immense resources needed for this programme can be generated only if education is related to productivity so that an expansion of education leads to an increase in national income, which, in its turn, may provide the means for a larger investment in education. Education and productivity can thus constitute a 'rising spiral' whose different parts sustain and support one another."

The link between education and productivity can be forged through the development of the following programmes which should receive high priority in the plans of educational reconstruction :

- science as a basic component of education and culture;
- work-experience as an integral part of general education;
- vocationalisation of education, especially at the secondary school level, to meet the needs of industry, agriculture and trade; and
- improvement of scientific and technological education and research at the university stage with special emphasis on agriculture and allied sciences."

Theodore Schultz (19.59-63) carried out pioneering work in the economics of education by analysing important issues which are given below :

(a) The Investment and Consumption Aspects of Education.

(b) The Optimum Expenditure on Education and the Methods of Financing such Expenditure.

(c) Factors Affecting the Private Demand for Education.

(d) The Optimum Structure of the Education System.

(e) The Relationship between Education and the Development of Human Resources and Economic growth.

The following methods are used in establishing quantitative education-economy relationships :

Residual Analysis—This method involves the establishment of a production function between economic output and capital labour and 'other' factors. Education is treated as the main contribution to the "other factors."

Input-output Methods—The basic idea on which input-output models are based is in establishing relationships between the outputs of each sector of the economy and the corresponding inputs to the other through the use of technological coefficients. Correa and Tinbergen (1962) were the pioneers of these methods. Almost all the input-output models used at the macro-level for educational planning have been formulated in conjunction with some other quantitative methods.

The studies concerned with input-output relationship in education primarily deal with the allocation of resources with a view to the maximization of returns. Such studies have been gaining importance over the years on account of the limited resources available for education. There are a variety of input-output analysis in education depending upon the nature of study as stated below :

(i) Factors of production measured in physical terms, e.g., cost quality studies, cost school size relationship studies;

(ii) Cost-effectiveness analysis regarding the relationship between costs of input and achievement of objectives, i.e., comparisons made between the alternative ways of achieving an objective in order to identify one with the lowest cost;

(iii) Rate of return studies/cost benefit analysis relating to investment appraisal— comparison of the cost and benefit aspects of education ascertaining thereby the economic profitability; and

(iv) Efficiency/productivity studies concerning with the measurement of efficiency of educational and outlays in providing the requisite manpower for economic growth in terms of quantity and quality.

Correlation Analysis – This method is used to correlate some aggregate indices of educational economic activities. Inter country (Cross-National) comparisons at the same point of time, inter-temporal (longitudinal) comparisons within the same country or even inter-industry and inter-enterprise comparisons can be made by using correlation analysis.

Development of Nation and Economics

There are usually two approaches adopted in the preparation of plans for national development. However the main objective of each approach is to get the most and best educational results for the effort expended and to maximize education's contribution to each individual and to the whole society.

Following are the two main approaches which determine the allocation of resources. Both, however are interlinked and one cannot be separated from the other.

Social Consideration – Under the first approach, the educational goals of a country are first determined with reference to its past traditions, comparison with advanced countries and the needs of the new society which it desires to create. The financial implications of these goals are then worked out, and an attempt is made to raise the funds needed for educational development. The usual experience in this approach, however, is that the finances required for supporting an educational programme which the nation desires to have, are not likely to be available in the near future, and in some cases, they are found to be even large than the entire public expenditure of the country in all sectors.

Economic Consideration – In the second approach, a beginning is made with the limitations of finance, and the first step is to ascertain the maximum financial resources that can be raised for education by mobilising internal resources through taxation or voluntary contributions in cash and kind and external assistance. On the basis of the resources that this seem likely to be available, three questions are posed : (1) What type of education can the country afford ? (2) How much or for whom ? (3) What should be the priorities of available funds?

The first of these approaches is dominated mainly by educational considerations, and the second by financial limitations. The ultimate solution of the problem would have to be sought in a realistic and wise compromise between these two approaches and that, in order to provide a good educational system to the Asian countries in the near future, educationists and economists would have to work together. In the process, educationists would become increasingly conscious of the new but significant science of the "economics of education' and the economists, in their turn, would become increasingly conscious of the significance of education in economic development. The major basic programme is to make an intensive effort to eliminate poverty and to raise the gross national product as quickly as possible. Programmes of increasing national income may have to be coupled with the programmes of population control as well. In the larger interests of speedy development, governmental expenditure on economic investment and development of social services, including education, should be increased quickly.

QUESTIONS

Essay Type Questions

1. "The relationship between economic growth and educational growth is like a chicken and egg." Elucidate this statement.
2. "The relationship between educational growth and economic growth is a two-way process—one of reciprocal

nature, other of mutual contribution." Explain this statement.

3. "Education is both the seed and flower of economic development." Amplify this statement.
4. Explain the nature of education as an investment.
5. What do you understand by human development ? What are its elements ? State the role of economy and education in this regard.
6. How is education related to economic development ?
7. Write an essay on 'Why Economics of Education' ?
8. Explain the role of economists in educational development.
9. Describe the ways in which education leads to productivity.
10. Explain the importance of social considerations and economic considerations in national development.

Short Answer and Objective Type Questions

11. Name any four foreign economists who have done a lot of work on the economics of education.
12. Name any two Indian economists who are associated with economics of education.
13. Study table and answer the following questions :
    (i) Which country has the highest per capita income?
    (ii) Which country has the lowest per capita income ?
    (iii) Which Asian country has the lowest per capita income ?
14. Write 'yes' or 'no' against each statement on the basis of data given in table.
    (a) U.S.A. has the highest per capita income. ( )
    (b) India has the minimum per capita income. ( )

(c) Life expectancy is the highest in Japan. ( )

(d) Infant mortality rate is the highest in Afghanistan. ( )

(e) Adult literacy rate is the lowest in Pakistan. ( )

15. On the basis of data given in table, write 'yes' or 'no' against each statement :

(i) Life expectancy is the highest in Kerala. ( )

(ii) Bihar has the lowest literacy rate. ( )

(iii) Maharashtra has the highest per capita state domestic product. ( )

(iv) Life expectancy is the lowest in Assam. ( )